Home
IMPROVEMENTS

Marshall Cavendish

Published by Marshall Cavendish Books Limited
58 Old Compton Street
London W1V 5PA

© Marshall Cavendish Limited 1972 – 1984

Printed in Yugoslavia

First Printing 1975
This printing 1984

ISBN 0 85685 094 2

This volume is not to be sold in Australia,
New Zealand or North America.

Introduction

If your home needs new sparkle or added style, this book has been designed with you specially in mind. It describes unusual and interesting home improvements carried out by architects, designers and builders, containing many original and striking ideas for giving your home – inside and out – an improved appearance and extra comfort.

Over seventy individual cases are looked at, from the sophisticated town house to a rural farm house. Hundreds of colour photographs show you how professional ideas and effort can result in beautiful decor and interior design.

Many of the ideas introduced require little money to put into operation, but the effects can be far reaching. Learn how to make the most of colour schemes or the best way of giving a small room a feeling of spaciousness. Or, if you're interested in antiques, you can find out useful ways of keeping them in good condition and how to arrange them for the most eye-catching appearance.

Some of the most common problems facing you when starting out on improving your home are dealt with, showing you how they can be overcome to best advantage. This book will give you inspired ideas and practical instructions on how you can make the most of your dwellings whether you live in the country or in town.

Contents

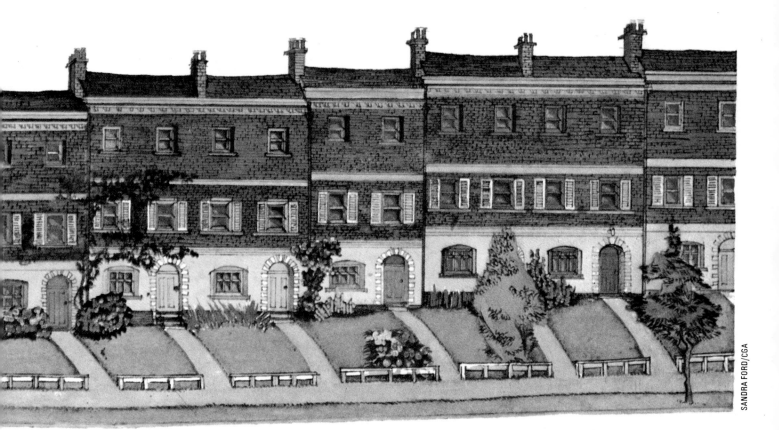

SANDRA FORD/CGA

Credits

Avenue – Daily Telegraph Syndication, pp. 52, 94
Bell, Peter, p. 98
Belton, Robert, pp. 110, 132
Benson, Mike, p. 70
Bernhardt, Jurg, p. 115
Bethell, John, pp. 12, 63, 86, 90, 120, 126
Beyda, Janet and Frank, p. 122
Boys, Michael, pp. 16, 42
Bull, Gunhild, p. 162
Broad, J. P./Macavoy, R., pp. 44, 150
Camera Press, pp. 78, 168
Coreless, Clive, pp. 50, 172, 174
Dunne, Michael, pp. 7, 134
Duns, Alan, p. 92
Elle/Photo Roger Gain/Transworld, p. 66
Ferrante, Leonardo, pp. 18, 26, 40, 57,
124, 140, 148, 176
Formica Ltd., p. 182
Francoise Rapin/Femina/Conzett & Huber, p. 2
Good Housekeeping, p. 160
Hargreaves, Nelson, pp. 72, 101, 108, 128, 153, 170
Henderson, Graham/Elizabeth Whiting, p. 96
Holly, Noel, pp. 75, 82
Howitt, David and Miriam, p. 88
Lambert, Sam, p. 131
MacLaughlin, Bill, pp. 36, 60, 164
Matheson, Rob, p. 180
McConnell, Sally, p. 54
Morris, Brian, p. 32
Myers, John, pp. 119, 136, 145
Neri, Grazia, pp. 38, 142
Peters, Bill, p. 29
Powell, Spike, p. 156
Seymour, John, pp. 68, 106
Simpson, Paul, p. 80
Tabbernor, Carol, p. 166
Transworld/Photo Roger Gain, p. 25
Tubby, pp. 47, 108, 112, 158
Tubby/Elizabeth Whiting, p. 10
Walters, R., p. 34
Watmough, Colin, pp. 14, 178
Wreford, Joyce, pp. 84, 104

MICHAEL DUNNE

Getting on top of a space problem

Although a mews house may provide ample living space for a bachelor, quite often it is considered barely adequate accommodation for a couple, let alone a small family. One such London mews house, however, was converted to accommodate a *large* family, with the help of architect Peter Wood.

When photographer Michael Dunne first bought his two-storey mews house, he had the stables on the ground floor converted into a garage-cum-studio, with a small flat above for himself, incorporating an office and dark room. Some years later he decided to stop commuting to and from his country house every weekend, and base his family in London instead. This

meant that his modest mews house now had to accommodate not only him and his wife, but also their five children, a parrot and a cat. The garage was to be retained on the ground floor, and some office space, however small, provided above.

This brief presented the architect with quite a problem, but it was obvious to him that the

7

MICHAEL DUNNE

Top left. *The extra floor, which scarcely rises above the roof line of the row of mews houses, is just visible from the street.*
Top right. *The black quarry-tiled entrance hall, where the spiral staircase starts. The red door leads to the garage-cum-studio.*

Above left. *A study area for Michael Dunne, which was provided by incorporating a section of the landing at the front of the house into the living room. His desk fits neatly into this corner without affecting the rest of the room. The whole house is now double glazed.*

Above right. *The laundry area at one end of the kitchen which, though smaller than before, is compactly planned. The concertina louvred doors close to hide all the washing debris when necessary. The slats in the ceiling conceal the air conditioning system.*

only way to accommodate all the family, in any degree of comfort, was to build another floor on top of the house. So the original valley roof was removed, the party walls raised, two steel beams slung across them, and a new roof put on top. The interior ceiling was covered in steel reinforced wood-wool insulation slabs sprayed with white paint, making it shallower than a

conventional construction while providing an interesting contour.

This top floor is devoted to the five children, so it was built with materials which withstand pretty rough treatment, and finished in bright colours. Constructed to look like a cabin cruiser, it houses three bedrooms and a bathroom, with an extra bedroom on the landing

which can be closed off by a louvred partition. In this way the central area, illuminated by rooflights, becomes a play space, with the bedrooms forming cellular units off it. The large sliding double-glazed doors on this floor open on to paved balconies at front and back, forming a continuous flower 'box'.

Two small rooms on the first floor were com-

Above. One of the children's bedrooms on the new top floor, with brightly coloured laminated blockboard cupboard and drawer units. Instead of a conventional joist construction, the ceiling is formed in steel reinforced wood-wool slabs sprayed white.

Top right. The main bedroom, with an attractive Chippendale four-poster bed hung with pretty fabric. The white laminate-faced Columbian pine fitted wall unit has sliding wardrobe doors and folding panels which hide the wash basin and vanitory unit.

Above. The bedroom was formed by knocking two smaller rooms into one, leaving space for a study area at the back for Mary Dunne. Rooflights—once the only light source in this room—were replaced by a large window. The wallpaper matches the bed hangings.

bined to form one large main bedroom with a study area at the back for Mary Dunne. A fitted vanitory unit incorporating wardrobes and wash basin was constructed along one wall, enclosed by white laminate-faced folding doors. Rooflights—once the only light source in the two old rooms—have been replaced by a large window in the back wall.

A dining area has been provided by enlarging the landing, at the expense of part of the large

kitchen at the back. The kitchen, now more compactly and efficiently planned, incorporates a laundry alcove, with sliding louvred doors which seal off the mess when necessary, and an informal eating area in one corner. The whole room is air-conditioned to remove unwanted washing and cooking smells.

The living room is much as it was, but the front section of the landing was incorporated into it to provide a study area for Michael Dunne.

A small lavatory and broom cupboard behind the stairs were converted into a tiny bathroom.

The original staircase running straight up from the front door was removed during the first conversion, and replaced by a spiral staircase constructed with a steel frame with teak treads. This was easily added to when the new floor was built on, and now runs straight up through the house from the small hall on the ground floor.

MICHAEL DUNNE

Flat with a first floor

Many houses built towards the end of the last century had vast proportions, with ceilings sometimes 15ft high or more. Such rooms have since been divided into two in modern conversions, but few people have thought of making full use of all the wasted space in the ceiling.

Designer Ian Rangeley's flat in the centre of London consisted of one large south-facing room, a kitchen and a bathroom. The large room obviously had to combine sleeping and living facilities, but it was the 13ft high ceiling that gave the designer an idea for a bedsitter with a difference.

By constructing a sleeping gallery over half the room area, away from the window end, he was able to retain all the floor space below for the living section, and still leave room for a dining area. The final layout allows 6ft headroom in the gallery bedroom and nearly 7ft below, and has the added benefit of separate living and sleeping quarters.

This room had already been divided into two in a previous conversion, and the partition wall created an awkward corner at the window end. Here a cantilevered desk has been tucked in, which helps to camouflage the ugly angles.

Two large sofas and two armchairs have been arranged to form a square conversation area under the sleeping gallery. A dining area has been fitted beyond it at the dark end of the room, next to the door to the hall and therefore handy for the kitchen. In this way, the door and circulation area do not break up any section of the room, but separate the dining and living areas. The vertical pillars that support the rear end of the sleeping gallery also mark the dividing line between these areas. The dining table is fixed to both the wall and two of these pillars.

A false ceiling had been fitted at this end of the room in the previous conversion, but the designer decided to construct another one 2ft below it to line up with the floor of the gallery. The space above it, which is accessible by removable panels, is used for storage, and the electricity meter and fusebox.

In another corner of the room, fitted shelves hold books, radio, record players and other leisure facilities. All the corners and alcoves in this room have been put to good use, and shelves and cupboards are fitted wherever possible to disguise the awkward angles.

Unlike many sleeping galleries, which are only just large enough for a bed, Ian Rangeley's is spacious, housing wardrobes and a dressing

table as well. He feels that rooms where every shelf and cupboard is enclosed look too clinical, so the hanging space and shelves here have been left open-fronted to reveal their contents. The sleeping gallery is L-shaped, and the cantilevered dressing table, with a mirror above, is fitted in the end of the L over the 'leisure' corner of the living room. Three horizontal rails act as a safety barrier at the edge of the gallery—a lighter alternative to a more solid 'fence'. No privacy is needed here, so this attractive open arrangement is quite satisfactory.

The tall windows light the sleeping gallery well, but the light in the living area below is somewhat subdued. However, the designer maintains that a lot of natural light is not necessary in a living room, as he spends so little time sitting in it during daylight hours. The soft colour scheme—off-white walls, cream furniture and pale green and pink upholstery—give a restful appearance. Enormous spherical paper lanterns hung apparently at random cast a soft light all over the room, supplemented by spotlights. A collection of plants at the window end improves the view over the fire escapes outside.

The furniture is one of the most economical features of this bedsitter; Ian Rangeley made it all himself, including the bed, in chipboard. He designed it on a module, based on the standard sizes available: 2ft 6in. x 1ft 8in. One sofa is 7ft 6in. long, and easily doubles as a spare bed, the other is 5ft. A large cube-shaped table provides additional storage to that in the bases of the sofas and chairs. He cut the foam rubber cushions by hand with a sharp knife, and covered them in a floral print.

Opposite page. *The sleeping gallery covers about half the area of the room, leaving 7ft headroom below. The structure is built from cheap softwood, sanded and finished with clear polyurethane varnish.*

Above left. *The view down from the sleeping gallery to the open area below shows the awkward shapes created by the partition wall erected in a previous conversion. A cantilevered desk fitted in an alcove by the window helps to disguise the worst angles.*

Below left. *A stepladder fixed at a slope leads from the living area to the sleeping gallery above. Bookshelves are fitted in a shallow alcove behind it, and a cupboard in the deeper alcove beyond.*

Above. *The furniture is made of chipboard, with storage space provided in the hollow bases. The foam cushions were cut with a knife to fit the sofas and chairs. Large paper lanterns supplement the spotlights fitted to the underside of the sleeping gallery.*

Below. *This sleeping gallery is larger than most, which have room for only a bed. Here, open-fronted wardrobes and a dressing table have been built into the L-shaped structure, which has 6ft headroom.*

JOHN BETHELL

A roomful of illusions

It looks spacious and expensively furnished but, that apart, there is nothing remarkable at first glance about this comfortable living room in Kensington, London. And that shows how misleading a first glance can be–for the spaciousness and opulence are illusions.

Designer Mary Gilliatt has taken a through-room of quite modest proportions – thousands of suburban semi-detached houses have one as big – and by a series of gentle deceptions made it grander than it really is.

How was it done? First, the fact that it is a through-room helps. A combined room like this, usually made by adding a living room and dining room together, nearly always looks 'greater than the sum of its parts'.

Then, Mrs Gilliatt used a carpet with a strong element of white to reflect the white of the ceiling. Together, they carry the light through from the windows at one end to those at the other, making the whole floor area seem bigger.

The furniture was chosen with the same idea in mind. Armchairs with low backs intrude far less than higher-backed ones would have done; you look over, rather than at, them. And their height corresponds, instead of clashing, with that of other furniture–result, a clean set of hori-

zontal lines through the living room 'picture'.

Similarly, although some bookcases were necessary for a family whose books already filled a massive bookcase in the hall, heavy-looking, wooden bookcases in the chimney alcoves would have been visually overpowering. The wall-mounted plate glass shelves used instead simply vanish into the background, particularly at night, when they are lit from below, leaving visible only the gleaming spines of the books themselves.

For the same reason, the heavy mid-Victorian mantel was removed, and replaced with a plain, white-painted mantel shelf.

In a room which is used for living, and not just for show, plenty of occasional tables are necessary. In this room they are simple Perspex cubes, turned on their sides – handy, because they double as magazine racks, but almost invisible until you start to count them. These were bought ready made, but you could easily make them yourself.

That is another aspect in which the room is deceptive: cost. Apart from some valuable antiques – a touch of extravagance, but not vital to the basic plan – the kinds of furnishing used are not inherently expensive.

The macaw-green wall fabric which sets the tone for the whole room, for example, is plain

*In the entrance hall, **above,** bright orange welcomes the visitor, while in the living room, **above right,** macaw green sets the scene for a comfortable stay. The Dutch grate and Thonet rocker, both early 19th Century, sit easily beside the square, plain ultra-modern Perspex log boxes.*
*The designer used a variety of techniques to make the room look larger. Glass bookshelves avoid the 'heavy' look of wooden ones, while Perspex occasional tables melt into the background and, **below right,** the whites in the carpet and ceiling carry a light, spacious look right through the room.*
*Suiting the height of other furniture, like the 17th Century chest, **below far right,** low armchairs help produce a clean, uncluttered look.*

felt. Laid over a conventional wallpaper lining paper (to cover minor flaws in the plaster), it is rich in appearance but, bought in 6ft (1.83m) rolls, less expensive than a good wallpaper.

The carpet, specially designed to pick up shades of the colours elsewhere in the room, is now a standard pattern. And the Roman blinds – they fold down concertina-fashion, rather than unrolling, to give a softer look – are in Indian cotton.

Mrs Gilliatt is a firm advocate of fabric wall-coverings in cheerful colours. In the sort of 'grey' light that you get in Britain, for example, pale shades can often turn insipid or 'washed out'. Bright colours, on the other hand, give living rooms and bedrooms a much cosier, more welcoming look.

12

Bright ideas for a new house

To be the first owner of a modern house is fun. You can choose your own colour schemes even before the house is completed, and all you need when you move in is your furniture and enough imagination to give the house a look of its own. Everything is so much easier than a move into an older house : no dry rot problems, no modernizing of the bathroom or kitchen—it's all there and all planned for practical modern living.

The owners of this modern Georgian-style house in London tackled their house in an unusual way. Rather than complete it slowly room by room, they concentrated on one particular aspect at a time. First it was the wall coverings, then the floors, next the furniture and curtains, then shelving, lighting and so on. Planning your home often means looking at each design aspect separately so you can give your whole attention to the particular problems involved in, for example, supplying each room with efficient and attractive lighting.

Here they decided that one of the best ways to give the house a different look was to use bright wallpapers combined with stripped and sealed floors in all the main rooms. Fitted carpets throughout would have been far too expensive, and stripped floors made the house seem much more spacious anyway. Apart from the wall-papering, which was done by the builders, the owners did all the rest of the work themselves.

Any family with two young children needs playspace and this is often hard to 'steal' in the average modern home. Here they decided that the play area would have to be on the ground floor within easy reach of help if needed.

On the ground floor are the garage, cloakroom, kitchen and dining room. Out of these, only the garage presented possibilities for conversion into a play area. It was carefully re-planned to serve as playroom and utility room and garage if necessary. It was given extra light by fitting glass into the top panels of the door, which was securely draught-proofed with a foam strip. Converting any area which was not primarily intended for living should involve meticulous draught-proofing or it will be impossible to stay in it for any length of time !

The main problem was the concrete floor—obviously too hard and cold for children to play on. The 'garage' might still be needed for the car from time to time, so a permanent lino or tiled floor was impractical. In the end they painted the concrete with deck paint which effectively sealed the dust in and gave a tough, durable finish. Then they put down inexpensive and attractive rush matting for the children to play on.

They painted the breeze block wall white, built in the electricity cables for safety and produced a workable multi-purpose room. There was enough room to house the home freezer, the washing machine and dryer. With the addition of toy storage trunks and some low seating, plus cheerful posters on the walls, the area took on a completely new look. And if they needed to bring the car in, all they had to do was lift the mats from the floor. This imaginative treatment for a garage proves that, even within the average family home, space used wisely can double its function without too much upheaval.

The small neat kitchen is well planned. The inset sink has a waste disposal unit. The storage cupboards are deep blue and fitted with a laminated worktop. The owners made some extra shelves—always useful in any kitchen—and spotlighted one to display an attractive set of deep blue and white china. Picking out particular treasures by using interesting lighting effects is an idea any home owner can copy.

The adjoining dining room shows what can be done with a collection of junk shop buys. An inexpensive old dresser was teamed with budget-buy table and chairs—and given a facelift. The owners shortened the legs of the dresser, cut down the high back, fitted brass knobs and then painted it white with a bright kingfisher-blue top, drawers and doors. The old table and new whitewood chairs were painted to match. One of the best, and cheapest ways of furnishing a home is to buy up furniture like this—with a lick of paint and some new handles it takes on a new lease of life, and fits most homes perfectly.

They found an old cast iron kettle on a rubbish heap, removed the rust with the sanding attachment on an electric drill, oiled it and gave it a new shine with boot polish. It now holds pride of place as an attractive and unusual plant holder. Old pots and pans like this are easy to find and it's a simple job to turn them into decorative objects in their own right.

A small side table with 'barley-twist' gate-legs was another bargain, and this was painted white, a colour that blends well with any decor. The blue and green sisal matting was bought as a remnant in a carpet sale—a sensible choice, being cheap and extremely durable. Carpet sales are ideal places to pick up bargains length of floor-coverings in a surprising range of colours —particularly if you're looking for a relatively small piece.

The wallpaper looks like hessian and is practical because it is easily wiped clean. This tones with the flower-patterned curtains in blue, purple and green.

The spacious first floor sitting room leads off a wide landing that has been utilized as a study—it always makes sense to use every inch of space. The easy chairs and sofa in the sitting room are the only large pieces of new furniture in the house—the rest is either renovated or made by the owners. And these chairs were chosen because they would give years of use. They are upholstered in a practical dark green—pale colours would only make extra work with young children around !

The pictures—all painted by the owner—are one of the main features of the living room. They offset the colour scheme which is composed of shades of purple. There is a large white shaggy mat on the floor.

The main bedroom which leads off the first landing has its own bathroom. This has a warm look with a mixture of bold pinks and purples, and a sanded and sealed floor. The huge brass double bed was a junk shop buy—so, too, was the attractive chest beside it. Originally covered with about six layers of paint, the chest has been stripped down to its basic pine finish, then sealed with polyurethane—the end result is well worth the effort of stripping and varnishing old furniture. Old furniture can often be bought for half the price of a modern counterpart and by the time it has been renovated may well be worth more. Getting a perfect finish takes time, but a good result is satisfying and looks attractive.

The main bathroom echoes the pinks in the adjoining bedroom and has pink fittings. The wall round the bath is sensibly tiled and the whole room is brightened by the pink, turquoise and green paper. Only too often bathrooms are the poor relation of home decor, looking insipid in pastel shades. In all colour planning, it is essential not to be afraid of experimenting – the results will probably be a success.

The children sleep on the second floor and the wide landing is used for extra playspace. Their room is colourful with bright wallpaper, and two old chests, one painted with bright green gloss paint and the other white, house toys and oddments. The owners made a useful shelving unit to give yet more storage space for further accumulations of toys. The rooms is completed with dark blue curtains patterned with daisies. A dark background colour like this is good for a young child's room because it doesn't let in too much light early in the morning and the child, hopefully, stays asleep longer !

With the minimum outlay on furnishings, and the maximum use of imagination, the owners have given their house a highly original finish.

Top left. The garage is transformed into a pleasant playroom with the minimum fuss and the maximum effect. The door panels are securely draught-proofed with foam strip.
Top right. A bold colour scheme flatters the whole of the first floor. Shades of pink and blue in combinations of plain and patterned wallcoverings make up the decor.
Bottom left. The dining room is elegant in its Georgian colours of green and blue. The sharp white bentwood chairs add a modern note, and provide an eyecatching focus.
Bottom right. The kitchen is a well-planned 'galley' shape, with everything easily to hand. The pink and blue wallpaper is unusual for a kitchen and effective.

COLIN WATMOUGH

Elegance in coffee and cream

Walls off-white, curtains and carpet off-white, even the sofa off-white: this is just the sort of room that, for a family home, sounds wildly impractical. But a living room in pale, plain colours can, in fact, happily play host to large numbers of guests.

To Mr and Mrs Peter Jay, the idea of an exclusively 'adult' room was first demonstrated at an exhibition called 'Living with Children' by interior designers Glynn Smith Associates. It showed how, if there is space elsewhere for a semi-partitioned kitchen plus breakfast room—the American 'family room'—a living room can be planned with a more sophisticated atmosphere. Both idea and exhibition appealed to the Jays, successful career people with two pre-school children; they asked Juliet and Peter Glynn Smith to convert their Victorian detached house in Ealing, West London.

The house was damp and dreary when the Jays bought it, as it had not been lived in for two years. The walls were covered in dingy cream and brown shiny paper, and there were still gas light fittings in some of the rooms. But there was plenty of space.

Given a completely free hand, the designers converted the separate kitchen and breakfast room into a combined kitchen-family area. The former reception rooms—covering a total of 403 square feet (37.4 square metres)—were thus free for improvement.

The two rooms were divided by a heavy screen infill partition and it was decided to combine them into one. The partition was cut away but the top corners of the opening were rounded, giving a visual link with the arched alcoves on either side of the two fireplaces.

The door from the hall into the former back room was removed and the space blocked in, leaving one door to serve the new living room.

The large sash window at the front was left, and heavy off-white wool floor-to-ceiling curtains now extend right across this wall. A sash window at the back was replaced by French windows, giving access to the large garden.

Since the living room now runs through the whole length of the house it offers wide scope for the arrangement of furniture. In winter the sitting area is concentrated round the open fire in the front part of the room, but in summer the furniture is turned round to face the French windows and the pretty garden.

The designers specified long low radiators, which are easily hidden from view by the careful positioning of tables, and do not spoil the clean, low lines of the furniture.

The designers' choice of lighting enhances the comfortable appearance of the room. Spotlights in the centre of the ceiling in each part of the living room give general lighting without glare. The front one points straight down on to a low white table in the middle of the room, and the back one is directed on to the chimney breast, reflecting light into the room. Two Italian Artemide lamps on low tables give a warm light in other parts of the room.

Above. *The ugly Victorian fireplace in the front part of the room was removed, and a chrome frame set into the chimney space to allow for an open fire. In the back, the old-fashioned grate was ripped out and the space blocked in.*

Below. *The top corners of the opening in the partition wall were rounded to tie in with the existing alcoves on each side of the two chimney breasts. The white-painted bookshelves in one of the alcoves at the back can just be seen.*

MICHAEL BOYS

Mr. and Mrs. Peter Jay's living room is decorated in cool, bland colours, and lit to give a relaxing appearance.
Above. *The walls are covered in off-white hessian, the carpet is off-white thick wool pile, and the big comfortable sofa is upholstered in off-white heavy wool matching the curtains.*
Below. *The interesting ceiling mouldings are accentuated by the use of colour. The ceiling and paintwork are white, and the cornice is picked out in beige.*

A cottage in town

Edwardian terraced houses can be seen in many London Streets. This one has a difference; it has an aura of a peaceful country cottage—a welcome feeling in an overcrowded city. This atmosphere was achieved through a well-planned conversion where ingenuity and visual imagination were applied.

The conversion took years to complete, and the house was lived in while the work was going on. To have finished the renovation before moving in was too expensive a proposition. Often temporary make-shift living is necessary if cash reserves have been exhausted by the first house payment.

Fortunately, the house was in sound structural condition. One of the first modernization jobs was to install gas central heating. Then the wiring and plumbing were brought up-to-date. Major structural alterations were not needed; the rooms—apart from the sitting room—had graceful and convenient proportions.

The sitting room had originally been two rooms: an old-fashioned parlour with a corner fireplace and a kitchen, complete with range. The fireplace and range were removed, and the partitioning wall knocked down and replaced by a rolled steel joist (RSJ) to support the floor above.

The original hatch was kept—for convenience —but the connecting doors to the old scullery were blocked up. French windows were put in at the garden end of the new room, to bring in more light and to help make a closer relationship between house and garden.

A common difficulty in combining two rooms into one is to give a natural look of unity. It was successfully done here by cleverly masking the pillars which support the RSJ. One blends in with the horizontal and vertical lines of a large built-in shelf unit. The opposite pillar is not in view; it was incorporated into the chimney breast.

The attractive shelf unit was made by first drawing a rough sketch on the wall itself, and then having a carpenter build the array of shelves. Although careful thought went into working out the best arrangement of shelves, the finished effect is deceptively casual with a beautiful juxtaposition of books and ornaments.

It's worth taking note of both the method of designing this unit and the arrangement of the items stored on it. It's an ideal example of how to use this type of shelving to best advantage. The weight should be evenly distributed— otherwise a support might give way and valued ornaments damaged or destroyed.

A second and common difficulty when embarking on a 'two-in-one' conversion can be the problem of different floor levels. Making the room into one level is a very costly undertaking. In this case, a less expensive and more imaginative solution was found through an unusual arrangement of furniture.

A handsome chesterfield was placed on one side of where the levels split. A small balustrade was then fixed around the sofa to prevent it from sliding backwards down the step immediately

LEONARDO FERRANTE

Above left. A dining room with a Wedgwood look. A striking contrast of blue and white is softened by warm hues of wood and rich gold upholstery. Paintings on the angular wall are effectively framed by white beading.
Above top. The house façade in pale yellow brick. A small group of shrubs and greenery give a feeling of privacy and seclusion.
Above. A 'two-into-one' living room on split levels. A balustrade around the chesterfield keeps it from sliding back and also serves as an ideal spot for displays.
Above right. An attractive and useful wall storage unit which has a handy hatch through to the kitchen. Once this lower level of the living room was a dreary and drab scullery.

behind. A ledge was put on top of the balustrade to provide a focal point for attractive displays.

A new fireplace was designed; the builders used the chimney originally in the room. The design didn't include a large mantelpiece—it would have made the room look too narrow. Instead, an imposing marble hearth was made, which wraps around the corner of the chimney breast. Other eye-catching features are the custom-made niche for holding ornaments and

a cast iron fire basket, made inexpensively at a local forge.

A period atmosphere pervades the room—a result of the wise selection of furniture, mostly acquired through junk shops, and the choice of lighting, mainly table lamps. The soft flattering light of the lamps help to create a restful atmosphere. The harsh overhead light is only used for sewing or close work.

The sitting room colours are an effective mixture of white, gold and orange. Rich velvet curtains enhance the generous French windows. In contrast, easy-to-care-for plain gold blinds are used in the windows at the other end of the room. Commonly seen expensive fitted carpeting hasn't been used. Instead, the floorboards have been sanded and sealed, and the luxurious patina helps to set off the large white rug.

The dining room is simply done in deep blue, with a sharp contrast in the white woodwork and cornices. The fireplace was removed, leaving an uninteresting small wall with little focal interest. It was livened up by building a large frame from white-painted beading. Inside the frame is an attractive collection of pictures and plates. The beading wasn't expensive or difficult to put up, and has added an unusual touch to the

room.

A neat serving corner was made, with enough room for a trolley to be wheeled in from the kitchen. Above the trolley park is a small wall cupboard, painted the same colour as the walls to blend into the room scheme. A light was fixed under the cupboard for use when serving meals.

The blue and white kitchen echoes the dining room motif. The room is small and every available inch of space is used to the full for storage. There are base cupboards under a working surface and wall cupboards above, plus extra shelves and hooks for all the vital extras needed for cooking.

A stable door leads from the kitchen out into the greenery of the garden. Motifs from the wallpaper were cut out and stuck to the cupboard doors—a successful and inexpensive way of adding pattern. The original coal hole was turned into a practical larder with a small fridge inside it.

The soft brown paisley patterned paper in the hall continues up the stairs and is used to great effect with a matching fabric. The fabric went into making the curtains under the stairs, which hide a storage area for coats. It is also used to conceal the hot water storage tank outside the

LEONARDO FERRANTE

Above. *Delicate touches of cane and lace give this dusty green and white bedroom a delightful air of elegant tranquillity.*
Inset. *The beds in the children's room were cleverly joined together with a cupboard unit which provides ample storage space, along with tiers of shelves.*

bathroom.

The tank is well lagged to keep the heat in, and curtained with a pelmet to match. In this way, it does not appear to encroach too much into the precious space of the landing. A built-in cupboard would have taken up too much room. Another technique for creating a sense of spaciousness was to remove every other upright on the stairs.

One of the main features of the house are the well thought-out corners. They house careful arrangements of small furniture, pictures and ornaments to attract the eye and give a pleasing visual effect. One such corner was made at the top of the stairs where a great deal of space was wasted by a large walk-in cupboard which had a window.

The cupboard was opened up, making the staircase and landing brighter due to the light from the previously covered window. The curtain over the window is looped to one side, and a small shelf underneath for books and ornaments helps to balance the area. An old comfortable cane-backed chair beside the window makes this into a pleasant reading corner.

The dividing wall between the original bath-

room and the next door lavatory was removed, making one reasonably sized room instead of two tiny ones. In went a new bathroom suite in primrose yellow, with matching blinds and curtains. A basin was built into a vanitory unit and a bath, which doubles up as a shower, was installed.

In the children's room, there is an excellent example of how good planning can benefit you in the future. At first there had been bunk beds. Now these have been turned into sofa beds which means the room can be used comfortably for both sitting and sleeping. There are neatly designed shelf units on the walls and convenient clothes storage space.

The main bedroom is a relaxing colour combination of dusty green and white. The bed has an attractive cane bedhead which goes across the old fireplace corner. Small alabaster tables

flank the bed on either side. The side lights are old brass candlesticks converted to take electricity.

A third bedroom was converted into a bed-sitter for overnight guests, and has a pine storage unit that incorporates a cupboard, bookcases and open shelves. There's a practical dark brown fitted bedspread and the room is brightly patterned with a flowery wallpaper and matching curtains.

Another attractive feature about this house is the front façade and garden, which is only a small plot of land between the house and the pavement. Instead of having a conventional front gate in the middle of a fence, leading straight up to the front door, there is a raised island flower bed to screen the door. The path curves up to the door on the other side.

More attractive flower beds help to screen the front window of the house. The selection of flowering shrubs and greenery is informal and creates a feeling of seclusion from the road. The brickwork, which was painted a pale yellow, offsets the garden well. This informal house front is an ideal way for breaking away from a more conventional look and also is very effective in creating a sense of privacy.

FRANCOISE RAPIN/FEMINA/CONZETT & HUBER

The flexible family home

It is vital when converting a house for a family not just to consider each person's activities and needs, but also to realize that they change over the years. The layout must therefore be flexible and capable of being altered as the family changes.

When architect Jean-Louis Reymond had the opportunity of converting an attractive barn set in a farm surrounded by green fields, he set himself two limits, one financial and one professional. He wanted to convert it cheaply and quickly, so that it would be a habitable home and studio as soon as possible; and he wanted

Above. The exposed roof timbers are complemented by the wooden platforms hung at different levels in this barn. The cross-shaped holes in the exterior brick walls cast a soft light over the entire area.

to design a layout that could be altered to suit subsequent changes in his way of life.

In order to make the best use of all the space in this high barn, wooden platforms are hung at different levels, reached by a complicated looking framework of ladders and bridges. The platforms, for beds and a conversation area, are suspended on chains fixed to the roof frame by means of simple bolted hooks. The height can be regulated if necessary, and the lowest one—for the baby—can be lowered completely to the ground when no-one is there to look after him. The sleeping galleries, bridges and ladders are made of ordinary softwood, nailed together in a simple construction.

An outstanding natural feature of the barn was the pattern of cross-shaped spaces left in the external brickwork, which provided constant ventilation for the freshly harvested corn. To avoid a strong draught, panels of clear corrugated plastic were fixed against the outside of the walls. This is scarcely noticeable, and even if the external appearance of the house has been affected, the interior has certainly gained in comfort. The natural light that is diffused through the pattern of holes in the wall creates a peaceful atmosphere.

The first floor area, accessible via an outside wooden staircase, has been converted into a living and working studio. The double front doors are fixed in the opening through which the sheaves of corn were once passed from the top of the loaded carts. At ground level is the entrance to the room where the oxen used to work the threshing machine. Provision has been made here for individual bedrooms to be constructed later for people who prefer solitude.

Inside the front door a small lobby has been enclosed by an island unit constructed from white-painted open-sided tea chests. On the lobby side these frame a coat cupboard, and on the other side they house records, drinks, glasses and china. As they are only piled on top of each other, the layout can easily be altered later according to current needs.

In the family part of the house, the two main rooms intercommunicate by means of a large round opening in the wall, which has a certain decorative value. One room combines kitchen and dining room, with fitted bookshelves on one wall. In the other room there is a large low divan bed, the baby's cot and a chest of drawers decorated with painted flower motifs.

Heating presented a major problem in this converted barn. A large fire was obviously needed to warm such a vast area, so a metal structure resembling a flying saucer was made and hung from the roof. This design enables the maximum area of sheet metal to radiate heat all over the house. The entire structure can also be moved in the future if the layout is ever changed drastically.

Throughout the house, the attractive wooden beams were given prominence by removing masses of plaster covering them. A coat of cement was laid on the badly pitted floor, and another coat of plaster on the walls, which were damaged.

The design scheme would not suit people who like well-divided areas and individual bedrooms. It is an unconventional layout, but it is fascinating to live in, and suits its present occupants.

Below. An island structure built from white-painted tea chests stands inside the front doors. The ladder leads up to the hanging platforms. Opposite page, top left. An external wooden staircase gives access to the first floor entrance. Clear corrugated plastic panels cover the pattern of holes in the walls to prevent draughts. Top right. A different way of linking two rooms—a round opening cut in the partition wall. Bottom. Looking through the hole from the kitchen/dining room to the nursery.

Elegant home from three rooms

A satisfactory and ingenious way of giving an old house or flat a new look is to remove all the unnecessary partition walls and restructure the remaining space to your needs.

When photographer Roger Gain decided to buy a flat in Paris, he wanted something a little different. While he was looking around the fascinating Marais district, he found an old flat comprising three large rooms, kitchen and bathroom.

By reducing the size of the bathroom, resiting the kitchen and making use of the wide corridor that originally lay between them, he turned it into an elegant and welcoming home, where his

*Opposite page, top. By digging out the walls on each side of the chimney breast, Roger Gain made deep alcoves for housing his hi-fi system and records. Plaster was removed to reveal the ceiling beams. **Below left.** The spare bedroom has a rich, dark Victorian appearance. **Right.** A floor to ceiling shelf unit in the kitchen holds herbs and spices.*

Below. A worktop-height double-sided pine cupboard unit acts as a low room divider between the dining room and the kitchen.

collection of modern and antique furniture blends well together against an old background.

To make room for a dining area at one end of the living room, a compact little bathroom was tucked into the front of the flat, with a fitted kitchen beyond it. A corridor now runs from the front door past the bathroom and kitchen doors, and through to the living room at the back.

The U-shaped kitchen is separated from the dining area by a double-sided pine room divider. This cupboard unit, with a working surface above, is most practical, as it provides easy access between the kitchen and the dining area and keeps the person cooking from feeling isolated in the kitchen. A wooden worktop with a double sink unit and a cooker fitted in it, runs round the other walls.

A timber false ceiling was constructed in the kitchen to improve its proportions. It also provides useful storage space above head height, and a frame for the recessed spotlights that light the kitchen.

A tall shelf unit at one end of the kitchen, reaching from worktop height to the ceiling, acts as an enormous spice rack. A magnetic bar at one side holds gadgets such as tin openers within easy reach of the working areas. Copper saucepans hanging on one wall provide an attractive display, and a cluster of

wooden spoons are arranged in a china jug like a bunch of flowers.

In the living room, a certain amount of 'excavation' work on the walls was undertaken. Alcoves on either side of the chimney breast were deepened and filled with fitted cupboards and shelves. When the ceiling plaster was pulled off, beautiful old beams were revealed and these have been stripped and left exposed throughout the flat.

A 13ft (4m) long sofa running along one wall provides the only comfortable sitting accommodation, but its enormous size prevents this from being a disadvantage and it can double as an extra spare bed when necessary. It is built on a hollow base, which is used as a huge storage space. The sofa cushions on it are covered in a print designed by William Morris in 1890, and roller blinds made in matching fabric colour the incoming light like a stained glass window.

The chimney breast has been faced in pine—a cheap wood used throughout the flat. Full use is made of the deepened alcoves on each side. Logs for the open fire are stacked in one; the dining table can also be pushed up into it. The other alcove houses a 'music corner'. An elaborate hi-fi system fitted on low level shelves can be hidden by removable louvred doors when not in use. A specially made rack for records was fixed at eye level on the wall above, with shelves for ornaments above and below. Fourteenth-century paintings bought mainly in England blend in well with the old ceiling beams, as well as the more modern furniture.

The two bedrooms were left much as before, and fitted wardrobes were built in along one whole wall of each. The spare bedroom has been equipped with a desk fitted in the recess of a blocked-in doorway. A black laminated board supported by two trestles provides an additional working surface. At the window, another roller blind in 1900s fabric, bentwood chairs, and white crochet bedspreads give a Victorian appearance to the room. The undeniably modern wardrobes are painted white, with their pine frames left exposed and varnished.

Roger Gain has collected furniture, paintings and ornaments from all parts of the world—many from England. An old English kitchen chest fits happily into his bedroom, frames from old English engravings now hold mirrors in the bathroom, and modern green glass lampshades light a model of an English boat in the spare bedroom. An American patchwork bedspread, a Mexican 'tree of life', Finnish glass vases, Swiss candlesticks, and Indian patterned wallpaper all combine to give this apartment an international flavour.

Surprisingly, however, the effect is not one of a hotchpotch of different styles and periods. Everything blends well to make it a comfortable and restful home.

TRANSWORLD/PHOTO ROGER GAIN

Cottage in the city

A cottage in the city lends itself to a variety of styles in interior design. At one extreme, it can have a modern look with a smart streamlined decor or, at the other end of the scale, a period flavour where antique furniture and a feeling from the past predominate. This London cottage borrows from both the past and the present, harmoniously combining the old with the new, to create a restful period flavour which nevertheless belongs to the twentieth century.

The Powells were tired of living in the high, predictable rooms often found in London houses. They wanted a change and began looking for a home that would offer them that change. The river had always held an attraction for them, but they found property too scarce and prices too high on the Thames. Eventually they came across a rambling seventeenth century cottage—near the river at Richmond—which they bought and then set out to renovate.

It had originally been two cottages, one large and the other very small. The rooms were pokey and drab; the cottage had no style or distinction. The outside, however, was unmistakable—it was painted a smokey pink and still dramatically remains that colour today. A large garden, badly in need of care and attention, spread out behind the house.

The job of converting began on the inside. An architect by profession, Mr. Powell made the decisions on the structural and interior design changes to the cottage. His emphasis was on restoring as much as on modernizing. The front door originally lead into a small entrance room which served little purpose and tended to be lost space. Beyond was a parlour which lacked the character to make it an interesting and appealing room.

The partitioning wall between the hall and parlour was pulled down and a necessary pillar

erected—precisely in the middle of the new and more spacious living room. It's often thought that a functional piece, like this supporting pillar, should be hidden from view in that it might look unsightly or arrest the visual flow.

Not so here. The pillar was made a feature rather than a structural object which had to be apologetically hidden from view. An imposing marble column was wrapped round the pillar, leaving a rather classical Greek look. Sometimes the boldest and most open treatment of functional items like pillars, pipes and radiators can have a positive impact. Many household pieces which initially seem unsightly and unattractive can be made intriguing with skilful use of colour or texture.

A further feature in the room, which adds both charm and character, is the oil stove. Again,

no attempt was made to tuck it away from sight. Its appearance is far more authentic and distinctive than a modern radiator. It was built into the back of a chimney breast and adequately heats the entire cottage—all three floors.

The main motif of this living room is casualness and simplicity, seen in decor both new and old. Adapting the room for comfort and convenience was combined with the Powell's intention to restore it. They didn't want to lose the cozy period flavour of the cottage. There are no fussy curtains or cushions, no carpet, and an absence of detail and knick-knack often seen in living rooms.

The floor was covered with rich brown quarry tiles, ideal for anyone shy of housework. The deep Edwardian fireplace was left with its delicate relief panel on the front. The hand-

Above left. A comfortable living room with an unusual feature—a classical Greek column. A modern ceiling spot over the sofa gives dramatic impact by night, while the oil stove at the back adds to the period flavour.
Above. View from the back garden. At the right, the lean-to kitchen, draped in abundant greenery, leads onto the patio.

made couch was chosen because of the low and generous lines; it invites the visitor to sit down and relax.

All the tables in the room are trunks—some stripped, some varnished. The bulky wood adds to the rustic flavour in the room and the trunks also serve as valuable storage space. Too often people hesitate to use simple, inexpensive items, like these trunks, which can be very effective as

27

LEONARDO FERRANTE

Left. A collection of Victorian jugs in subtle pastel colours makes a feature of the fireplace. Brown quarry tiles save the striking white decor from a sterile look.
Bottom left. Imposing ships in oil set a rich tone for the cozy dining room. The 'chandelier' was simply made from a steel frame and gathered beige calico.

the hall and stairs and then on to the dining room, and the other directly into the dining room. This room is small and cozy. An impressive oil painting of sailing ships, with a gilded frame, imposingly spans one wall. A white brick fireplace, which tends to dominate the room, will be removed at some point in the future and replaced with a large expanse of glass to open out the room.

The 'chandelier' over the table is an eye-catching—and economical—creation. A steel ring about a foot in diameter was strung up to the light flex hanging from the ceiling and then covered with beige calico, brought together in tucks. The effect is a soft gentle light which adds warmth to the room. Many fabric lampshades are quick and simple to make and the materials are usually available at any good department or handicrafts store.

Between the dining room and the adjoining kitchen are the original outer wall and windows, which were left intact. The effect is unusual and interesting; it allows light to pass between the two rooms but gives the kitchen a separate entity as well as preventing cooking smells from filtering into the dining area.

Built in the nineteenth century, the lean-to kitchen, with its gracefully sloping roof, has been equipped with all the modern conveniences. Perhaps one of the nicest changes is the long sliding glass doors which replaced part of the brick wall facing the back garden.

On warm sunny days, the doors are left open, giving a close relationship between the interior and out-of-doors. The garden is magnificent; many things are growing there from strawberries and grapes to roses and irises. The beautiful landscaping includes a graceful pergola and, at one end of the garden, there is a swing and tree house. The patio was made by Mr. Powell with York paving stones. The atmosphere is secluded and remote and seems completely detached from the concrete and steel of the surrounding town.

Moving up to the first floor, there is a warm pine-clad floor which leads on to two bedrooms and a bathroom. The floor above this originally had two rooms. The ceiling was so low that an average person couldn't stand up straight without hitting his head. The ceiling was raised and a dividing wall put up in one of the rooms. The wall comes directly up to the centre of a casement window so each side of the partition has one opening window. In order to visually increase the sense of space, mirrors were put along the partitioning wall to reflect the window which gives a greater feeling of light and openness. Mirrors are magnificent accessories in small rooms.

The Powell's rambling cottage now has an air of charm and comfort, resulting from a harmonious combination of restoration and modernization, the old and the new.

long as they suit the general mood of the room.

Effective decorative impact and cost don't necessarily go hand-in-hand. A good eye, imagination and willingness to try out new ideas play a big part in making a room come alive. If you're on a slim budget, you still can produce a striking and memorable decor, if sufficient effort and imagination are applied.

Like the 'trunk' tables, the inexpensive multi-angle lamps, used in many rooms of the cottage, are an economic way of lighting a room while also adding to the visual impact. Conventional lamps with porcelain bases are generally used in more formal and elaborate rooms. Because of the streamlined theme here, these modern lamps fit in very well. Their flexibility is also valuable in that they can be angled to highlight different parts of the room as required.

The main ornamentation is on the mantel, which has a lovely nineteenth century collection of jugs on either side of an old mahogany clock. The soft pastel colours of the jugs don't intrude or distract from the soft beiges and browns of the rest of the room.

Opposite the mantel, on the other wall, is a fitted bookcase with a fascinating feature. Hidden among the books is a built-in film projector which can be operated from the other side of the wall with a small hatch for viewing. A ceiling hook in front of the fireplace is used for hanging up the screen. The Powells find they watch home films and slides more often now because they don't have to undergo the bother of setting up a projector. It's an ingenious idea.

Two doors lead from the living room, one into

Farmhouse conversion

Converting an old barn and farmhouse into an attractive home requires a great deal of imagination, ambition and effort. This early Victorian barn and farmhouse was in a sorry state before it was transformed into the gracious and appealing home it is today. Equipped with all the modern conveniences, it still retains a flavour of old world charm.

Originally built by a Scotsman in Glen Roy on the Isle of Man in 1836, the site for the farmhouse and barn was ideal. The sturdy rock strata eight feet down created a firm foundation; a nearby stream provided a convenient source for drinking water; and the mountainside location gave protection against strong prevailing winds.

Further shelter came from large graceful trees on the mountainside, eventually leading to the name Brundal House—'house in the trees'. Despite the sheltered location, World War II bombing razed the barn to the ground and left the farmhouse totally uninhabitable.

Attracted by the magnificent scenery on the Isle of Man, insurance broker Roy Watkin and his wife Pat found and purchased the ruins of Brundal House. The beauty of the sweeping panorama surrounding the house compensated for the dilapidated state of the buildings.

After obtaining planning permission, the Watkins produced a balsa wood scale model for the proposed home and then called in a local architect, Graham Jones, to draw up plans, using the model as a guide.

Several major difficulties had to be dealt with. The many different levels presented obvious problems in converting. A further difficulty arose —the barn and farmhouses were separated by a

Above. A derelict barn and farmhouse now transformed into a spacious and attractive home. The raised swimming pool on the right is on the site of the old barn. The timber and slates came from a cotton mill demolition site.

22ft. (7m) road. At one point the Watkins thought it might be feasible to demolish the farmhouse, concentrating their efforts on the barn. They rejected this idea, however, feeling that the farmhouse belonged to a past era, and would add character and old world charm to their new home.

This is an excellent example of making the most of existing structures in a conversion. It would have been very easy for the Watkins to create a totally modern home, losing completely the original period quality. Although more effort and money were needed to salvage and convert

both the farmhouse and barn, the resulting home retains an appealing aura from the past.

A small labour force worked on the house. It consisted of a skilled joiner, who doubled up as site foreman, two local building workers, a brick layer and his labourer, and Roy Watkin. Specialized work such as electricity, plumbing and plastering was contracted out.

A clever move was made in obtaining two essential materials—heavy timber and roof slates—which would help to keep the period flavour. It involved buying high quality, second-hand materials from cotton mill demolition sites in Lancashire, and transporting them to the Isle of Man.

Rich pitch pine beams, rolled steel joists, thousands of 'Bangor Blue' slates and tons of timber for floor and ceiling joists were purchased at a fraction of their original cost and shipped over to Glen Roy. Although the delivery fees were high, the overall saving was considerable. It's this type of well-conceived operation which can help to make your money go further.

The second-hand beams were then spruced up. They were passed through fire to remove ugly machine oil, cotton waste and other unwanted substances that may have collected over the years. By using a wire brush, the original hue and grain were revealed. The beams were then treated with a waterproofing agent to seal in the natural oil of the timber—a measure taken to prevent staining from concrete, mortar and other building materials.

The treatment of the timber represented many hours of tedious work, but it was a good long-term investment. The beams, which play a large visual role in the house, have a luxurious finish, setting a handsome tone to the decor. Because of the waterproofing, the timber will also last for many years to come without the worry of its decaying.

The majority of slates brought over from the cotton mill were used on the roof. About a quarter of them had hair cracks—these were used for the kitchen floor tiles or as hardcore for the driveway and parking area. Roy Watkins made certain no materials went to waste.

Conversion work broke down into four sections: bedrooms, lounge and kitchen, the 'new' area, and the swimming pool. The old farmhouse became four luxurious bedrooms—all fitted out with convenient showers, attractive vanity units and built-in wardrobes. At the opposite end of the house, over the garage, a large L-shaped lounge was built. Joining the 'garage' section to the bedrooms is a totally new area, including a reception hall, stairway, television lounge and office.

Finally, there is the swimming pool, inventive-

Above left. A dining room with a grotto-like atmosphere, featuring unusual ceiling light fixtures. The graceful curve of the window is echoed by the roughly rendered arch. Centre left. The roomy kitchen richly clad in abundant pine. The arch creates an intriguing and eye-catching frame for the room, setting off the modern fittings.
Bottom left. Looking from the lounge to the swimming pool beyond. Simplicity of both colour scheme and furnishings adds to the visual appeal and rustic flavour of the room.

ly built within the old thick walls of the barn. All sorts of features complement the pool—sauna bath, dressing room and promenade. Few do-it-yourself swimming pools can be set in such scenic surroundings.

A major problem—damp—frequently common to old buildings, was then tackled. First, heavy gauge polythene was put under the concrete floor and then run up the walls. This succeeded in overcoming the rising damp. Next, the walls were rendered with waterproof concrete, then treated with a tar based compound, and finally covered with sand.

The finishing touch—a fascinating rendering —gives an old world look to the walls. It's a technique that goes a long way in creating a different look. While the plaster was still wet, a trowel was used to make a rough, irregular surface, reminiscent of stone which has been whitewashed many times. A final coat of plaster was applied, much as if it were paint.

Graceful arches were built during the conversion. One appears between the dining room and downstairs lounge, creating an intriguing grotto-like effect. Another, born of necessity, is found in the bedroom as a special, eye-catching feature. The walls in this room are 6ft. (1.8m) thick with a fireplace so firmly built into the wall, that any attempt to remove it meant re-building a complete wall. Instead, the chimney was used as the foundation to the new and unusual arch.

It's important to be flexible when converting. If you are firmly set on one line of action and then discover it requires too much money or time to execute—as with the treatment of the bedroom fireplace here—explore other avenues of action. Your alternate course could easily turn out to be more exciting than your original plan.

Many features add to the charm of Brundal House. Bow windows with bull's eye glass create a variety in the external wall surface. Warm, rich wood is seen in many places— parquet flooring, pine-clad kitchen and bath-rooms and, of course, the beams. The liberal use of white contrasts well with the heavier look of the wood.

Two colour motifs tend to dominate—cool blues, accented with gold, and warm orange and rust, trimmed with rich aquamarine. The overall feeling is one of casualness and spaciousness. This effect was achieved by keeping furniture to a minimum, lines simple and decor streamlined.

This large and lovely home, set in the rolling countryside, had its beginnings in old buildings, caught in the grips of decay. Today it is a comfortable and attractive home, owing to the energy, hard work and imagination that went into its transformation.

Above right. *The television lounge accented with deep purple and gold. The imposing timber ceiling and parquet floor give a rich and rural tone to this cheerful room.* *Centre right.* *A bedroom in restful blue with brilliant splashes of gold and purple. The bow window makes an attractive feature along with the wooden beams and louvred doors.* *Bottom right.* *The other end of the bedroom tailored for convenience, with a tiled shower, vanity unit and built-in wardrobe. No fussy details clutter up the streamlined look.*

Bold ideas—and effort

Sometimes the charm of an old house can be lost through over-zealous modernization. If, like designer Mary Gilliatt and her professor husband, you are lucky enough to find an 'antique' farmhouse, you may find that it needs 'de-modernization' to rediscover its full appeal. Often money is only half the story—it takes bold ideas and a fair amount of effort to turn a shabby house into an unusual home.

The Gilliatts discovered the farmhouse in an area of Suffolk, England, where they had already decided to live—and immediately decided to buy the house, despite its obvious need for extensive alteration. It was really two cottages, one Tudor and one Victorian, which joined at right angles. Both were in fairly bad condition, with leaking roofs, birds nesting in the attics, and some dry rot. Attempts had been made in the past to modernize the whole house, with unbecoming results.

The problem was to recapture the original character, and to add some personal touches, without making the house impossibly old-fashioned. Being a designer herself, Mrs. Gilliatt already had some ideas on what to do. but she also called in designer Paul William-White and architects John Abbott and Ian Hamilton-

Penney to help make the most of the house's considerable potential.

There were enough rooms to cater for the family and for a reasonable number of guests (and their children); there were some fine old brick floors which needed little upkeep and very little in the way of floor covering; upstairs, there were wide elm floorboards, and exposed oak beams everywhere. The price of the house was reasonable enough to leave money for quite ambitious alterations.

The existing scullery, a poorly-constructed, leaky lean-to was knocked down to make way for a modern kitchen with sliding glass doors giving on to a courtyard. The old kitchen—which was at right angles to the new one—was divided up into a utility room and a partitioned-off washroom and cloakroom.

The designers built a larder in the middle of the new kitchen to act as a room-divider—one side of the room is now used as an eating area—while the preparation and cooking of food takes place at the other side, out of sight. Because the existing floors were in fairly good condition and so attractive, they decided to find matching bricks to continue the expanse of floor out into the courtyard. One type of flooring 'flowing' from one part of a house to another always makes it seem more spacious.

They knocked through the wall between the

sitting and dining rooms, but left the fireplace between them standing as an unusual focal point, which could also effectively block out most of the view from one half of the room into the other, while the whole area could be used for parties.

Upstairs, in the Victorian part of the house, the master bedroom was large enough to allow for a second bathroom to be cut out of it. The Gilliatts had to remove a pretty Victorian fireplace which would have been in the way of one of the new bathroom walls. But throwing it away would have been wasting a valuable asset and the fireplace found a new home in the nursery immediately below.

One of the bedrooms already had a washbasin in it, and this was turned into a vanity unit incorporating a wardrobe. In this way, it could be closed off behind cupboard doors for extra privacy and tidiness.

The staircase was rotting when the Gilliatts moved in, but to their amazement, they found that a whole new staircase—built for looks—would cost less than they had budgeted for a top-quality stair-carpet! One problem here was integrating the new open-riser staircase visually with the heavier-looking exposed oak beams and generally 'solid' look of the interior. Mrs. Gilliatt decide to brighten up the hall by painting the staircase with a clear red polyurethane stain, which would be both durable and cheerful.

To give a clear view right from the hall through the eating area of the kitchen to the hills beyond, an old window, which had originally been bricked up when the old scullery was built, was restored. The 'resurrected' window was extended down to floor level and filled with plate-

Opposite page, left. *An inviting sitting room with an open fire as focal point. The red trestles and Magistretti chairs echo the red motif throughout the house. The beams, unusually, are picked out in white.*

Top, centre picture. *The rustic-looking dining area. The orange walls tone well with the furniture, and the white paintwork and fabric blind add a note of contrast. Crockery on display gives interest.*

Above. *A handy 'tunnel' under the eaves. Notice how the pipes are painted the same colour as the surrounds, as camouflage.* **Below.** *The outside walls have been painted in a good stonepaint, in a warm colour.*

glass shelves to show off a collection of decanters and attractive wine bottles. In this way, it was made to serve the double purpose of affording a view and being a pleasing focal point in its own right.

The structural alterations were limited to the necessary minimum to preserve the essential character of the house. Once the heavy work was over, Mrs. Gilliatt could employ her skill as an interior designer in planning the decor.

The exposed ceiling beams throughout the house have been painted in rich 'earth' colours— a deep red in the kitchen, for example. This gives them a note of distinction which would not have been possible with traditional black beams against a white ceiling. The new kitchen has been given a natural look with whitewashed brick and pine matchboarding on the ceiling.

The living room continues the rich earth colour scheme with nutmeg-brown walls; the hall and landing have been painted a deep mustard, which tones in well with the red open-riser staircase and the dark beams.

The walls in the master bedroom are orange, but a fine Tudor fireplace uncovered by the builders has been left unpainted. Fabric blinds are used throughout the house, some roller blinds but mainly Roman. In the master bedroom they are of green-and-white fabric which matches the bedspread exactly. The ceiling between the beams is papered with a vivid

green and orange print.

Furniture throughout the house is a mixture of antique and very modern. Old houses can often benefit from the clean lines and bright colours of contemporary furniture, and the complete contrast between the intricate surfaces of old furniture and the plain lines of twentieth-century pieces can look stimulating and flattering to most interiors.

When the decoration was finished, red was very much in evidence—not only on the beams but in other striking features throughout the house: for example, there is a desk on red trestles with a matching chair designed by the Italian Magistretti, and the walls of the son's room are painted with a glowing pinky-red. When starting from scratch with a new home, or redecorating an old one completely, a unified colour scheme or a 'motif' of this kind running through several different colour schemes can hold the whole appearance of the house together.

Other striking features include black-lacquered sofas with yellow vinyl cushions, specially designed by Paul William-White, a gold-coloured Afghan rug, and brightly coloured fibreboard furniture.

With a lot of imagination, skill and respect for the farmhouse, the Gilliatts have managed to turn a dilapidated building into a welcoming and attractive home.

A home from two cottages

Converting a derelict cottage can be a discouraging undertaking. It means dealing with problems of dampness, decay and deterioration, and once these have been coped with, consideration must be given to interior design. This early nineteenth century pair of semi-detached cottages were in a state of dilapidation when they were bought, and have now been transformed into a livable and attractive home.

When the Hedderwicks first set foot in these two semi-detached Somerset cottages, they were damp, chilly and unattractive. The wall paper was faded and peeling; the plaster was blistering and flaking; the atmosphere was heavy and dank. Major renovation was badly needed, but the site and price were so ideal that the Hedderwicks decided to go ahead with a conversion.

Rising damp was the most formidable problem; an architect advised the Hedderwicks not to tackle it—the effort and expense would be too great. A damp proof course wasn't feasible in such an old building, so another method, although expensive, was decided upon. It is based on a theory that dampness is assisted by static electricity, and can be prevented if the static is earthed.

To earth this electricity, an unbroken copper strip was inserted throughout the external walls, covered with cement and then attached to 6ft. (2m) copper rods which extend out from the building underground.

Although this method of overcoming dampness was expensive to install in the cottage, it has proved to be very effective and a good long-term investment. A damp house is an expensive liability as dampness can cause deterioration and decay, as well as personal discomfort for the people living in it.

Originally there had been two small workmen's cottages; these were knocked into one. Neglected vegetable patches sprawled over the front garden, making it drab and featureless; the land has now been transformed into a beautiful and imaginative garden.

Curving steps, surrounded by abundant foliage, lead down a steep incline from the road to the front door which was built into what had originally been the back of one of the cottages. On entering, the eye sees several floor levels, low doorways leading into various rooms, and an expanse of clover coloured carpeting. The wooden doors are painted white with wrought-iron hinges and handles.

From the entrance hall, two small steps lead into the sitting room. This had originally been two rooms—a smallish parlour on one side and a decrepit kitchen and scullery on the other. The partition was pulled down, the kitchen complex gutted and the old front door blocked up.

The resulting room, measuring 11ft. (3.3m) by 22ft. (6.7m), is long and rather narrow and initially presented problems in design. Mrs. Hedderwick cleverly coped with this 'narrowness' by creating two areas in the room

—a comfortable sitting area and an area surrounding the fireplace. This division was done by strategically grouping the chairs and couch in one part of the room and by using a large oriental rug in the front of the fire which sets it off and makes it seem like a separate unit.

If you're having difficulty in arranging furniture in a long or narrow room, try to 'open out' the space by making more than one area of interest. This can be done by grouping chairs and tables in one part of the room or by creating a separate visual area through the use of paintings or, as in this case, a fireplace and rug. By having more than one area of focal interest, the eye can be distracted from the shape or narrowness of the room.

Two functional and attractive beams, rescued from a builder's yard, support the bath above. A durable asphalt surface was laid over the old flagstone floor. The room was then enhanced by lowering the tiny windows; the panorama of the garden can now be viewed while sitting. Mrs. Hedderwick was advised to have modern double glazed windows, but she decided to have leaded windows instead, to match up with the windows still in use upstairs. The period look was not impaired by modern styled windows.

The hamstone fireplace is one of the most imposing features of the room. An old and sooty cooking stove was removed and a wrought-iron screen, made by a Devon blacksmith, put in its place. Spanning over the fireplace and creating an impressive façade, is a large clavel-

R. WALTERS

Above. Major renovation was needed to convert a pair of damp, chilly and unattractive semi-detached nineteenth century workmen's cottages into this livable and attractive house in a Somerset garden setting.

Above. The living and dining rooms have been enhanced by enlarging and lowering the tiny windows. Now the panorama of the garden can be viewed while sitting. Lead windows match up with the original upstairs windows.

stone, found by the owners in a stone maker's yard. Three china plates fill in the space between the fireplace and the ceiling.

Moving away from the eyecatching fireplace, there is an attractive grouping—an unusual looking Edwardian corner chair, covered in muted damask fabric, and a dainty inlaid Edwardian table. Other period pieces include a Queen Anne chair and a Georgian table which show how effectively a variety of different period pieces can work together to make a harmonious whole. Too often people think that antique furniture should be kept to a single period. Mixing different types together can be more interesting visually—as long as the proportions, quality and design are right—and less of a strain when buying.

The hand-made couch and chair have proved to be a good investment; they have held up well over the years. The spinning wheel in the corner adds a note of interest—it was a wedding present, which means it's been under the owners' roof now for almost fifty years. The period look is also helped along by the wall fixtures which have an antique finish and the rich-looking beige curtains which are an antique velvet. Every item has been carefully thought out; no one item dominates the room, either in colour or in size, and none of the furnishings suggest a modern look.

The colours in this room—as well as in the rest of the cottage—are soft and delicate shades often found in the surrounding countryside.

When going from the garden outside into the cottage, the eye needn't adjust, the inside and outside are an integrated whole. The floral upholstery on the couch, for instance, has subtle shades of terracotta, blue and green with hues of yellow which are then picked up in the carpet.

The clover carpet, echoing the grass and greenery outside, carries through the passageway—made interesting by its variety of levels—into the dining room. Here the carpet is the same colour, but is a practical hair cord. The original cottages were virtually mirror images of one another and the present dining room and kitchen correspond to the living room on the other side. Lovely French doors leading out to the garden have replaced the former front door.

Some of the old beams can still be seen in this room, where the main motif is brass and wood. A beam spanning over the fireplace houses some eyecatching brass pieces: a chestnut roaster, a cream skimmer and a bed warmer. Also in keeping with the motif are the horse brasses which hang from most of the wooden beams.

A small Welsh dresser doubles up as a useful sideboard—a good idea for a room with limited space. A Georgian dining table, made of oak, is just the right size for this cosy room. Soft shades of ochre and olive green in the curtains contrast effectively with the rich-looking pink velvet of the armchairs.

The dominant colour in the adjoining modern

kitchen and larder is white. A practical breakfast table neatly fits under a leaded window which looks out on the garden. The southern exposure here is ideal, especially on sunny summer mornings.

The subtle and delicate colours found on the ground floors are repeated upstairs in the three bedrooms and bathroom. All the rooms share in common a floral pattern and a magnificent view to the garden. A sloping roof adds an unusual touch to the first floor landing.

Throughout the cottage there is a black and white motif seen in the white painted wooden doors and the wrought-iron handles and hinges. This certainly contributes to the period flavour. It's these little consistent touches in a house which can make the difference between an average looking home and an outstanding one. A modern, up-to-date fixture could completely spoil the period effect.

Before embarking on a home conversion, it's important to decide what look you want—a modern twentieth century look or a period one. Once this initial decision is made, all the changes made or the furnishing bought should be in keeping with the theme you've chosen. Although there is every modern convenience in this cottage, a period flavour remains. Contributing features to this look are leaded windows, low door-frames and period pieces in the furnishing.

It would be impossible to look at this cottage without taking note of the garden; it really is an integral part of it. A mill river runs through the full length of the garden which is filled with a variety of plantings including primulas, irises and mecanopsis. In the seven years that Mr. Hedderwick has been working on it, it has changed from a forgotten workman's vegetable patch into a restful and charming garden.

Calm amid the storm

How to escape from congestion, traffic fumes and foot-wearing concrete pavements is a problem which exercises the minds of many city dwellers. The charm of the real countryside is, for many, outweighed by the drag of commuting—not to mention the non-existence of late-night transport. Hence the growing popularity of the houseboat, which offers something of the countryside's atmosphere without its remoteness.

Candy Coloured Tangerine, a butterscotch painted houseboat on the River Thames at Chelsea, was built by The Chelsea Yacht and Boat Compnay. The steel hull and wooden superstructure comply with their basic design, but the owner had the inside built according to her own specification.

Life on the river is unconventional, and so the fact that the front door of this houseboat is on the upper deck and the bedrooms below is not surprising. However, this arrangement has the advantage of making the living room, which covers the entire upper floor, very light and sunny. It opens onto a fibreglass-covered sundeck which overlooks the river, and is decorated with pot plants and creeper-covered trellises.

The 20ft x 12ft (6 x 4m) living room has an interesting shape from the positioning of the staircase and water tanks. A conventional staircase would have taken up a lot of valuable space, so the owner bought an old iron spiral staircase, had it cut in half, painted white, and fitted in one corner of the living room, leading to the dining room below. Down here an anthracite-burning boiler which heats both the houseboat and the water counterbalances the weight of the staircase.

On the lower deck there are two bedrooms, dining room, kitchen and bathroom. The main bedroom is below the sundeck, with windows all round giving panoramic views of the river. The delicate turquoise paint is enhanced by the light reflecting off the water outside. Fitted wardrobes were built in both here and in the spare bedroom, which is tucked in next to it, behind the dining room.

Top left. The large windows at the back of the houseboat lighten the first floor living room and give a broad view over the river. The spiral staircase leads to the lower deck.
Left. Feminine touches have not been confined to the inside of the houseboat; plants in tubs and painted flowers on the superstructure liven up the sundeck.

BILL MACLAUGHLIN

Above left. A compact dining area has been provided by building banquette seating in one corner of the lower deck. The boiler heats both the water and the houseboat.
Above right. Beyond the wrought iron spiral staircase, the bright red kitchen is enclosed by a hanging shelf which holds cookery books and casseroles.
Right. The bathroom, tucked in beside the kitchen, has been given the atmosphere of the ocean bed by swirling green and pink marbled paper covering the walls and doors.

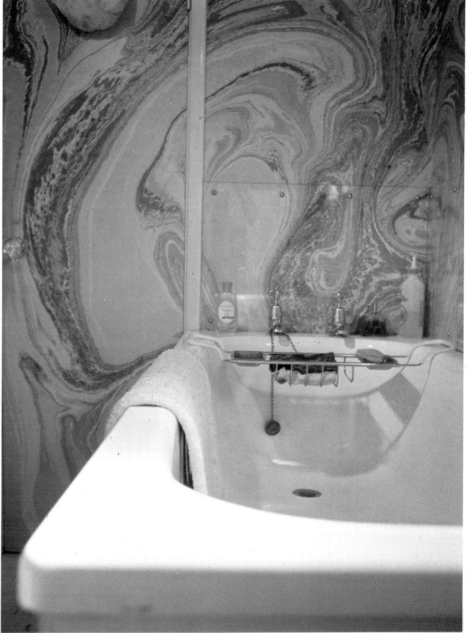

As the plumbing on a boat should really all be at one end, the kitchen and bathroom are next to each other, below the water tanks. A green swirling marbled wallpaper makes the compact bathroom look as though it is on the ocean bed—the only wild diversion from conventional decor the owner allowed herself.

The kitchen is separated from the dining area by a hanging shelf suspended on chains from the ceiling. This holds cookery books and casseroles, and swings gently with the rocking of the boat. Bunk seats fitted in one corner of the dining room are a practical and space-saving idea. These are supplemented by ladder-back rush-seated chairs standing at the pine dining table. The whole dining and kitchen area is painted bright red, which glows warmly at night, the pure white spiral staircase in the corner standing out like a beacon.

Houseboats are clean, civilized dwellings, but all the same, deep pile carpets would be out of place on the river. Instead the floor is covered thoughout in rush matting, which provides no opposition to all the gay colours used in the paint and upholstery.

Candy Coloured Tangerine is owned by a young woman, and its decorations are undeniably feminine, proving that floating homes do not have to have a nautical look. Throughout, small items like shells, cameos and enamel boxes give away the hobbies and interests of its owner. There are always fresh flowers in the living room, complementing the purple, turquoise and yellow of the furnishings, backed up by pretty patchwork cushions.

GRAZIA NERI/PHOTO NINO LO DUCA

Simply brilliant

Strong colours and modern furniture can transform an ordinary flat into a stunning apartment, without necessarily involving major structural alterations.

Architect Piero Castellini was called in by the owner of an art gallery to convert her Milan flat, where she lived with her two young daughters. The proportions of the flat were good, with interesting vaulted rooms off the main living area. The owner specifically asked for these to

be retained, and highlighted if possible with a white finish. As the flat, built in 1950, was in reasonably good repair, with only certain plaster work needing to be made good, the architect's job was primarily a decorative one. However, because it was all on one level, part of the floor in the living area was raised to make the contours more interesting. A terrace was constructed outside to take advantage of the view.

The first striking feature is the small entrance hall, painted bright tangerine, a colour which

dominates the entire flat, giving it a sunny appearance. The large living room is divided into three sections; a square conversation area, with a dining room through an arch at one end, and a study area at the other, both with coved ceilings. These two vaulted rooms are emphasized by white gloss paint, with tangerine appearing on the end walls.

Two large sofas at right angles to each other frame part of the conversation area, with a carpeted dais covered with cushions on the third side. The cream upholstery and soft brown carpet are a perfect background for the strong

Top. *The square conversation area in the living room is framed by two large sofas. The dining area is in the alcove beyond, with sheer white curtains at the windows.*

Above left. *Dark blue gloss paint and a matching carpet give the small television room a dramatic appearance. White cupboard units hold drinks, radio and television.*

Above right. *Sage green predominates in the girls' bedroom which is decorated in a more conventional manner. Fitted shelves built along one wall enclose a bed.*

colours used and the hard, bright finishes of the accessories. Tables, lamps and ornaments are almost all simple and modern, mostly made of glass, acrylic or steel. In contrast, an antique desk sits happily in the study area, and in other rooms modern and antique furniture have been effectively combined.

Cushions in black, red, orange and yellow scattered over the sofas in the living room and study add bright splashes of colour to these areas. Sheer panels of white curtaining hung on rails at all the picture windows, let in a soft light which enhances the furnishings.

The girls' bedroom has a less austere appearance, with practical features such as a wall completely covered with shelves, pinboard panels, and a large wardrobe. A steel and glass trestle table acts as a desk, and the curtains are in sage green.

An unusual but very effective colour scheme was chosen for the small television room. The walls are finished in dark blue gloss paint which matches the carpet, and all the paintwork is picked out in white. A sage green sofa is scattered with dark blue and white cushions to complete the scheme. Two specially made white

lacquered cupboards were designed for this room. One holds glasses, bottles and a television set; the other is fitted with a radio, record player and refrigerator. Modern steel and glass furniture adds a crisp bright appearance to this room.

French windows lead out from here on to a small terrace, with its view over the rooftops of Milan. Covered with rampant plants, it has an atmosphere of freshness and tranquillity that is rare in the centre of a large city. Enamelled steel chairs covered in green and white printed fabric blend in well with the surroundings.

Above left. The spacious living room is given a homely atmosphere by the choice of an open fireplace.
Above. Attractive and sturdy design is maintained with all the house's furniture—both old and new.

A terrace house refashioned

Many people in Britain buy small Victorian terraced houses because they are relatively cheap and offer so much scope for improvement. They are generally solidly built and will stand up to a good deal of structural alteration—you can even gut them completely and refashion the interior to suit your needs.

This house in Hammersmith, London, looks deceptively tiny from the outside. Only a new bow window and small porch give any indication that any changes have taken place, but the house inside has been completely reshaped.

If you have decided to make structural changes to your home and have the necessary money it is a good idea to be bold with your plans. Half measures will often result in a house where the new work clashes with the old structure and the overall effect is awkward and 'bitty'.

In this house only the original stairs remain—the interior has been completely rebuilt. Downstairs a combined parlour and kitchen and the front sitting room were changed from two cramped rooms into one larger room, which can still be divided up by handsome louvred doors. New wide french windows give on to a neatly-kept garden. Here, an old chimney is featured as an unusual plant container, from which luxuriant ivy grows up to camouflage the cement-rendered garden wall. Even the commonest garden plant can be made to look exotic if its container is out of the ordinary, and it is well worth spending some time and thought on ways of displaying your plants to advantage.

The french windows in the kitchen half of the through room and the new bow window in the other half provides the interior with plenty of light. The bow window is vacuum double-glazed to keep heat in and noise out. The new porch was built out into the front garden to save space in the original tiny entrance hall.

The whole house has been treated to new floors and ceilings, and downstairs the partition walls—which were originally lath-and-plaster—have been rebuilt in sturdier brick. A steel girder which had to be incorporated in the new ceiling downstairs has been used to make one half lower. The space above now conceals cupboard space.

This is an excellent example of putting every inch of space to good use. Cupboards don't always have to be in conventional places as long as their contents don't spill out on to your head and you can get at them without slipping a disc. The average house wastes a fair amount of space simply by bad organization.

The rich glow of natural wood is much in evidence downstairs—the ceiling and floors are in matching boards, and the floors are sanded and sealed for extra shine.

The protruding chimney breast has been rebuilt to half its original size, following the path of the flue, to scale in with the room.

LEO FERRANTE

Previously it dominated the room and all the furniture in it. The whole of the chimney wall is painted off-white, and the opposite wall is a deep matt green, hung with Victorian racing prints in formal groups.

There are blinds in a vivid green and blue fabric over the french windows and green covers on the comfortable easy chairs and settee. The colour motif is repeated in a large green and blue shaggy rug which contrasts elegantly with the polished board floor.

The kitchen section of the through room has green and blue Italian tiles on both the floor and the walls for extra effect.

Any interior benefits from a strong line in colour, and a consistent colour scheme which might be carried from room to room throughout a whole house. Colours from the same part of the spectrum make excellent partners—especially if you are doubtful about your ability to mix opposites sucessfully. Here blue and green, two close colours, make a recurring theme throughout the downstairs room, and blue is carried on into the upstairs decor. Red and pink; purple and indigo; and yellow and orange would all harmonize perfectly in similar schemes.

The downstairs bathroom has a 'sauna' look, with timber cladding on the ceiling and halfway

Above left. The rich wood panelling seen here is used to good effect throughout the house. Above right. The house looks deceptively small from the outside, yet the white paintwork and bow window achieve a look of elegance.

down the walls. The rest of the walls and the floor are tiled in fawn and grey patterned Italian tiles.

Upstairs the emphasis is on shades of blue. The master bathroom is completely decorated in soft blue—even the sanitary fittings match the tone exactly—and there is a whole wall of mirrors to make the room look twice the size. The small window is set off by Italian carved shutters painted white.

The master bedroom has floor-to-ceiling cupboards along one whole wall—solving storage problems in a room with limited space. They are painted an electric blue and have a brass knob to highlight each cupboard door. There is a blue bedside chest of drawers fitted with attractive blue and white patterned china knobs, and the blue is re-emphasized in the fabric of a lampshade and on the window wall (where the radiator is camouflaged by being painted the exact shade as the wall behind). To

save space, there is a sliding door between the bedroom and bathroom,

The focal point of the bedroom is a huge white bed with a brass bedstead piled high with giant Indian-style cushions made by the owner's wife. The floor is sanded and sealed.

All the furniture in this house is solid, unpainted and dating from the Edwardian era, and most of it was picked up from inexpensive furniture markets. Plain pieces—perhaps relieved by brass ring-pull handles—look good with almost any decor, and prove to be extremely serviceable.

Originally the house was 'two-up, two down' —now there is the large through room and bathroom downstairs, and upstairs the space has been re-divided into two bedrooms and another bathroom.

There are many houses where space is badly organized. Intelligent planning and alteration could make them considerably easier to live in. Sometimes householders consider adding on instead of simply reorganizing the space they have, often an easier and much less expensive operation. This house proves it. It has been opened up by skilful re-shaping and is both more spacious and more convenient to manage as a result.

MICHAEL BOYS

The low-down on a nursery

As babies and small children view life from a lower level than adults, nurseries should be designed with the focal points lower than usual, to provide visual stimulation at a baby's eye level.

Michael Boys' work in decoration photography, and his wife Pam's experience as a photographic stylist, give them a head start when faced with a design problem. The Victorian house they bought in Kensington, London, was in an unbelievably bad condition, complete with black beetles and peeling paint.

It was on a corner site, so the rooms at the back were irregular shapes.

The old workroom chosen for the nursery was no exception, with a mass of alcoves and awkward angles, and the high ceiling made it a very unfriendly room for small children. The designers' aim was to incorporate cupboards and other facilities into a practical design without adding to the irregularity of shapes already there.

The first job was to reduce the height of the room. At the window end the ceiling was left its original height, then sloped down to the top of

This page, top and left. This shabby room has been transformed into a bright nursery. Above. Cupboard unit with shelves at the end; the stable door can be seen at right. Opposite page, above. Play box holds the baby's toys, her clothes hang above a nappy changing flap, and the blackboard is within reach. Below. Play bench under the window, with a sink in the corner beyond the cot.

the door frame and levelled off. This gives a feeling of intimacy to one end of the room. This false ceiling houses two concealed spotlights, which supplement the central pendant. A sheet of glass covering each circular hole can easily be slid to one side to change the bulbs.

The problem of giving the room a more conventional shape and making a success of the decoration was solved by another problem—the need for storage space. Cupboards were built in the top half of an alcove at the side of a cupboard jutting in from the next room. The space below was left for a radiator, which provides warmth for the baby's clothes on the slatted shelves above. At one end, below the hanging space, a flap table opens down on hinges to provide a surface for changing nappies. The soft sponge cushion has a loose cover made of towelling. Pinboard was fixed on the top part of the back of the protruding cupboard, with a blackboard at floor level. Bookshelves were fitted at the end of this unit.

The alcove at one side of the chimney breast was filled in, and the ugly mantelpiece ripped out. The remaining fireplace recess houses a 'play box'—a large open-topped box with round holes in each side—which serves as a toy box and climbing frame. Castors underneath enable it to be pushed around easily, and it is weighted at the bottom to prevent it from toppling over.

A play bench was built along the wall under the window, and in the remaining alcove next to the chimney breast. This bench was designed so that a toddler can hold on to it while walking along, and later clamber on to it and look out of the window. An abacus was adapted to fit underneath, where a child can sit on the floor and play with it.

In a corner next to this bench a round flat-bottomed stainless steel wash basin was fitted, with animal motif tiles around and a cupboard underneath. This shape is most practical for 'dunking' older babies, as they can sit on the bottom without slipping. Later they can stand on the bench and wash themselves. ·

The decorations were designed to give visual emphasis at the eye level of a small child. White laminate 3ft 6in. (1.07m) high was fixed all round the walls, providing a child-proof surface at a uniform height to link the cupboards, basin unit and window at the same level. A decorative wood trim, covered in the curtain fabric, provides a focal point for a baby and makes the whole scheme hang together. A mobile hanging low from the central light gives an extra diversion for a small child.

Since the nursery was to be decorated to a budget, bright yellow emulsion paint was used for the irregular walls above the handrail, and white on the ceiling. The floor is covered in grey vinyl sheeting scattered with ochre-coloured washable shaggy rugs. The original sash window was left (the bottom half is never opened) and curtained in bright cotton. The Tiffany lampshade is covered in matching fabric.

The original panelled door was cut in half horizontally to form a stable door. Beading along the join gives draught and sound protection. Normally the bottom half is closed for safety, as the room leads straight on to the stairs. The open top half prevents the baby from feeling shut in, and enables the parents to hear her if she cries. At night the top is left open and the landing light left on for comfort.

The baby's cot is kept against the door wall, and her playpen is stored in front of the radiator to act as a guard. For safety the light cord hangs high out of a child's reach, and the power points are 'hidden' in the back of a cupboard.

A stable/barn conversion

Conversions don't always arise from old houses. In this case, an eighteenth century barn and stables were totally transformed into an unusual and modern home. Major renovation included re-building the barn roof and replacing the stable walls. More impressive changes, however, took place in the reshaping of the interior.

When research psychologist Tim Jordan and his wife began house hunting in the Oxford vicinity, they found the prices staggering. The money they had to spend simply couldn't buy the kind of house they had in mind. Then an eighteenth century Cotswold farm caught their eye. It wasn't in a livable state, but the price was within the Jordan's means. They decided to buy, and then embarked on a total and remarkable conversion.

Dr. Jordan decided on a scheme of attack and a new layout, and then had an architect draw up the plans. These were submitted to the local authorities who gave planning permission as well as a building grant. It took ten months to complete the conversion, and Dr. Jordan spent a great deal of that time working side-by-side with the builders.

The farm was built in a T-shape, the barn being the central section, with matching stables stretching out on either side to make the cross-bar. The high barn became the main living area with bedrooms and a bathroom above. The stables remained on one level with the kitchen/dining area and spare bedroom on one side and the study, utility and work rooms on the other.

The thatched roof over the stables was in good condition. The Stonesfield slate roof on the barn, however, was poor and in need of repair. In re-doing it, the style of the building was kept. Concrete tiles were used which blend well with the Cotswold stone. Felt, with a glass-fibre backing, was put between the tiles and the fibre board on the inside for extra insulation.

The street side of the house was left in stone; the original character remains, which is one of the most attractive features of the house. The walls of the stables facing the back garden, however, were changed when a necessary damp proof course was installed.

It was a laborious task. It meant supporting the thatched roof while the foundation was broken and the damp course installed. Further details and instructions on damp proofing can be found in most home DIY manuals. The walls were then built with Thermolite blocks and covered with rich cedar boarding, which adds a warm and effective contrast to the stone.

When converting an old building, it's important to select materials which will harmonize well with the original materials. In this case, the cedar walls and concrete roofing tile do not clash with the weighty stone and attractive thatched roof. The old and the new blend well in colour and in texture.

Once the damp course was installed and the

Above. *Street view of a home which hasn't lost its distinctive character through conversion. The stables on either side of the barn have their original thatched roofs. The windows in the barn are a new addition.*

Below. *Stairs leading to a gallery and bedrooms above contrast with a stark white wall. High barn doors, covered in rich pine, and an original and imposing door, add to the countrified atmosphere of the room.*

barn roof re-made, work began on the inside. The high barn ceiling lent itself to building a floor above. Dr. Jordan didn't want to lose the barn effect so he struck on a successful compromise. Stairs were built against one wall leading up to a gallery which lead, at one end, to the master bedroom and, at the other end, to a bathroom and spare bedroom.

An open well of space reaching from the floor to the eye-catching angles and beams of the ceiling is most impressive. At the same time the low pine ceiling supporting the gallery and main bedroom reduces the amount of space, giving a more intimate and cozy feeling which centres around the fireplace.

A compromise is often the best solution to problems which might arise in interior design. If you're re-doing a large, high room, consider the possibility of creating different levels for living, thereby changing the concept of space from one part of the room to another. A gallery or platform bed, for instance, can add interest and variety to a room, as well as providing further space for living.

The 'staircase' wall was constructed from Thermolite blocks and then painted white. The Jordans decided not to plaster the wall; they thought the rough surface texture was in keeping with the rural flavour of the rest of the house. Money was saved by not plastering, and the desired appearance was achieved.

The inside stone walls required a great deal of attention. They had originally been whitewashed, and the painstaking task of stripping this had to be done. The owners thought the natural stone would enhance the room. It was a tedious job which required patience and tenacity. Friends came around to help with the job. Once the stripping was complete, all the crevices had to be re-pointed. This laborious wall 'face-lift' paid off in big dividends. The irregular pattern of the stones and their natural hue are the main tone setters of the room.

Cotswold stone was also used in the construction of the fireplace, which seems to emerge from the wall itself as an appropriate focal centre to the room. It was designed by Dr. Jordan. He first set up a model fireplace and tried placing it in different parts of the room to see where it would be most effective.

The corner was found to be the best location visually and practically—the angle of the fireplace throws out the heat better than if it had been flush to the wall. An interesting arrangement is created with the varying size of the natural stone used. After scouting around for buildings being demolished, the Jordans found one, where they purchased the handsome elm beam spanning the grate. The core of the fireplace is brick.

The stones used in building the fireplace came from the openings in the walls made for the windows. This is a good example of how materials can be successfully re-used. The heavy wooden door leading into the barn was also salvaged from another part of the building, and now makes an imposing entrance. In the study a leaded window, saved from the stable, now creates an eye-catching detail as a window in one of the inner walls of the hall. 'Re-cycling' materials can be effective and money-saving.

J. P. BROAD/R. MACAVOY

From the fireplace mantle there are a series of stone steps, providing shelf and storage space, which lead down to the floor-level bookshelf. The small openings in the wall above add an unusual note, especially when the sun shines through the yellow and blue perspex glass inside. These openings were built to allow rods to be inserted into the barn to check the temperature to avoid spontaneous combustion of the stored hay. Little touches like these add an aura of authenticity.

The wide windows and sliding glass doors face the south, which means the room is flooded with light on sunny days. Beyond these is a quiet and private garden. Only a few windows in the house have a northern exposure. All the rest take advantage of the southern aspect.

The furniture in this room is unusual in that jumbo-sized cushions replace the more conventional couch, chair and coffee table combination. The Jordans decided on this furniture scheme partly for aesthetic reasons and partly for practical purposes. They had lived abroad for six years before moving to Oxfordshire and hadn't accumulated large pieces of furniture.

Floor cushions can create a luxurious and comfortable atmosphere in a room. Too often people feel tied to an unimaginative couch/chair

Above. *The sanctuary of an inner garden which faces a more modern looking timber and stone side of the barn. Glass doors and windows maximize on the sunlight which floods into the rooms from the south.*

gathering. Especially if you're starting up in a new home without much money or are undecided or uncertain about what your style of furniture will be, cushions can be an inexpensive way to 'furnish' a room as an interim measure. It also means that you can do a lot more experimenting with colours and textures.

The handsome trunk by the door was bought in a California junk shop and used for shipping items back to England. The ugly oil cloth covering it was removed, and then the surface varnished. It serves as both a functional and decorative piece.

The high, imposing barn doors were covered with rich pine. A set of small windows run along the top to allow for more light. Like the small 'rod' windows, these doors are integral to the barn motif. They could also be helpful for moving if the Jordans ever decide to buy large pieces of furniture.

The spotlights in this room help to highlight the texture and interplay of shadows on the

stone wall. In one of the hallways, fluorescent lights, partially covered with a strip of wood, throw out an indirect light which also heightens the viewers awareness of the rough wall texture.

Moving through the heavy wooden door of the barn, the long 'stable' passageway leads to the kitchen/dining area. A clever room divider was used here. A large unit of storage cabinets —blue laminate on one side and pine clad on the other—were placed in the centre of the room. A central section was cut out, and provides counter space as well as a serving hatch. The flow of space continues, but there is a distinct feeling of two separate areas.

The dining table—an old refectory table— overlooks the garden. On one wall there is an iron hay rack which curves generously out from the wall. It now holds a multitude of brightly coloured paper flowers. The kitchen is fully equipped with modern conveniences. Flagstones were left in the area around the sink to eliminate spills and stains on the carpeting.

An outstanding feature in this home is its variety. Each room has a different shape and feel about it. The layout, also, is unpredictable, largely due to the fact that this attractive home emerged from a barn and stables once used for storing hay and housing animals.

TUBBY

An artisan's cottage

You can't always judge a home by its exterior. From the outside it may look small and uninteresting but it is the interior that reveals the character of a home. This point was proved by actors James and Carol Lawrenson when they converted this small Victorian artisans cottage which was built in 1873, on a council estate in South London. Today it has been transformed into a charming home, equipped with modern conveniences while still retaining a period flavour.

In the 1870's when the population of London was expanding, Lord Shaftesbury designed and built a mile-square estate south of the Thames River in Battersea. Built on pastoral land, it was planned to accommodate 'worthy workers'.

The estate is characterized by row after row of houses. They look the same at first glance but one feature which distinguishes the individual houses is the differently shaped door arches, designed according to the trade of the original inhabitants. The Lawrenson's home is the same as any other in the street until you enter the front door—and discover an interior that is both modern and Victorian in appearance.

The original entrance passage, parlour and dining area were converted into one large room. One of the original fireplaces was left and it now houses a late nineteenth century iron stove—rescued from a house that was being demolished in Notting Hill Gate. White tiles with a delicate blue pattern line the fireplace, contrasting in both colour and texture with the heavy, dark stove.

A second fireplace was successfully converted by building in a useful and attractive pine cupboard—a good technique for taking full advantage of a superfluous fireplace by gaining

storage area without any cost to space in the room. This is just one thing you can do with fireplaces you no longer need. There are many other unusual ideas for utilizing an unused fireplace such as installing a hi-fi unit.

Shelves for storing china were then built into the recess made by the 'cupboard' fireplace. The wooden table nearby serves as both a dining table and a desk; its location under a window makes it an ideal place for working during the day.

A Victorian paraffin lamp—made in France and purchased in Cornwall—adds character to the setting and its unusual blue colouring ties in with the luxurious velvet covering on the rocking chair.

In the kitchen, attention is immediately focused on rows of red brick which sweep up from the stove to the ceiling. The bricks are a superb camouflage for the unwanted gas stove which was originally there, and they provide an effective backing for the copper pots and pans which hang in front.

Perhaps the most eye-catching item in the room is the original beams. They are arranged in an irregular pattern, close to each other. The effect is unique and one that probably couldn't be reproduced with modern beams. Always try to maximize on features already present in the home, like the beams here, when you embark on a conversion.

A rather clever idea—inspired by the Lawrenson's—was to take an old cupboard and divide it horizontally into three parts. The bottom section serves as a cupboard, the middle section as an area for the refrigerator—conveniently located at waist level—and the top section is tailored to hold cookery books.

The Lawrenson's spent quite some time looking for a refrigerator which hinged on the

Above left. A kitchen given character through eye-catching beams, an array of copper pans on brick and a rounded antique mirror.
Above. A living room with a Victorian flavour. The fireplace became a focal centre using delicate tiles and a heavy, dark stove.

left-hand side—most hinge on the right. It may seem a small point but if you spend a lot of time cooking efficiency is an important factor. If the refrigerator door had been hinged on the right, it would have meant extra steps and a longer reach when taking items out. Attention to details like this make the difference between an average house and a comfortable and convenient home.

During the planning stages of the conversion, the Lawrenson's sketched out their proposals. As the conversion progressed from day to day and as they began to get the feel of living in the cottage their plans altered, expanded or were abandoned altogether. An advantage to living in a house during the conversion is that you can alter your plans as the new home begins to take shape.

A consistent theme running throughout the cottage is the use of pine and brass. The pine louvred door to the bathroom opens on to one of the richest looking rooms in the house. Pine has been used here wherever possible—on the ceiling, walls, sides of the bath and lavatory and for the cupboard. The curtain railing and door knobs are brass—a small touch which adds a great deal of visual enjoyment.

A low window at the end of the room frames the garden outside. It also created a superb focal point as you enter the house, carrying the eye from the front door, through the differently shaped rooms to the vivid colours of the garden. A second and higher window helps to give a feeling of openness, as well as providing a good spot to display healthy plants.

A large mirror makes the small room look much larger—a technique which can work wonders in any room suffering from lack of space. Tiles above the bath house the central heating radiator—a clever place to put it since here it doesn't distract from the wood panelling. The only touch of colour in the room comes from cheerful stripes in the bathmat.

Throughout the ground floor, easy-to-clean cork floor tiles, with a polyurethane finish, have been used. The Lawrenson's had a special reason for doing this. They knew that coal and dustbins would be dragged back and forth between their back and front door on a fairly regular basis—treatment that most carpets couldn't withstand. The durable cork tiles were the answer. They tie in well with the pine and, if a touch of colour or variety is needed, a bright rug can be used.

The only carpeting in the cottage is a deep shade of brown leading up the stairs into the master bedroom, also carpeted, in a light beige. The motif in this room is Victorian. The bed dominates the room with its delicately curved iron bedstead, topped with brass knobs. The lace bedspread, oyster coloured curtains and carpet give a wonderfully light feeling to the room.

In order to fit the four wardrobes into this room, the door frame had to be moved over six inches. The wardrobes now span the full width of the room, giving lots of much needed storage space. Other eye-catching features are Victorian lights over the bed and an ornate table mirror—touches that can give special character to a room.

In removing the old wallpaper, the plaster in the master bedroom was found to be in very bad shape. Rather than undertaking a major replastering job, the walls were coverd with extra thick anaglypta paper, which sufficiently camouflaged the rough plaster. The anaglypta paper was then spruced up with glossy paint.

A number of noteworthy accomplishments—both functional and decorative—were achieved in this conversion. Storage space was developed to maximum capacity as seen in the 'fireplace' cupboard, the three-tiered kitchen cupboard and the long bedroom wardrobe. The Victorian theme was maintained by a careful selection of furniture and decorations; and similar materials were used throughout—like wood and brass—which gives a sense of continuity.

Above right. The other half of the living room: Here the fireplace was converted into a china cupboard lined in rich pine. The old 'lamp' table comes from a dentist's office.
Centre right. The tiny bathroom, given a luxurious look through using warm pine wherever possible. A large mirror over the sink adds a further dimension to the room.
Bottom right. A bedroom conceived in whites and creams. The Victorian look comes from touches like the delicate lace bedspread, adjustable wall lamps and an ornate mirror.
Far right. The house exterior, dating back to 1873. Built by Lord Shaftesbury as part of a council estate, the people living there now still enjoy the benefits of community living.

TUBBY

An adventure in colour

Above. *A living room with a modern look—the key is the geometric pattern on the couches and abstract shapes in the painting.*

Colour—the key to success in this modern home—is used boldly and imaginatively. The often seen whites and the neutral colours of natural surfaces have been eliminated. The cold and clinical impression, frequently associated with the 'modern' look, has been done away with because of the exciting and original colour treatment in this English country home.

Maroon is the dominant colour of the house and whether used all over, as in the dining room, or lightened to a colour wash of shocking pink, as in the main bedroom, it gives a feeling of warmth and friendliness.

Interior designer Christopher Galloway was given complete freedom in choosing his scheme. His brief was to design the most up-to-date, exciting house imaginable, and this is exactly what he has done. It is worth noting that he has used colours with effect, turning what could easily have been a plain modern home into a striking and cosy place that comes alive with colour.

The house is mainly on one level and built in a T-shape, surrounded by an attractive courtyard and garden. All the bedrooms, apart from the main suite and the spare room, are on the ground floor. The feeling of space has been

preserved through the use of glass and the closeness of the garden.

Where white is used on walls and ceilings, the finish is white sand cement rendering—a good idea because it does not need a fresh coat of paint every year. The surface should stay bright for some years and will only require washing. The colours are bold primary ones—pastel shades are not seen anywhere.

Lighting is totally up-to-date, with downlighters, spotlights and kinetic lights for effect showing discriminating use of some of the many forms of lighting available today. Dimmers have been used to give added adaptability to the lighting schemes. There are no standard lamps in the house and only one table light, on the study desk.

The totally modern feeling starts at the front door which is made of stainless steel. All the hall doors are faced in stainless steel with matching architraves, and white sand cement rendered walls and ceiling. The colour comes from a collection of bold avant-garde prints in stainless steel frames.

Entering into the sitting room, there is a feeling of openness and spaciousness. The huge windows link the interior to the garden outside. A generously cushioned seating pit in the centre of the room is closely carpeted with a white shaggy rug. The jumbo cushions are covered in linen with a geometric pattern of maroon, black and white.

At the far end of the seating pit is a rectangle of stainless steel, set into the floor. This is the lid to the hi-fi system, cleverly concealed underneath it. The system is piped throughout the house. The idea of building the hi-fi literally into the floor is a good one, because the records are easy to change from the nearby seats and the

CLIVE CORLESS

Below. *The original and bold colour treatment in the garden room leaves a decisive and unforgettable impression. A mini-kitchen and fitted cupboards are neatly concealed behind the louvred doors.*

equipment does not clutter the room with extra furniture.

The outside perimeter of the room is covered with brindle-coloured quarry tiles. At the end of the room, in two arched recesses, are large fitted mahogany bookshelves with cupboards below. The arch on the left side is a concealed door. The whole unit can be swung open easily and it leads into the exciting garden room. The reason for a concealed door—besides being a good topic for conversation!—is that it makes the garden room into a private, quiet place. It also means the room can be effectively shut off in cold weather. The huge door is built on the same principle as a bank safe door. Being heavy, it is supported on three stainless steel strap hinges. The leading edge of the door is on a roller which runs on a stainless steel track.

The garden room is a kaleidoscope of colour with cheerful zig-zag stripes painted along two walls. The louvred doors conceal fitted cupboards on one side and a Beekay mini-kitchen on the other. The kitchen is equipped with a small sink, fridge and boiling ring, making an ideal place for serving drinks, brewing coffee or heating snacks. One remaining wall has glass windows, and the other is covered with mirrors. At night, kinetic lights reflect off the white ceiling.

In contrast to the striking appearance of the garden room, is the open plan kitchen-cum-dayroom. The large stainless steel bar, echoed by the roomy bottle rack above, divides the cooking area from the eating and sitting area. A number of useful items have been built into the stainless steel counter top—two bowls for washing up, a circular pastry slab of marble, and an electric cooking hob. The raised oven and fridge have been fitted into a storage wall filled

with cupboards and drawers, finished with a red laminated surface.

This kitchen unit is a superb example of the benefits of a well-planned layout. Although it is contained in a small space, the kitchen is efficient, easy to work in, and visually appealing. It is wise not to let a kitchen 'evolve' in a haphazard fashion—a great deal of thought should be given to the arrangement of storage units and appliances, ventilation, and plumbing as this area in particular should be above all, well planned and pleasant to work in.

Above. The kitchen-cum-dayroom. The vinyl floor and stainless steel surfaces make it a good room for children's play.

CLIVE CORLESS

Below. A dining room with a grotto-like effect. The perspex chairs and glass-topped table add to the sense of spaciousness. The bold pattern of the carpet contrasts smartly with the solid maroon walls.

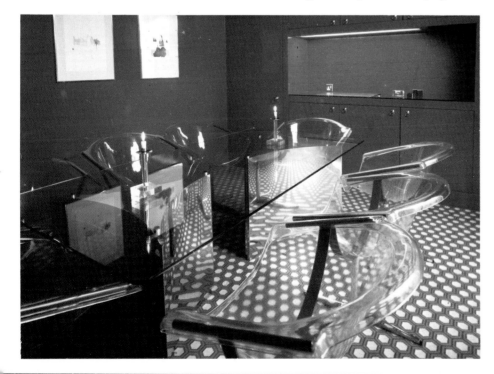

The step down to the main part of the room is effectively set off by the touch of red laminated skirting. The centre of the room is used for family meals and as a play area for the children. The Provençal pattern floor is made of vinyl which is a time-saver when it comes to house keeping. In rooms where eating or children's play is going on, a vinyl floor is a boon to any housewife.

The dining room is yet another splash of colour with walls painted in maroon gloss. Instead of curtains, there are floor-to-ceiling shutters, also painted in maroon gloss, giving the room an almost grotto-like effect. Although the room is not a particularly large one, the choice of furniture gives a sense of spaciousness. The glass-topped table is on a stainless steel base. The transparent perspex chairs are visually unusual and also very practical because of their washable surfaces. The red-fronted cupboards are useful for serving and have the added attraction of inset stainless steel hot plates for keeping food warm.

If a house needs cheering up or you want to get a new look without spending a great deal of money, think carefully about changing the colour scheme. The widespread use of maroon with the contrasting greens, yellows and oranges in this house work together to produce a striking and individual effect.

Dutch treat

Bold, bright colours aren't an essential ingredient for a warm and welcoming home. Simple colours—applied with imagination and intelligence—can create a dynamic effect. This one-room house in Holland does just that. The gracious and elegant appearance emerges from the simple use of black and white.

Having only one room to work with can be difficult, especially if eating, sleeping and entertaining areas must be included. It means a great deal of advance planning and an effective colour scheme to unify the room.

On entering this Dutch house, there is a feeling of stark and striking beauty coupled with luxury and style. The different structural levels and shapes give variety—the eye constantly moves from one plane to the next. There is no one focal point, but a well-integrated and well-balanced total effect.

There is no place for unnecessary pieces. Every item must be functional and yet in keeping with the overall design. The first consideration is where to begin. In this house, the central island unit became a focal point. It is functional because it houses the open fire, the central heating boiler and the cooker—these being the

only sources of heating for the room. The hearth effectively brings together the living area.

The sitting well centres around the black carpet—a perfect colour for a carpet when you don't have too much time for housekeeping. A surprising number of people can sit and relax on the black and white sofas. The cushions add an air of casual comfort. Attention to detail such as throw cushions—their colour, size and texture—make a big difference to the atmosphere of a room. It is a touch that can be done inexpensively, but can go a long way to enchancing a living area.

The flat surfaces, cleverly arranged at different levels, and the centrally-placed low table, are laid on a plywood covered wood frame that has a rough plastered finish. Surface space is essential in a sitting area and you can create an original look by experimenting with various table types and heights. It is too easy to buy matching side tables where contrasting tables could be much more visually appealing. A low table at one end of the sofa, perhaps, with a cocktail cabinet at the other—you still have the same amount of surface space, but you've gained new storage area and leave behind the more old-fashioned 'balanced' look.

A consideration to keep in mind, if mixing

Above left. *Bird's eye view of a streamlined kitchen. Rough rendering adds a delightful Mediterranean touch.*
Above. *A living area in striking black and white. The large oblong slabs, used as*

unmatching furniture, is that at least one aspect in the design has to link the items together. Colour can do this, as in this home. Shape is another method; a technique also used here. Note how all the furniture is cubic—the few

inspired and logical way. Suspended in the whiteness of the low white stone walls, white tile floor and white central unit, are two large worktops. The oblong slabs of black create a dramatic contrast and save the room from a clinical look. The tables have many uses—drawing, typing, writing, sewing and hobbies. The thick worktops are made from black stained wood, covered with black laminate. The built-in drawers are white. The rough plastered pedestals supporting the wooden slabs are found again in the kitchen area.

The table tops could have been left as natural wood but the owner didn't want to break up the black and white motif by introducing a new colour tone. Every last detail has been thought about in terms of colour, from desk lamps to ashtrays. In a small room, it's a good idea not to use too many colours (although a variety in tone can be exquisite)—there simply isn't enough space. The flowers and table fruit are the only items which contrast with the black and white motif.

Tucked away in two corners of the room are relaxing-cum-sleeping areas, surrounded by low white walls which create a sense of privacy. A screen or cupboard unit can also be effective as a room divider; they also can be changed without major reconstruction.

Enormous windows are fitted into nearly all the external walls. The rose garden can be seen by opening the vertical blinds. A change in the angle of the slats alters the view of the garden. Again the choice of 'curtains' is in keeping with the rest of the decor. Rather than using bright colours or soft fabrics, easy-to-clean slats are fitted into the windows. The straight, simple lines of the blinds echo the simplicity of line throughout the rest of the house.

The kitchen-cum-breakfast area is the most enclosed section. Black shelves, serving also as a working surface, have been built into the waist-high walls. The black and white theme is carried out in the refrigerator, washing-up machine, oven and hob. The table, like the large oblong desks, is supported on a cubical pedestal and easily seats eight people.

One of the most interesting details in the house is the rough rendering of the white surfaces. It suggests a slightly Spanish flavour and also eliminates the white-walled hospital look. The great expanse of white is broken up by the rough finish—far more restful to the eye. This finishing technique needn't be done by the professional. It simply requires taking gypsom plaster, such as Artex, and spreading it on the surface. Then, using either a stippling brush or a spatula, the rough design can be made while the plaster is still wet. It's easy and gives an original touch. Dirt won't show up as much either.

Many ingredients work together to make this Dutch house attractive and comfortable. The most important factor in creating a sense of harmony and co-ordination is the use of colour. The restriction to black and white—except for the ornamentation—is the key to success. Before planning the design for any room, make certain your colour sense is being used to the best advantage—it can make the difference between an ordinary decor and a vibrant one.

table tops, effectively break up the large expanse of clinical white. Touches of colour come from the ornamentation only, leaving a feeling of stark beauty. Unseen sleeping areas are cleverly concealed in two corners.

exceptions being the decorative items such as the lights and the sculpture. A harmonious and co-ordinated look is not a matter of luck. It means a great deal of advance planning with particular attention to the colour scheme.

The tiles covering the raised hearth in front of the open fire tie in with those on the floor surrounding the seating area. The advantages of using this type of material is obvious—no need to worry about stains on the carpet and the annual carpet shampoo can be a thing of the past. The low white walls break up the area around the central island unit, depending on their various functions.

The problem of combining working and living in this one-room house is solved in an

Comfort with economy

Money isn't the only key to successful redecorating. Good ideas and effective methods of execution are equally important. This house lacked style and comfort when it was bought, but through imaginative ideas and a great deal of energy, it has turned into an easy-to-live-in and attractive home.

This Australian house was drab and dreary looking when Don and Marina Gutteridge bought it. Built in the late 1940's and made of brick and tile, it is a typical design of that period. Dutch born Marina Gutteridge decided to redecorate the house. Her budget was limited but through the use of colour, imagination and interesting 'Dutch' touches in the decor, an attractive and distinctive home has emerged.

The front door opens directly into the living room which had been awkwardly shaped, dark and unwelcoming. By introducing light colours into the room and by using light pieces of furniture, the room now has a bright and airy appearance. The walls were covered with a fresh looking green and white patterned wallpaper. The ugly fireplace was painted olive green, along with the skirting boards, window and door frames, to tie in with the wallpaper.

The choice of colour was a good one. Olive green is neutral—it blends easily with other more vibrant colours—and is restful on the eye. Before choosing the main colour for a room where you spend time relaxing, consider its versatility—will it be a good background for your upholstery, paintings and curtains, and will your eye tire of it over a period of time? Soft colours generally are the best choice and also help to lighten up a room. Leave the more striking colours for rooms where you spend less time, or for decorative touches.

The olive green divan couch, which conveniently doubles up as a bed for overnight visitors, was given a more stylish appearance through the use of cushions which lie abundantly and casually on the couch. Often, clever use of items like cushions can improve what might otherwise be an ordinary looking couch. Cushions aren't expensive to buy and, if you're handy with a needle, not difficult to make, and they can go a long way to enhancing any room.

The couch sits under a window in an alcove which has been turned into a cozy area for chatting and relaxation. Space was saved by removing the arms from a two-seater settee. A white shaggy rug, which ties in with the dainty white wrought-iron side table, brings the grouping together.

The room now gives the feeling of lightness because of the colour treatment and because none of the furniture is heavy looking or over-

SALLY McCONNELL

Opposite. Making the most of a small living room alcove. Delicate furniture and light colours eliminate a cluttered look. A petit-point chair depicts the family crest.
Above. A verandah turned sunroom/dining room, as shown by the slanting roof. The furniture was resurrected from a junk shop, stripped and refinished by the owners. Bright café curtains add a festive note.
Right. A cooker fits neatly into a tiled alcove in this colourful and compact kitchen, where bold rusts and browns dominate.

bearing. The straight-back armchair, for instance, isn't bulky and has been enhanced by the petit-point upholstery which depicts the Gutteridge family crest. Two similar armchairs with graceful lines, and placed in front of the fireplace, are also covered with a delicate petit-point floral pattern. There is an absence of heavy cumbersome furniture which contributes to the spacious and airy feeling.

Contrasting to the bright and fresh appearance of the living room is the 'heavier' look in the

sunroom-cum-dining room. The furniture here is darker in colour and mainly wooden, which gives a far more 'weighty' effect. The attractive dresser, table and chairs were bought at a junk shop, stripped and refinished. Money, as shown here is not a prerequisite to a visually appealing room. The furniture in this room was not expensive to purchase—the most important ingredient that contributed to the rich finish was the effort that went into re-doing it.

Further effort was put into making the curtains which give a lovely Dutch flavour to the room. Rust-coloured hessian café curtains, reaching to the ground, hang on a brass rail. At either side there are full length curtains with an old fashion floral print. The overall effect of the window tends to give the room a distinctive character and the café curtains give privacy and style without blocking too much of the light.

A single item, like the café curtains, is sufficient to set the tone of a room. Finding one item which has distinctive character can be a very effective technique for creating a motif in a room. The main thing to remember is that once your central item is established, keep the other furnishings in line with the theme which has been introduced.

The Dutch flavour of the dining room carries through into the kitchen where similar shades of rust and brown are seen. The colour design here was bold and inventive. Originally the walls had been white, which only accentuated poor lighting from the one window. The high ceiling was painted a chocolate brown, to lower it, and then the walls were brightened up with patterned wallpaper with the woodwork in a matching orange.

Orange café curtains are effectively used again. Rather than buying a cooker in conventional white, the Gutteridges bought one in a bright red which fits neatly into a tiled alcove. An old sink was removed from the opposite corner and a new stainless steel one put under the window.

Although this room is small, the use of dark colours has not limited the sense of space. Other techniques for creating spaciousness were applied: the stove was put into an alcove, a freezer was stacked over the fridge, and a suspended counter was built into the wall, allowing more room on the floor.

There are really two methods of 'expanding' a room—one is done visually through the use of colour or mirrors and the other, as in this room, is done through careful and clever planning of equipment. If a sufficient amount of time and thought is given at the design stage of a kitchen, more efficiency and space can emerge at the finished stage.

In contrast to the Dutch flavoured kitchen and sunroom, is a light and modern master bedroom. The decor is simply done in stark white; the only colour is seen in little ornamental touches. The dressing table, which had a sombre green stain on it when bought, was stripped and painted white. The mirror was detached and hung on the wall—a clever idea if more surface space is needed on a dressing table. The floors were given a face-lift with sanding and polishing which is another example of how effort, more than cash, can give an attractive result. The bedhead was livened up with patterned contact paper.

It's interesting to note how the various rooms in this house have different looks which do not distract from or overpower one another. The period flavour of the sunroom, for instance, harmonizes well with the streamlined appearance of the bedroom. House design needn't be consistent from room to room.

A far more appealing approach to decorating, which can result in a more dynamic and attractive home to live in and to look at, is one where rooms have different characters, colours and appeals. If each room can capture an individual mood or feeling, then you can pick the surrounding that suits you most as your mood changes. Never limit yourself to total consistency; variety in design can be exciting.

In the children's room, there is a cheerful and bright mood. The citrus colouring is not overbearing because it was cleverly broken up with a lively print wallpaper which stretches from one wall onto the ceiling. This effect is good because the floral print is not confined to one wall only—as is often seen—but continues on so

Above. A simple decor in stark white makes this bedroom striking and streamlined. The mirror was detached from the dressing table to give more surface space. Patterned contact paper livens up the bedhead.
Left. Bright citrus colouring creates a cheerful atmosphere in the children's bedroom. Decorative flowers pasted on the cupboard were cut out from left-over wallpaper.
Bottom left. Once an entrance hall, now an attractive wc. A superb example of how space can be utilized to best advantage.

the eye isn't abruptly stopped as it moves up the wall. With the right techniques and materials, wallpapering a ceiling is not nearly as difficult a job as may be imagined.

The bedspreads, curtains and cushions were made in a matching citrus. The café curtains are particularly practical in this room. They keep out the strong afternoon sun so the children can nap. They also provide privacy while still allowing light in when required. The flowers pasted on the cupboard add an individual touch; they were cut out from some of the left-over wallpaper.

The lampshade was made by Mrs. Gutteridge by taking an olive green string and methodically winding it around a wire shape. Bamboo rings decorate the hanging flex. This attractive lampshade cost very little to make, but succeeds in adding another individual element to the room. If you're interested in making your own lampshades, wire frames and covering materials are available at most good department stores.

Another ingenious innovation in this home was executed when the wc was built. There had been no wc inside, so a side entrance leading from the garden into the hall was blocked up and the necessary plumbing installed. A small entrance hall often becomes a catch-all for items which are haphazardly left there. In this case, the space was put to good advantage by building a wc into it. The archway to the hallway can still be seen which adds an unusual note. The greatest advantage in devising this wc scheme was that it didn't reduce space in any other part of the house.

This Australian home had once been drab and characterless. It now reflects the taste and style of its owners and, for a modest cost, has been turned into an attractive home.

SALLY McCONNELL

Victorian conversion

Above. *A living room in rich brown with a smart visual accent in constrasting beige railings. A three-wheeled antique invalid's chair makes an eye-catching corner piece.*

A late Victorian terrace house is not an uncommon sight in London. What is more unusual is an impressive interior; one which reflects good taste and originality. This home in south London lacked beauty and comfort when it was bought. Within ten weeks, an attractive and distinctive interior design emerged.

Ugly tiles covered the ceiling in the parlour when interior designer Gerard Knuvelder and his wife moved into their house. The floors were in a ruinous state, the bath was embedded in the earth on the kitchen floor and the bathroom ceiling leaked incessantly when it rained.

Mr. Knuvelder's experience as an interior designer, however, made him realize there was potential for a successful re-conversion. A good approach when buying a house is to decide first whether you want a modern, well equipped one or an older one, which may be in poor condition, but lends itself to effective redecoration. The second alternative requires a good eye and imagination.

Coming through the front door into a passageway, covered with a gold and brown boldly patterned wallpaper, there is a turning into the sitting room. Originally this has been two rooms —a smallish dining room and a parlour. The 'two-into-one' conversion was carefully planned. A district surveyor was called in to approve major changes.

Often, opening out two rooms into a through room is done by pulling down the partitioning wall. In this case, about a five foot opening was built into the wall. The owner decided the room would be more interesting because of the angles provided by the extra wall.

The interplay of space between rooms can be very effective. The flow of space is not stopped —merely detoured—by having walls on either side of the opening. The movement of space in this room was further reinforced by carrying the same colour scheme from the front part of the room through to the back.

The walls and ceilings were painted a rich chocolate brown. The railings were not removed, but used rather as a contrasting beige accent on

the expanse of brown. This small detail is very effective in breaking up what could possibly have been an overwhelming area of brown.

When it came to re-doing the floor, the owners were practical. A geometric patterned tiling in pale shades of grey were laid on the floor. It's easy to clean, and large parties and small children are no longer a threat to an expensive carpet. The tile also helps to cool the room on hot summer days.

With dark brown walls and ceiling and a pale grey floor, it's natural to think that the curtains, upholstery or paintings would have to be in dynamic colours to brighten up the room. Not so here. The roomy couch and matching chair are black leather—a good long-term investment in furniture material. It's not difficult to look after, there are no cleaning bills, and the texture stands up well.

The curtains are a soft mixture of brown and cream—they do not fight with other colours in the room. The old panel fire was removed and replaced with a simple marble fireplace. Still there has been no introduction of vibrant colours, although there is a feeling of warmth.

LEONARDO FERRANTE

Above. The 'Chinese' lounge. The couch had been a child's bed—generous cushions now give it a quality of comfort and luxury.
Above right. The side tables in the living room are an ingenious and inexpensive idea, made from luggage racks and slabs of glass.
Right. A kitchen given a distinctive air by bringing eighteenth century marble cupids from the garden inside to perch on a ledge.

One extremely ingenious idea is the concept of the side tables. A London Hotel which was being demolished was selling luggage racks, made of chromium plated tubing, for well under a pound. Four were snapped up by the Knuvelders. Then they bought slabs of glass (also inexpensive), put them on top of the X-shaped legs of the luggage racks and now they have four smart tables which cost them very little indeed.

Two canary yellow lamps with bases made from Victorian vases sit elegantly on the 'luggage rack' tables. Here is the first suggestion of a bright colour. Next to the fireplace is a three-wheeled French invalid's chair, dating from the Regency period. Unlike so many homes where antique pieces are 'off limits' and meant for viewing only, this invalid's chair is used along with the rest of the furniture.

A home where antique furniture isn't used like the ordinary everyday pieces, is often an uncomfortable home. If you buy a period chair or table which serves only as a showpiece, you're reducing the comfort and convenience of a room where you spend time relaxing. If a piece of furniture is so delicate that it can't be touched, then make certain it doesn't occupy a prominent part of a room where you spend time lounging.

In the front and back of the room, on the centre of the ceilings, there are clusters of three spotlights. These help to set off the Victorian crewel work tapestry hanging on the wall, the fireplace, or other items that warrant highlighting.

The lighting is really the key to the warmth of the room. Often it is colour or texture which creates a sense of warmth; here it is the subtle use of versatile and flexible spots. A shower of soft difuse light gives a relaxed atmosphere, removes any harshness, and provides an interesting interplay of light. Spots also have the added advantage of being adjustable—an aid if you rearrange your furniture or decide to highlight a new piece.

From the rich chocolate of the sitting room, through the passageway, there is a sharp contrast in the clean light colours of the kitchen. Ugly linoleum was removed from the ceiling; the old bath, which has been embedded in the earth, was disposed of; the fireplace was blocked up, and a new floor laid down. The Knuvelders wisely chose the same geometric flooring used in the sitting room—an effective technique for bringing rooms together.

White walls and ceiling brighten up the room. The lighting, again, is a cluster of ceiling spots and, over the dining table, there is a Victorian gas lamp (now converted to electricity). The table was bought for about four pounds and the chairs, also, for a reasonably small sum. The owners then covered them with an antique gold velvet. The effect is elegant; the cost was nominal.

Old cupboard space was put to good use—it now houses the washing and drying machines which are stacked on top of one another. Making use of old cupboards like this is an excellent idea; the machines do not intrude on other valuable space in the room.

The eighteenth century cupids, perched on top of the blocked up fireplace, add an unusual and eye-catching note. They originally sat in a garden, but the Knuvelders have always found an appropriate place for them—inside. Sometimes the most unexpected items—like marble cupids!—can make fascinating focal points which can give character to a room. If you're in an expansive mood and have a little extra money to spend, it's not a mistake to buy an exceptional or unusual object—it could bring you pleasure over the years and probably be used effectively wherever you live.

The colour motif of the sitting room is carried up the stairs and into the master bedroom in the deep brown wall-to-wall carpeting. This room has a Victorian flavour. The floral French wallpaper has subtle shades of muted pinks, pale yellows and soft browns. A delicate white lace bedspread, delicate pink floor-length curtains, spanning one wall, and mock gas lamps add to the general motif.

Turning off the first floor landing is a spacious bathroom. High cupboards are conveniently located along one wall. The bottom half of the

LEONARDO FERRANTE

window was blocked up for privacy and also so a mirror could be attached to it. A suspended sink unit and a shower were installed.

Originally there had been tedious water leakage from the floor above. The previous owner had used—unsuccessfully—soft board to prevent the leakage. In re-doing the ceiling, a large opening had to be cut to allow the water tank to be lifted into the loft above. Mr. Knuvelder decided to make the most of this and, instead of covering up the opening, he had a white wrought-iron staircase installed which now leads up to the study.

Once an old loft, the study is now strikingly done in total white: floor, walls and ceiling. The angular ceilings break up the expanse of white and touches of colour come from a healthy floor plant, a seventeenth century chair used at the drawing board, and a delicate collection of Victorian glasses on a glass shelf spanning one wall. No heating is necessary here; the central heating rises sufficiently to heat the room. The only lighting is a single spotlight.

This room is a good example of the effectiveness of simplicity in decor. It can also be seen in the lounge of the first floor where the motif is Chinese, elegant and unforgettable. There are very few pieces of furniture: the two main items are a magnificent eighteenth century Chinese lacquered chest and an unusual couch made

Above left. *A magnificent lacquered chest, dating back two centuries, makes a handsome piece in this elegant 'Chinese' lounge. No attempt was made to conceal the railings; painted a vibrant red, they dramatically accent the rich yellow walls and ceilings.*
Above right. *Looking down from the spiral staircase into a bathroom, livened up with floral French wallpaper. The stairs lead up to the 'loft' study above, totally conceived in stark white. The opening for the stairs was first made for hoisting up a water tank.*

from a nineteenth century Chinese child's bed. The only additions to this piece are the back and arm cushions in a fragile yellow print. A smooth marble-topped table stands in front.

All the items are in keeping with the Oriental motif including the vases, figurines, bamboo plant stand and an antique Chinese chair. The colour scheme is exquisite. The rich yellow walls and ceilings are set off by the Chinese red railings—the same technique used in the sitting room where, instead of trying to conceal the railings, they are used for a visual accent in colour. The beige carpeting in the 'Chinese' room doesn't distract from the delicate colouring and the air of graciousness.

The success of this room lies in its simplicity—both in furnishings and in the colour scheme. A

large room needs only one or two major pieces to fill it up. It is usually better to under-furnish a room, rather than clutter it up with too many pieces. The main items should be visually appealing and, where applicable, comfortable (as with the couch in this room). The colour scheme is also relatively simple—variations of yellow and beige with an accent of red. Too many colours can spoil the feeling of harmony.

If you're lucky enough to have a spare room, it's worth adventuring into unusual decor. It needn't be expensive; only a few pieces of furniture are required and an outstanding result can be achieved. A foreign motif such as Spanish, Dutch or Chinese could be exciting, and it's something you're not likely to find cropping up in a friend's or neighbour's home.

Moving up to the second floor, there is a colourful children's room with walls covered in curtain material. The sloping ceiling is painted canary yellow and the floor is covered in a practical linoleum. The adjoining bathroom is lined in plastic mirror paper—a clever and inexpensive way of making a small room look bigger.

Every room in this converted home reflects originality and imagination. The rooms may be similar in shape and size to thousands of others in London, but the visual impact is far more memorable.

Above. The front of the mews house, with its large bow window. The old carved wooden door was hung on pivots rather than hinges, and is framed by a section of plate glass.

Bringing the country to town

A family house in a London mews doesn't sound like a horticultural haven or a nature preserve. However, barrister Pat Turner and his wife Debby have achieved an effective blending of art and nature throughout their house in the centre of London, which has no conventional garden.

The house, built on three floors in 1815, was once a grocer's shop and then stood empty for a number of years before the Turners bought it. A growing family brought the need for more space, and with limited resources their only solution was to expand. A sloping roof which reduced the third floor to an attic was removed, the back and front walls extended and made vertical, with a flat roof above. This now provides two adequate bedrooms for the two children and a nanny.

The first distinctive feature about this house is the entrance. A large old carved timber door has been hung on pivots set about a third of the way along, so that it opens both out and in at the same time. To make an even more striking focal point of the entrance, the door was framed by a specially made section of plate glass.

Above. *In the dining room an ornate grille screening the front window serves as both a trellis for plants and a burglar deterrent. An aviary in the corner houses foreign birds.*

Just inside the front door, and visible from the street through the plate glass, is a collection of small pictures illustrating the recent history of Belgravia. The large ground floor room acts as a hall and dining room, with a kitchen/breakfast room behind. The large bow window at the front is screened by an ornate grille, which is not only an attractive trellis for climbing plants, but also acts as a burglar deterrent.

To add the sounds to the sights of nature, an aviary was constructed in one corner of the dining room. Made of twill weld (a heavy wire mesh), it encloses a selection of foreign birds.

As in many town houses, the first floor holds the living room. It is an attractive L-shaped room, formed out of two smaller rooms, with French doors leading to a flat roof over the kitchen below. The Turners decided to create a roof garden here which would flow out of the living room and provide a feeling of openness. To avoid having to close the French doors leading on the the roof garden, it is enclosed in acrylic panels which let in the light in winter and can be removed in the summer. This garden—called the 'salamandery' after its three reptile occu-

pants—is a jungle of plants, creepers, sculptures, earthenware jugs and coloured lights for evening illumination.

In one corner of this raised back garden is an enormous deep acrylic fish tank, tinted green and filled with goldfish. Its sides are reinforced with aluminium struts to withstand the pressure of the 120 gallons of water it holds. A landing window was enlarged so that the tank is visible from the stairs and a spotlight behind it illuminates it at night.

The main bedroom on the second floor has a little room off it that has served variously as a dressing room, nursery and study. Now it houses Mr. Turner's extensive collection of art deco,

Above. *A roof garden enclosed in acrylic panels leads off the L-shaped living room on the first floor, where oriental rugs cover the smart wood floor. A back-lit aquarium is visible through the enlarged landing window.*

Above right. *A small room off the main bedroom resembles Aladdin's cave, with its rich collection of art deco, reflected and enhanced by a mirror on the wall behind. More ornaments adorn the bookshelves.*

Below left. *A concertina door between the two children's bunk beds closes to separate them at night and folds back when necessary.*
Below right. *The solarium and roof garden provide a rural retreat on top of the house.*

and its enlarged window lets more light into the main bedroom. A compact bathroom is off the landing on this floor.

The two children were happy to share one of the third floor bedrooms, but needed somewhere to store all their belongings. This was solved by building the beds on stilts, each with a private play area underneath. A hinged plywood door closes to separate the two beds at night, so that they do not disturb each other, and also to divide the untidy child's territory from that of the tidy one. A concertina screen door closes off the whole room completely when necessary.

An aluminium staircase leads up from this landing into a heated solarium and roof garden. The solarium houses tropical plants and is enclosed by sliding glass doors which give on to the flat roof. Opaque reinforced glass panels provide wind protection and privacy to this enclosed garden with a rooftop view of London.

Not only are both flat roofs used to advantage, but the basement, which is lit from the area, has also been put to good use. Access was made easier by removing the door and replacing the awkward curved staircase with a straight one. As well as a laundry-cum-playroom, there is

also a store room, and the old coal hole now provides cold storage for food and wine. A lavatory and sunken shower cubicle were fitted into a tiny corner under the threshold with a fascinating modern stained glass window, designed by Mr. Turner, casting coloured light in from the area. A spotlight behind it illuminates it at night.

Mrs. Turner decided not to use curtains, as they obscure valuable daylight; instead she chose Roman blinds for all the windows. Made in fabrics to match the other furnishings, they look attractive even when folded up, and give privacy when pulled down at night.

A riverside home

Rats and rot would discourage most people from buying a decaying riverside house. At first sight, this derelict house seemed beyond rescue; it was condemned for demolition by the local council. But a determined buyer spotted it and recognized its potential for a successful conversion. The council decision was fought and obvious obstacles in renovating were surmounted, and today it emerges as one of the most attractive homes in London.

This Queen Anne house is one in a row of terraced houses which stretch along the River Thames at the East End of London. Several hundred years ago, they were lived in by seafaring captains who could enjoy an expansive view both up and down river because of their strategic location in the middle of a generous curve in the river.

As times changed, so did the nature of these terraced houses. Sadly, they were turned into warehouses and then, around the turn of this century, they were abandoned altogether. During the Second World War the terrace was bombed, leaving some of the houses mere shells. The local council finally gave the order to demolish them.

The houses hadn't been completely ignored by the public though. Dr. Barraclough, a physician, had been on the look-out for a house and was immensely attracted to the idea of living by the river. He found these Queen Anne houses and was impressed by their superb location on the river and by the sense of character which still pervaded them, battered though they were.

There were two problems of large proportions to be dealt with before Dr. Barraclough could consider making one of these homes into his own. First the council's decision to demolish had to be reversed and secondly, the many inherent problems in rebuilding a collapsing river house, infested with rats and damp, had to be tackled. The redeeming features of the terrace —its location and character—outweighed any apparent drawbacks in Dr. Barraclough's eyes, and so he set out to buy one of the houses.

A group of interested citizens, including Dr. Barraclough, and set on saving the terrace, went to the council, asking them to cancel the demolition order. The houses, the group felt, represented a period from the past and if they were destroyed, there was no replacing them. The efforts of the group paid off and now the council has issued a preservation order for the terrace.

If you're interested in buying an old house for the purpose of converting, don't be put off by what appears to be an irreversible decision or set of circumstances which could prevent you from purchasing. Sound reasons and determination, combined with a unified front—as in this situation—effectively overcame the obstacle which threatened the very existence of this terrace.

Above. *View from the Spanish 'well' into the dining room and kitchen. The spiral staircase stretches through five floors from basement to skylight. The rich timber came from the pier commemorating the Festival of Britain, bought for a very nominal cost.*

Below. *Looking over the 'well' in the opposite direction into the living room. A skylight above and sliding glass doors overlooking the river add to the spaciousness, while graceful trailing plants and a ship's lantern give a feeling of casual graciousness.*

JOHN BETHELL

With the first hurdle behind him, Dr. Barraclough embarked on the long haul of rebuilding Only the skeleton of a house remained. The brick street wall was intact, but the walls between the houses were flimsy plaster board, and only a remnant of the brick wall facing the river was left. Any existing floors were rotten and crumbling.

The shape of the house is unusual; it's long, tall and narrow. It's about 60ft (18m) long, five stories high and varies between 11 and 13ft (3·3 and 3·9m) in width. The main problem was to get light and space into the house to avoid its appearing like a dark 'corridor' house. The problem was solved in two ways. First, sliding glass doors were put on every floor of the house facing the river, leading out to a balcony, and secondly, wherever possible, skylights were built into the different levels of ceiling, allowing light to filter through the various openings. Horizontal space was expanded by capitalizing on the magnificent river view and vertical space was emphasized by creating varied 'gaps' in the ceiling.

Within the house itself, space was also allowed to circulate freely and irregularly. There is no feeling of five standardized floors with predictable rooms one above another. Between the ground and first floor is an open 'well'—based on the idea of a Spanish court with all the rooms surrounding it. The 'well' literally is an open space in the floor which divides the living room from the dining room, provides a good place for hanging plants, and creates a surge of space from the ground floor upwards.

Another magnificent effect—both from a visual and a practical point of view—is the spiral staircase which stretches from the playroom in the basement, past the ground floor study-cum-studio, to the first floor living room, dining room and kitchen, and then on to the next two floors where there are bedrooms and baths. A single pole, the full height of the house, supports the wooden stairs which wrap round it from the depths of the basement to the skylight at the top.

A spiral staircase has many positive aspects. It's visually appealing; its graceful curves and lines add interest and character to any room. It also takes up less space than an ordinary staircase where the area under the stairs usually becomes a featureless catchall or simply wasted space. And, as in this house, it still allows the eye to move through the house without being cut off in any way.

Perhaps one of the greatest practical coups of the conversion was the way the timber was acquired for the house. A pier had been built on the Thames over twenty years ago to commemorate the Festival of Britain. Word came to Dr. Barraclough through 'river pirates' that it was to be sold. Dr. Barraclough made a bid—a very nominal one, indeed—and found himself the buyer of the pier. It was pulled down, taken down the river and cut up in a timber yard across from the Queen Anne terrace. The wood in the house is a relic of the Festival of Britain. Today the same amount of wood would cost well over thirty times as much as was paid for it seven years ago.

This pier purchase is an exception, but there are many other channels of action to take to help your finances when rebuilding. Find out where local demolition is going on and perhaps you'll

*Opposite page. Waterfront property rescued from rot, rats and demolition. Glass doors and balconies make ideal river viewing. **Above left.** A studio-cum-study featuring an imposing marble floor, a richly timbered ceiling and eye-catching pieces from the past. **Above.** The master bedroom leads out onto a balcony where the atmosphere from the majestic sweep of the river can be captured.*

find beams, boards, cornices, brick or whatever you need, at a very reasonable price. It may take a period of time to find what you want, but it can be a great financial aid.

The overall impression in the house is one of brick—some white, some red—rich wood and abundant and natural plants. The white brick contrasts well with the green plants and these are highlighted with ceiling spotlights or soft diffused light which comes up from the floor. The wood used for ceiling, floor, stairs and doors gives a warm and handsome appearance. The wood, incidentally, used on the living room furniture was found in the river.

The decorations are also in keeping with the nautical motif which dates back to the time when sea captains lived in the house. On one wall there's a graceful piece of driftwood; on another a brass ship's clock. There is also a lantern and a life saver, both suggestive of river life.

It's difficult to imagine that this unusual and captivating home was once condemned to the demolition squad. It was only through Dr. Barraclough's determination, perseverance and colossal effort that it has been transformed into what it is today.

Above. *Foam-covered mattresses provide seating in the living area, where a shelf unit on one wall disguises the roof slope.*

'Blind' loft into glamour home

A flat with no windows can easily look dark and bare if the design scheme lacks imagination. However, the additional space provided by the 'blind' walls can be exploited to advantage, with fascinating results.

When a young French couple were flat-hunting, they saw a large loft tucked under the roof of a house in Bordeaux. They immediately decided to convert it into a flat, even though this meant that they had to forgo the views through windows that are a valuable feature of more conventional homes. Architect Michel Sadirac was asked to transform the loft, with its nooks and crannies, beams and shadows, into a light and cheerful living space.

The long irregular loft space divided quite easily into living and eating areas at its wider end, with the kitchen, bedroom and bathroom

in the narrow part. The original criss-cross roof beams, which separate the various areas, have been picked out with white paint, but not emphasized so much as to break up the large open spaces. The original floor was very uneven, so it was levelled and covered throughout in natural coconut matting.

There are no windows anywhere in the flat, so daylight has been 'captured' and directed downwards through deep rooflights which let in shafts of light all over the flat. The light is diffused by the predominantly white colour scheme, which has been cleverly distributed by means of different finishes: rough-textured white on the plastered walls and partitions, brilliant white on the gloss-painted beams, and smooth white for the worktops and shelves.

Against this plain background Michel Sadirac has set a range of strong toning colours: splashes of red, orange and yellow on a mid-

brown floor. All the furniture has been adapted to complement the original structure; it is unobtrusive and functional, and made to measure to save space. Plain mattresses cut from 10in. thick foam and covered in dark brown fabric are arranged round the edge of the living area, with bright scatter cushions on them. The simple coffee tables are plain white-painted cubes.

A practical and attractive feature of the flat is a long bookcase fitted along one wall, which conceals the roof slope on one side of the living area, and continues past the dining area and into the kitchen, where it forms a useful shelf unit.

The compact dining area was also made to measure, with furniture reduced to its simplest form. White-painted cube seats with dark brown cushions stand at a table consisting of a white laminate top on a simple base. Panels of insulation board fixed to the beams that act as a room divider separate this area visually from the kitchen; openings are left in it for use

*Above left. In the bedroom, a geometric mural painted on the doors of the wardrobe comes alive when they are opened. **Above right**. Red-painted shelves cover the wall right up to the ceiling above the units on one side of the kitchen, lit by a rooflight. **Below right**. The compact dining room is tucked between the living and kitchen areas. Enormous black lettering livens up the otherwise dull radiator. The main living spaces are divided by natural open partitions formed by the criss-cross roof beams.*

as serving hatches to the dining area.

White laminate units along one wall in the kitchen house basic equipment such as a stainless steel sink, electric hobs and a small refrigerator. A red-painted wall unit of uneven pigeon holes climbs right up to the ceiling and is tailored to the slope of the roof; it provides visible and accessible storage for everything arranged on its shelves. A white laminate worktop similar to the dining table has been fixed to the partition between the two rooms, where it is easily accessible through the openings in the room divider.

The wildest splashes of colour appear in the bedroom, where a geometric design in red, orange and yellow has been painted on the wardrobe doors. It comes alive when the doors are opened, revealing a vast storage space behind. A low white-painted shelf runs the whole length of the wall behind the bed, and continues into the bathroom, where flexible spotlights pick out the pure white of the walls and fittings.

The ever-accommodating town house

When a family grows, a major decision has to be made—whether to move to a larger house or to extend the existing one. Quite often it is cheaper to add to the present house, and make provision for using the additional space later when the children have left home.

When architects Francis and Charlotte Baden-Powell bought their three-storey terraced house in Chelsea, all it lacked was adequate sanitation. They had a 'sanitary tower' constructed at the back, which housed a basement bathroom, a ground floor kitchen, and a first floor bathroom. This arrangement enabled the main house to be used for living in, unaffected by plumbing, except for the water tank, which was fixed in the attic above the stairwell. The house was now quite large enough for them; in fact they were able to let off the tiny basement as a self-contained flat. They lived on the upper two floors, comprising a large living room (which was once two rooms), kitchen, two bedrooms and a bathroom.

When their family subsequently grew to five, with the arrival of two children and a nanny, they needed a lot of extra space, which the basement alone would not provide. They therefore had to choose between buying a larger house or adding extra rooms on to their present one. They were reluctant to leave their house in a quiet terrace in Chelsea, which was thought to have been built as temporary artisans' dwellings for the workers on the Crystal Palace. They finally decided to stay put, and Francis Baden-Powell commissioned his wife to 'make' the extra space by converting the basement and attic and adding a small extension at the back.

The V-section roof was removed, the party walls and chimneys were raised, and a flat roof constructed. The steep staircase leading to the small attic was replaced, and now rises into a room which covers the entire top floor of the house, providing a splendid bedroom and play area for the two children. In designing this room Charlotte Baden-Powell took into account the fact that growing boys at one stage would want their own bedrooms, so the construction easily lends itself to the erection of two partition walls. This would form two little cabin bedrooms and still leave a play space directly accessible from the stairs.

The straight parapet was kept, and new dormer windows were set back in the mansard roof to keep the front of the house as unchanged as possible, also to be acceptable to the local authority. In order to avoid having an ugly downpipe on the front of the house, a gutter was fitted behind the parapet. It runs across the front and along the side, taking the roof rainwater and leading it into a downpipe at the back of the house, now well covered by creeping plants.

Although a dining table in the living room had

JOHN SEYMOUR

served adequately when the Baden-Powells were only two, a separate dining room now became a necessity. The obvious solution was to fill in the space at the back formed by the L-shaped house. There was room here for a structure housing a 9ft square ground floor dining space and an extra bedroom in the basement (there was a back area already, so no excavation was necessary).

In order to gain enough headroom (8ft) for the basement bedroom, the dining space above it had to be raised. Two steps lead up to it from the living area, providing an additional seating platform 15in. above floor level. The height was an important safety factor, as Mrs Baden-Powell felt that one step could go unnoticed and therefore be dangerous, whereas a 15in. dais was clearly visible.

The regulations in Britain governing windows stipulate that one tenth of a room's floor area must be glass (not window frame) and that one twentieth should open. This presented a small problem in the new basement bedroom, but it was solved by building a false bench seat at the back of the dining area above. The wall directly below the top of the seat houses the high level bedroom window, which is above ground level, so avoiding the need to dig out the ground at the back. The garden comes right up to the back of the house, with no space wasted by an area.

Even though the dining area is raised, 8ft headroom was possible here because no rooms were built above it. The sloping roof is of fixed clear patent glazing, which lets in a good deal of extra light over the now elongated room, and

throws it back into the living area. Aluminium-framed sealed units fitted at the back of the dining area slide three-quarters of the way open to give a visual link between the house and the garden. The window space at the side of the kitchen was retained, and now acts as a hatch to the dining area.

A great deal of London was constructed on a kind of 'split level' system. By artificially raising the roads by half a storey, space was provided under them for sewers, services and coal holes. The original ground then became basement level, with the ground floor half a storey above the road (except for mews, where the road is taken down to the natural ground level). The front of this house adheres to the system, with the front door half a storey above road level, but the back garden is at ground floor level (ie: half a storey above the road, and a whole storey above the original ground level). This is most unusual in this type of London development, but in this case it proved to be an advantage, as the kitchen leads straight into the back garden, without the need for steps down.

Above. The original ground floor space is now all living room. **Opposite page, top left.** The dining platform overlooks the back garden; the kitchen runs beside it. **Top right.** The attic was converted into a children's bedroom which can later be adapted to provide two cabin bedrooms and a play space. **Right.** The back of the house has been altered considerably, with the addition of a sanitary tower (right) and dining area.

Kitchen-diner in a mini-space

The architects of those enormous Victorian houses must have placed little importance on the value of cooking, as —in marked contrast to the large reception rooms—the kitchen quarters are often meagre.

When designer Liz Goldfinger was asked to modernize a poky kitchen in a basement flat in North London, she realized that the curved inside wall separating it from the corridor had to be knocked down in order to incorporate an informal eating area. This would not only increase the space available, but also enable light from the kitchen window to spread over the whole area.

The corridor leading from the front door and running along the middle of the flat separated the kitchen from an alcove opposite, which was to become the eating area. At the back of this alcove were doors to a broom cupboard and a staircase leading to the ground floor. This staircase was removed and the space used to enlarge a wardrobe in the bedroom behind. The broom cupboard became a walk-in larder, whose door was incorporated in a false wall faced with pine boarding.

To make the most of the small eating area, a bench seat was built along one side of the alcove, with a cushion covered in red plastic and a pine backrest. The freestanding white laminate-faced table has a cantilevered top, as legs would get in the way.

The kitchen is now open on the corridor side, with only a worktop/cupboard unit and an open shelf above dividing it from the eating area, creating a 'bar' effect. The cupboard opens on both sides, so that china can be put in from the kitchen and taken out from the other side when needed for meals. There is no kitchen door—

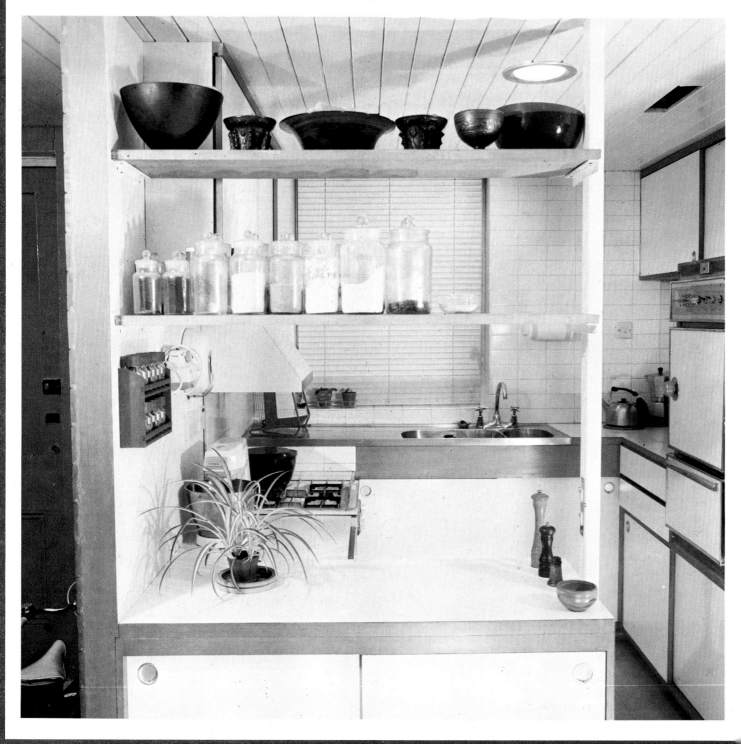

just an opening large enough for access.

The small square kitchen had to be carefully planned to make best use of the existing area, and provide adequate storage space. The white laminate-faced cupboard and drawer units were specially made to accommodate the hob, oven, large refrigerator and double sink unit. All the cupboards have sliding doors, so as not to waste space. They are suspended on plastic track and have simple recessed handles.

Liz Goldfinger designed the wall cupboards particularly shallow. She finds them more practical than deeper cupboards, as bottles and jars stored two or three deep on a shelf tend to get knocked over when someone is reaching for something behind.

The stainless steel sink unit runs under the window, which has a washable Venetian blind, and the wall around is covered in white ceramic tiles. The recess for the refrigerator was made large enough to provide adequate ventilation space above and behind it. A metal vegetable rack was specially designed to slide out on tracks below the food preparation area.

The worktop surrounding the separate hob is covered in heat-resistant tiles. A large hood over the cooking area encourages fumes up into a false ceiling, and an extractor fan in the outside wall dispels them. Two small openings in the white painted tongued-and-grooved wood ceiling help serve the same purpose.

Electric wiring is housed in ducts in the false ceiling, and a specially made steel tube supporting the shelf above the 'bar' unit conceals wires leading to the light switches.

Pale grey vinyl floor tiles are coved up at the edges to make cleaning easier—just one of many features which make this kitchen practical. There is plenty of storage space, with room high up for those things that are seldom needed, and everything is easily accessible. The white finish on the units, light-coloured flooring and pale wood all help to create a feeling of space in what was once a small, badly planned kitchen.

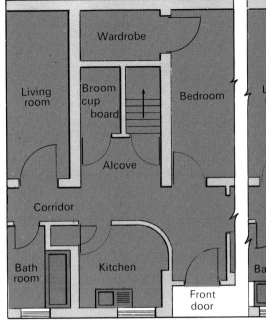
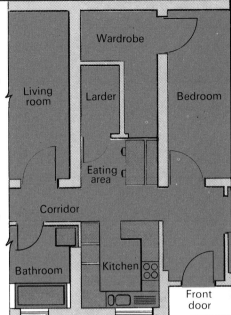

Above. Floor plans showing the area before (left) *and after conversion* (right). *The stairs were removed, an informal eating area fitted in the remaining alcove, and the corridor wall of the kitchen knocked down to link them.* **Opposite page.** *The kitchen is light, spacious, and fitted throughout. A false ceiling holds all the electric ducts, and the steel tube supporting the open shelves conceals wires leading to the light switches at the bottom.* **Below left.** *Looking through the doorway into the kitchen. The worktop next to the hob is covered with white heat-resistant tiles, with a sliding vegetable rack beneath.* **Below right.** *View from the kitchen through the 'bar' unit to the eating alcove on the other side of the corridor.* **Right.** *The fitted bench seat saves valuable space in this small area.*

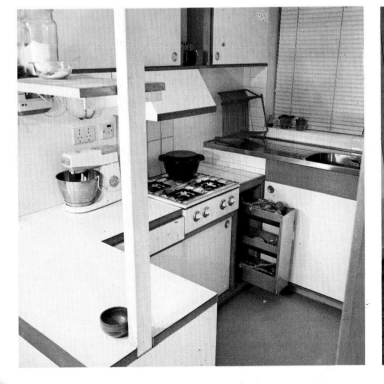

Converting without fuss

When Art Editor Sally Downing decided to look for a house to buy, she had settled ideas about what type of home she wanted. It should be as near the centre of London as possible, adaptable, light and airy, and a good long-term investment. A career girl, she wanted a home that was tailormade to suit her life-style, or at least one that could, with the minimum of fuss, be converted into her ideal.

Finally she found a house in Fulham, one of the inner London suburbs, which was in many ways her idea of what a home should be—a simple, two-storey terraced house, dating from the Edwardian era, of solid construction and with rooms of naturally good proportions. When she bought it, the individual rooms were too cramped for her needs, so she first let off the ground floor to a sitting tenant, and then set about converting the top floor, which was to be her apartment.

Two smallish rooms at the front of the house were given the illusion of being one by the simple technique of knocking a large door-shaped hole in the dividing wall, giving the effect of spaciousness while still retaining the separate identity of the two rooms.

There was no upstairs lavatory, and the bathroom was tiny. All modern conveniences were to be installed but space was a problem. This was soon solved by taking out the bath and replacing it with a small but compact shower area, leaving enough room over for a toilet and washbasin.

The kitchen at the back of the house was a decent size, but valuable work space was lost under the eaves where the Edwardian builders had put a pantry. Its dividing wall was knocked down, leaving enough extra space for a fair-sized table and two benches—a handy corner for folding clothes.

All the fireplaces in the flat were taken out, and the walls filled in, smooth and elegant. The recesses on either side became useful as shelved alcoves for storing records, housing night storage heaters and an impressive collection of books.

Once the flat was converted structurally, Miss Downing turned her artist's eye to the decor, and total 'look' of the place. She hates 'fussiness' and wanted somewhere that was easy to keep clean and tidy, and that could look stylish with the minimum of effort.

She chose white, off-white, creams and beiges as the background colours. They are sophisticated, subtle and easy on the eye—she works at home on painstaking artwork and needs a restful environment.

Right. Brightness in an up-to-date sitting room where luxurious, jumbo cushions are complemented by the bold zig-zag patterns and colours of a prayer rug from the Far East.

Throughout the flat, the floor is covered in a good quality haircord carpet in a warm light beige. It is fitted in all rooms (except the bathroom) and covers the stairs, too. In her main living-area a large prayer rug from Kelim, in the Far East, provides a splash of colour with its oranges, browns, pinks and reds—though none of these colours is too dominant, and together they please the eye rather than tire it.

The colour of the fitted carpet is echoed in the beige of the large, comfortable settee, piled high with homemade cushions. Designed to emphasize the deep comfort of the settee, Miss Downing made the cushions incorporating patchwork pieces to add interest to the otherwise unbroken expanse of beige.

Cushions are becoming increasingly popular, both as aids to cosiness and as fashion pieces. Their full shapes and colour can provide a simple room with all the accessories it needs.

More cushions—this time giant floor cushions—make even the floor inviting. Their restful green was chosen carefully as a direct contrast to the brilliant red in the huge poster above—showing a London bus in meticulous detail.

The room is mainly uncluttered by furniture but what there is, is chosen to be in keeping with the tone of the room. It is often better to buy one or two expensive pieces that you won't tire of, than fill a room with an assortment of nondescript furniture that gives little style or character.

The main pieces here are a large, sturdy table with a serviceable top in white plastic laminate and modern-looking chrome legs, and a wide chair—seat and backrest in soft black leather, and legs and arms in tubular chrome. Both are instantly recognizable as up-to-the-minute and help to set the tone of the house.

Small details also help to create the desired impression: a chunky black clock with gold figures and a special flick-over address book set on chrome legs add interest to the wide expanse of table top. Also, there are tall, spiky plants in old earthenware plant pots. At night they look even more impressive silhouetted against the white roll blinds.

A large colourful poster, bought in the States and framed under glass in London, rests against one wall, on the floor. This is an unusual place for a poster but Sally felt it was right—the people sitting low down on the floor cushions need a focal point, and the glass makes it too heavy to kick over or damage.

A cluster of tiny but powerful spotlights are fixed to the old ceiling rose, which has been painted over, but still has charm. The spotlights pick out points of interest in the living-area and the bedroom beyond, and provided both rooms with softer lighting than the ordinary central pendant light which cast harsh shadows—and she was able to achieve the effect without major alterations to the existing wiring.

The bedroom is simple and functional. Miss Downing made an eye-catching patchwork quilt from the same material as the cushions in the living room—this helps to give the two areas a sense of continuity. Her drawing board, with its black-painted steel legs manages to look like an 'art form' itself and—a nice touch—her brushes and pencils are kept in a battery of earthenware plant pots.

The whole bedroom and living room area is a study in modern living. It serves its purpose well; it is easy to maintain; it is stylish—and

Above left. The brick exterior is livened up by sharp white trim, a wrought iron fence and decorative stained glass door panels.
Left. A pantry turned into a convenient and cosy breakfast alcove. The simplicity of the table, benches and rush matting gives an uncluttered look to this well utilized area.

NELSON HARGREAVES

splashes of colour keep the total effect from being over-clinical.

The new shower room is tiled with terracotta-coloured quarry tiles. There is no conventional shower-curtain to make the space seem even more cramped. A raised 'mini-wall' of tiles defines the shower-area, and a row of tall, robust plants in pots make a stylish and original 'shower-curtain'.

The kitchen maintains the overall style of the flat: there are ultra-modern fitted kitchen units in immaculate white, all with plastic laminate tops for ease of cleaning; the floor immediately in front of the units is tiled in rubber, then comes a carpeted area—the same beige carpet that covers the rest of the floors.

The multitude of plant pots holds cutlery this time; a huge pinboard on one wall dominates the room, and prevents the kitchen, the most functional of rooms, from being merely serviceable. A pinboard is a good idea in all kinds of rooms—kitchens, nurseries and work-rooms benefit from having a surface where you can pin memos, posters and anything that adds a personal, colourful note. Here a giant calendar—with a different primary colour for each month—and blown-up pictures of exotic Tarot cards mix with the more usual bills and recipes.

A small airing-cupboard occupies the space where the fireplace used to be. A subtle mushroom-coloured storage heater fits in neatly, and an antique rail holds clothes over it to air. This rail used to be part of a passengers' hand rail in one of London's first omnibuses. Above it, on the wall, is an antique clock found in a junk shop.

A final note of originality is the stained glass of the front-door panels. This came with the house but, with its vivid colours and Art Nouveau design, contrives to look ultra-modern.

Miss Downing's house is hers—not just because she has bought it, but because her taste and imagination have given it a personality of its own and made it truly a home.

Above left. *A tiny bathroom with a compact shower effectively set off with terracotta tiles. A graceful potted palm serves as a stylish and original 'shower-curtain'.*
Top. *This spacious kitchen is spruced up with a giant-sized pinboard, featuring a bold* red London bus.
Above. *A view from the sitting room into the cheerful bedroom. The patchwork bedspread adds a colourful note. Abundant light and space make it an ideal spot for detailed work at the drawing board.*

NOEL HOLLY

Above. *A living room with tall, elegant arches—once a solid unambitious hallway wall. Geometric patterns in the brilliant red rug complement spacious French doors.*

Design in narrow confines

A narrow piece of land can present problems for house design. It requires an intelligent arrangement of rooms and well-planned placement of windows in order to take full advantage of outside light and space. This Australian home, built on a block measuring 33ft by 16ft (10m by 4.8m) was converted and extended, making an asset, rather than a drawback, of its 'narrowness'.

When Professor Bolton and his wife bought their narrow plot of land, the pre-World War I house standing on it was badly in need of renovation. Their first inclination was to pull down the old house and build a modern one with all the up-to-date conveniences. On closer

inspection, however, and with advice from an architect, the Bolton's decided to alter the old house, taking advantage of the existing assets.

The façade had character which would contribute to the attractiveness of the home. The main rooms were situated at the front of the house which faces north—the exposure which benefits most from the Australian winter sun. More accommodation was needed—bedrooms and a play area for the children and a bedroom and study for the parents—but it would be possible to provide these through converting and extending. And so the work began.

The exterior was given a face-lift. A new corrugated iron roof came first. Then attention was given to the brick walls which had an old-fashioned look because the lower half had

been painted. The paint was stripped off, the entire wall re-pointed and then a splash of white trim added to break up the expanse of brick. A heavy iron-roofed verandah, which had blocked out valuable light from the living room, was pulled down and replaced with a more delicate pergola.

Some privacy was desired, but a high wall would have cut off the attractive view across the road. The solution was a shoulder-high brick wall which was gracefully designed in a circular fashion. A small garden was built up, styled for people who have difficulty in 'finding time' for gardening. Instead of a lawn requiring constant attention, there are wood chips, and the plants, which will eventually grow much larger, are native to Australia and don't require much watering. The stepping stones leading to the

back of the house have been positioned in a rather whimsical and graceful fashion.

It's very easy, when embarking on a conversion, to put all your energy into fixing up the interior and forgetting about the exterior which really is equally important. A shabby or forlorn façade is a most unwelcoming sight and is a poor recommendation for the interior to come. Make certain the outside of your home is not neglected—it's a reflection of you.

Once the cumbersome verandah was removed, allowing more light into the front rooms, renovation began on the living room. Originally there had been a long, narrow and uninspiring hall, running adjacent to the living room wall. It really served little purpose, so it was 'treated'— three tall and graceful arches were built into it.

The arches add a note of elegance, open up the space of the living room, while still suggesting the feeling of a hallway. Arches can be effective and decorative room dividers. If you're in the process of renovating and want an original touch in your home, a plastered arch

or curved wall can be used to add decorative interest and bring a new dimension to almost any room if used imaginatively.

The small front windows were replaced by large French doors which lead out to a pergola. A brilliant red rug with stunning squares gives a rich tone to the room. The furniture is a harmonious mixture of antique and modern. Ceiling spots highlight the 'hall' bookshelves at night, creating a dramatic effect.

The dining room had been a rather dreary back bedroom. It was extended by raising the ceiling and lowering the floor. The drab fibrous plaster ceiling was taken out, leaving the natural slanting line of the original ceiling which then required replastering. The exposed wooden joists were left which create an appealing visual effect. The floor boards were removed, which substantially lowered the level of the floor, and replace with 9in. (228mm) brick tiles.

A small tiled ledge, running along one wall, conceals limestone footing and a damp-proof course. The original floor had been the height of

this ledge which now serves as a handy shelf for display. Often features which emerge out of necessity, like the 'camouflaging' ledge here, turn out to be eye-catching focal points in a room.

If your home requires a camouflage or disguise for ugly pipes, meters or radiators, consider making a feature of the 'disguise', rather than trying to hide it apologetically from sight. You could also consider drawing attention to such an item by painting it with a coat of brilliant glossy colour.

The spaciousness of the dining room was further increased by making one wall almost completely of glass. The French doors and surrounding glass panels don't arrest the eye and help to bring the greenery of the patio from the outside into the dining area.

Two good techniques for making a room look larger have been used in this room. The first was to increase the actual amount of physical space available by raising the ceiling and lowering the floor. The second was to visually expand the

NOEL HOLLY

Above left. Attractive wooden joists, spanning a slanting ceiling, and a lowered brick floor open out this once confined room.
Inset. An imposing teak wardrobe serves as a functional room divider with a bedroom on one side and a studio on the other.
Above right. The handsome extension, made from pine and brick, with a rustic kitchen fitted out with modern conveniences.
Inset. The 'face-lifted' exterior, characterized by a rounded brick wall, white contrasting trim and a delicate pergola.

space by opening out the view with glass, carrying the eye out to the patio.

A third technique for making the most of space was used in the bedroom-cum-study. Originally this had been the sitting room and back bedroom. A new and clever arrangement was worked out. The partitioning wall was knocked down and replaced with a large dark teak wardrobe which also serves as a room divider. One side is the study and the other, the

bedroom, with wardrobe doors opening out on either side with a section for books spanning between.

If you're creating different areas to a room, make certain you use appropriate room dividers. Plants, screens, arches or wardrobes are all likely possibilities. It's important that the dividers appear to be an integral part of the room, whether it be decorative, functional or both. A room divider which doesn't blend in with the rest of the decor tends to detract rather than contribute to the beauty of a room. The wardrobe here adds a rich tone to the room and also has a practical and appropriate function in the room.

The colourful motif in the bedroom begins with the bold red and orange flowers on the bedspread. The iron bedstead gives an old world charm to the room. On the other side of the wardrobe, the atmosphere is 'booky' because of the desk and bookshelves, but the wardrobe ties the two parts of the room together. A small bathroom leads off the study.

Having successfully converted the existing rooms, the Boltons set out to build an extension. The narrow land ruled out building on to the sides of the house. At the back of the house there had been an asbestos lean-to. This was knocked down and new kitchen and family room erected, with children's bedrooms and a bathroom upstairs. The advantage to this set-up was that the children could play in their section of the house without disturbing the parents who might be entertaining in the main part of the house.

The new extension was made mainly with brick and handsome pine. The wood adds a feeling of warmth while the brick helps to keep this area cool on hot days. An attractive brass rubbing hangs on the brick wall and a light Japanese-type lantern hangs from the ceiling.

The Australian house is a delightful and unified living area. The narrowness of the land, rather than being a limit to the 'growth' of the house, has added to the appealing decor and layout.

77

Design for compact living

Life in modern cities is becoming increasingly cramped, and most householders feel they need more living space. Even if there is enough room for the family to move around, space for storage is often limited, and what room there is seems to shrink as time goes on. In flats the problem is accentuated—with fewer rooms there are fewer odd corners which can be put to good use.

This flat in the centre of old Helsinki, Finland, is extremely small. Its total area is only 40 square yards (or metres), but it has been skilfully adapted so that it provides a family of four with adequate living and storage space. The Huhtamaa family chose this particular flat because it was inexpensive and presented possibilities for future re-planning when the budget allowed.

At first it seemed impossible to make the tiny living room meet their needs. Then they hit on the idea of using the height of the room to best advantage, and built a sleeping platform at one end of the room. Bedsteads take up a surprising amount of room, so they spread out two thick mattresses on the platform, covered with a bedspread and scattered with cushions to provide splashes of colour during the day. Both the parents have to write a lot, so they dragged an ancient writing desk up onto the platform,

Opposite page. The owners used the height of the room to advantage and built this sturdy bed platform where they sleep and work during the day.

Above. The door to the children's room is fastened back during the day and a shelving unit used to bridge the gap. Primary colours are used to effect.

Above. The main living area is under the bed platform. The chairs have been collected gradually and are of different styles, but blend together well.

where they could work in peace. A narrow unobtrusive shelf holds a few reference books and angled reading lamps.

A narrower platform was built in the nursery which acts as a 'guest room', and later on it will be the older child's private province. Altogether the balconies have effectively added 10 square yards (or metres) to the living space of the flat which would otherwise have been wasted.

In Britain, for example, rooms in Victorian or Edwardian houses tend to have very high ceilings which, to the modern eye, make the rooms seem chilly and unwelcoming. But the extra height makes them ideal for balconies or platforms. Hobbies rooms or children's rooms especially benefit from an extra level, particularly if storage is a problem for hobbies equipment or books. And if a room is shared by children of different ages, a bed platform might provide the necessary feeling of privacy for those not frightened of heights, and the extra living space can be well worth the effort involved.

Here the living room, small though it is, has to be flexible enough to accommodate a number of activities—sleeping, eating, working and entertaining. So they made a storage shelf system to take their numerous books and equipment—again building the units upwards using the height of the room to compensate for its small floor area. Part of the shelving system bridges the door between the living room and the children's room. During the day the door is fastened back so that the parents can keep an eye on the children as they play. It is always a good idea to provide small children with play-space near the kitchen so they can be under supervision without feeling they are being spied on.

The shelving system was deliberately made so that drawers and doors could be added when needed to hold all shapes and sizes of storage. The vacuum cleaner is kept behind one of the flap-doors, and its cord is just long enough for it to reach all over the flat.

The owner built a multi-purpose table in front of the window. It is a folding table with three hinged parts, made of chipboard and covered in plastic. One end is attached to the window sill and the other is supported by a leg made of bent metal tubing. When the table is not needed the leg is detached and the whole table folds flat against the radiator. It looks modern and very expensive—well worth the effort of designing and making it at home. Generally, purpose-built furniture is prohibitively expensive unless you make it yourself. Many DIY home carpentry manuals supply the necessary information on how to make your own.

The sitting area is concentrated under the main sleeping platform in a cosy corner. There is a classic settee with a magnificent fur rug thrown over it, and a group of chairs of different styles which have been collected together over the years. The varied styles look well together even in an ultra-modern environment, Properly used, a mixture of styles can add a great deal of interest and charm to a room.

The round table is again made of chipboard and covered in plastic, with a sturdy round base of toughened cardboard. The owner's wife made a multi-coloured rya rug in an abstract design which takes pride of place as a wall hanging. This lounging corner looks welcoming and stylish despite the limited budget.

The flat has one room in the shape of a small circular tower which is now the kitchen. The

cooker, fridge and one cupboard are the only standard fittings which the Huhtamaas bought when they first set up the flat. They made most of the kitchen furniture themselves so it would fit snugly into the unusual circular shape. Again, by making as much furniture as they could, the owners saved a great deal of money and ended up with a kitchen tailor-made to suit their particular needs. They fitted up cupboards wherever there was a gap, and a worktop circles the whole room. In fact the curious circular shape turned out to be an advantage because all the equipment and fittings are readily to hand.

The nursery doubles as a store-room for the family's clothes and linen. Because every square inch counts, the cupboard space was actually planned. If you decide in advance exactly what you want to store in your cupboards, and list the objects according to size and shape, you can then divide the cupboards up into segments which will store your belongings without crushing them and without wasting any space. Here chrome tubes were used as hanging rails, and there are innumerable little shelves in one section for small things. Toys are stored in an old bookcase with the glass front removed for safety, and the room is left as uncluttered as possible to provide ample play space.

The hall is just big enough for one guest to step in from the street and for a cupboard which has one section reserved for adult-sized coats and a lower rail for children's. This is another example of how every inch was made to count.

The flat is an ingenious solution to a tricky modern problem. The bed platforms and home-made built-in furniture make living in 40 square yards not only feasible, but attractive.

Above left. *The exterior of this weatherboarded school assembly hall was not altered very much by the conversion. The rear section of the roof was raised and tipped up to make room for a gallery bedroom. A brick wall encloses a paved garden at the back.*

Staying in after school

The cost of ready-to-move-into houses has risen so much over the last few years that more and more people are looking for an unlikely building—whether it be a barn, windmill or shop—which they can buy cheaply and then convert into a comfortable home.

Architect Anthony Teale needed somewhere to live and base his practice in Kent. Nothing that was on the market suited his needs, so he decided to tackle any suitable unconverted building he could find. A local preparatory school had been disbanded a year before and the main building sold, but he managed to buy an assembly hall next to it. It had been built six years before from old bricks that once formed a garden wall running between the main school building and the adjoining property.

Although it had stood empty for a year, the single-storey structure was in good condition.

The inside, however, which was just one large space, was clad with orange-painted blockboard. The first job was to remove this ugly panelling and replace a block of lavatories at the back with a fitted bathroom. Then the architect set about converting the bare hall into a practical and comfortable home. He has succeeded in using as many natural materials as possible in the scheme, while incorporating necessary modern comforts such as central heating.

Apart from the usual living, cooking and eating areas, the architect needed two bedrooms and a self-contained studio. As the building was only 20ft (6.1m) wide, the problem was one of creating a feeling of space. The original 9ft (2.7m) ceiling gives an impression of openness, while dividing walls enclose certain areas where necessary. The kitchen is screened off in this way by a 6ft 6in. (2.0m) partition wall. The maximum width has been retained by having no

space-wasting passages or corridors, and the final design combines the atmosphere of open plan with the privacy of enclosed areas.

A split-level design was the obvious solution to the height problem, so the architect decided to construct a sleeping gallery. By raising part of the roof and lowering a section of the floor below, he was able to fit a full height gallery bedroom at one end of the building. This improves the proportions of the house, while leaving the maximum amount of usable space on the ground floor.

The studio was built at the front so that the living quarters should be as far away from the road as possible. This front room, and the adjoining cloakroom, can be closed off to separate the office and living accommodation.

A corridor kitchen leads from the studio to the living areas behind. The original floorboards here were found to be in good condition, so after the floor was raised by 6in. (150mm), they wer

PAUL SIMPSON

Opposite page, right. A corridor kitchen at one side leads from the studio at the front to the living room. The dining table is in the corner nearest the kitchen, and the remaining L-shaped area provides ample living space. Sliding glazed doors lead to the back garden.

Above left. A low brick dividing wall separates the dining space from the sitting area round the open fire, where enormous floor cushions take the place of armchairs. The spiral staircase leading up to the sleeping gallery is just visible on the right.

Above right. The sleeping gallery, fitted with built-in wardrobes, runs the full width of the back of the house above the sunken part of the living room. Louvred doors fitted in the sloping wall fold open to look over the living area, and close for privacy at night.

refitted, sanded and sealed. Modern laminate-faced units in olive green tone well with the natural bricks. The lighting is arranged so that the living room is not affected by the strong lights needed for working in the kitchen at night.

There is a spare bedroom next to the kitchen, and the remaining half of the house is taken up by a living room with dining area, and the gallery bedroom above. The partition wall dividing the spare bedroom from the living room is 3ft (0.9m) thick. Running halfway along the middle of the house, it acts as a service block, incorporating meters accessible from outside, hot and cold water tanks, a recessed vanitory unit in the spare bedroom, an open fireplace in the living room, and a linen cupboard. The block was arranged so that tradesmen need not go through the house to read meters or service the boiler house.

Most of the living room is at the original floor level, with a sunken section below the gallery

bedroom to give adequate headroom. Sliding glazed doors lead out to a small paved and walled garden at the back. The living area is L-shaped, with a dining table near the kitchen completing the rectangle. A low brick retaining wall at the side of the dining area is used as a back rest for the enormous floor cushions that take the place of armchairs. The hearth in front of the open fireplace was covered with old quarry tiles taken from the kitchen of a demolished farmhouse.

The original high level windows were retained along both side walls, and provide ample light while maintaining privacy. The blockwork wall along one side was lined with old bricks, which have been left exposed. The wall on the other side has a complex construction. On the outside, the original breeze block was covered in building felt as a moisture barrier, and boards. Inside, a grid of 2in. x 1in. (50 x 25mm) timber encases a 2in. (50mm) layer of compressed

fibreglass and provides a fixing for foil-backed plasterboard.

The sunken area below the main bedroom is 6ft 6in. (2.0m) high, with a door to the bathroom behind. A striking feature of this house is the spiral staircase leading up from the living area into the bedroom above. Its parana pine treads are screwed on to cantilevered supports of square-section steel. The staircase is an obvious space-saver in a small house such as this. A timber beam was slung across the building to support the bedroom; two vertical steel stanchions take its weight.

The inside wall of the 8ft-deep gallery bedroom is sloped, with louvred doors which fold open to look out over the living area below. They give more light and depth to the living room when open, and close at night for cosiness and privacy in the bedroom. High-level windows in the raised sloping roof make the bedroom very sunny.

Left. Dramatic impact in a hall created through bold colours and a dynamic design. *Above.* A living room furnished with junk shop 'finds' including the luxurious chaise longue and roomy chairs and couch.

Combining old and new

Interior design can successfully combine 'old world charm' with a modern look. It doesn't take a great deal of money, but it does require careful planning and imaginative ideas. This converted home in Australia effectively combines the old with the new. It took time and energy, but the costs were kept down to a minimum.

This small brick house was built about the time of the First World War. Over the past five years, it has been renovated by journalist Robbie Burns and his wife Sue. The house was given an old world charm through the imaginative use of colour, a wise choice of wallpaper, and an inexpensive collection of Victorian furniture.

The colourful entrance hall sets off the tone for the rest of the house. Originally it had been dark and unwelcoming. It was livened up by the deep red walls and the bold black and white floor tiling. The oval sepia photograph over the door frames and the wooden hat rack and table add to the period feeling. From the hall the eye carries on through the other rooms, which are cleverly accented by a contrasting white door frame, luxurious red velvet curtains and a bright canary yellow door.

Often, using bold clear colours in sharp con-

trast to one another can have a dramatic impact. The main thing to keep in mind is that the larger the area, the more effective this application of colour contrast should be. The black and white floor here, for instance, would probably make a small bedroom or bathroom too hectic—a softer pattern is more successful in a small room.

The hall motif is then picked up in the living room, which combines a luxurious period flavour with a modern one. The abstract painting over the fireplace, for example, does not clash with the rich velvet chaise longue which seems to emerge from the past—the colour tie-in eliminates this possible incongruity.

If you're mixing different period looks in your decor, try to find one element which serves to co-ordinate your scheme. This can be done by using similar textures—leather or tweed, say— or by the clever use of colour, as in this house. A rich red holds the various items together and integrates the different styles and textures.

The furniture in the living room was bought from a junk shop, and then 'face lifted' by the owners from the re-upholstering to the stripping and re-varnishing. The old varnish was stripped by taking a pad of steel wool, saturated in methylated spirit (paint stripper was also used if the lacquer was too heavy), the old finish removed, and then the surface re-finished with a mixture of linseed oil, lemon juice and methy-

lated spirit. Many fine old pieces of furniture can be bought quite reasonably because the surface is in poor condition and although restoring can be tedious, it can provide some attractive furniture economically.

In contrast to the clear bold colours of the living room, are the more muted and subdued colours of the study. The wallpaper here is the tone setter—the delicate pattern set against an antique gold background sets off the oval mirror and carved wooden fireplace.

Right. Two features in the dining room: A Victorian high chair and swinging louvred doors—designed for ease when serving.
Below. Old world charm exudes from this warm kitchen, centred around the hearth.

It's very important to select the 'right' wallpaper—it can enhance a room tenfold or, if badly chosen, distract from every item in the room. Before choosing your wallpaper, consider what your central colour theme will be, how the pattern will affect the furniture in the room and, lastly, will it be a colour and design that you can live with over a period of time. The eye quickly tires of a busy pattern.

The graceful arch of the fireplace is accented by the white plaster strip which contrasts well with the deep hues of the wooden surround. The bricks have been arranged in steps to allow a recess for a potted palm plant. As in the living room, the pieces of furniture here are junk shop 'finds', restored by the Burns. The rush matting on the floor as well as the shaggy rug are good selections because they're in keeping with the general colour tones of the room.

The same old world charm is found again in the bedroom, mainly inspired by the floral wallpaper. The attractive brass bedstead and delicate lace curtains also add to the period look. The heavy Victorian dressing table doesn't make the room look overly dark because of the light walls and carpeting.

The flower picture above the bed was made by Mrs. Burns, using felt and wool. The colours and design cleverly echo the wallpaper. The handsome red and blue bedspread also suggests a floral pattern. All the co-ordinating colour and design elements were carefully planned down to the last detail, including such touches as the deep red of the bedstead to the dainty painting of red flowers next to the window. Attention to details can go a long way to improving the appearance of a room.

Leading off the living room is a bright and lively dining room which had once been a dingy back room. The saffron wall is an effective backdrop for the multi-coloured tapestry hanging on the wall. It's a good idea to break up large expanses of bright colours; it's more restful on the eye. To get additional light in the room, a window was built into the wall. The leather covered high chair adds an unusual touch—it dates back to Victorian times.

Perhaps one of the nicest features is the swinging louvred doors linking together the dining room and kitchen. They were made from old railway carriage window shutters. Swinging doors make carrying dishes from one room to another easier and the louvred slats provide ventilation. The wood tones complement the yellow walls.

Moving into the kitchen, there is an old world atmosphere, too. The wood stove and brick-tiered chimney were retained—the stove is still used in winter. Tartan paper was put over the asbestos walls. The low wood walls, which were painted white, the delicate white curtains and red check table cloth and cushions all add to the atmosphere. Again, the cheerful touches of red tie the room together.

At the back of the house a playroom/television room was added. A bathroom and laundry room are just beyond. A nice touch, which sets this part of the house apart, are the wooden steps leading up to it. Raised or lowered floors add interest to any room—they cause the viewer to stop and take note. Other eye-catching features are the leather chaise longue, the brass railing, and the old fashioned trolley. Potted plants are another feature which add to the period flavour.

A final look at this house shows how an effective and atmospheric decor can be attained without spending large amounts of money. Points to bear in mind if you're converting are finding a suitable colour scheme, selecting versatile wallpaper, and locating junk shops which have attractive furniture with potential for restoring.

Keeping your cool in the sun

Although buying a holiday house sounds a straightforward proposition on the face of it, the price of isolation is often a lack of amenities, causing unforeseen hazards when you want to convert it into a 'dream house'.

When design journalist Joyce Wretord and her husband decided to buy a cheap house in the sun and convert it for holidays, they undertook more than they bargained for. It took several summer holidays on various Mediterranean islands just to find a simple house of the right kind. It must be isolated, but not cut off, they decided, and within easy reach of a quiet beach. It must have water (either from mains or a well), electricity, and land suitable for a septic tank. It must have (or have space for) three bedrooms, a living room, bathroom, kitchen, and a large, shady terrace.

The process of choosing the ideal island was fairly lengthy. The Riviera was too expensive and too crowded; Majorca was ruled out because either water was lacking or the owners of houses seemed never to be found. The country houses in Malta were usually huddled together in groups, making solitude impossible. Eventually, the Wrefords settled on Menorca, with its friendly people and uncrowded beaches.

After much searching, they found an unconverted farmhouse, or *finca,* built in three-quarters of an acre, with a potato field at the back. There was no indoor sanitation, and no mains power, an old windmill on top of the roof being the only method of generating electricity. Several small rooms could be greatly improved if made into larger ones, but this would leave a shortage of bedrooms. However, a granary on the first floor was large enough to house three bedrooms and a bathroom, so provision was made on the ground floor for a self-contained

This converted finca *in Menorca is now a cool summer retreat. The windmill on the roof was once the only means of generating electricity.*

Left. Two rooms were knocked into one to make a large living room, with a wide arch formed in the old partition wall. Gnarled pieces of driftwood complement the simple decor.
Above. *White-painted walls and ceiling, quarry floor tiles and pale furnishing fabrics combine to make the bedrooms look cool.*
Below left. *Solidly built furniture gives the kitchen a rustic feeling.* ***Below.*** *Vines and bougainvillaea trail up the bamboo canopy shading the terrace, which would otherwise be an uncomfortable suntrap.*

suite of bedroom, bathroom and small sitting room.

The land that came with the house was too large for the Wrefords, so they arranged with a neighbouring farmer to exchange their prickly pear field for a strip of his land, which was needed for the septic tank. Electricity was brought in, and an electric pump was fixed to the outside cistern to take the mains water to a tank on the roof.

In planning the alterations, Joyce Wreford tried to interfere as little as possible with the character of the *finca.* When the large living room was made out of two smaller rooms, a wide arch was formed in the old partition wall. This arch is typical of the local architecture, and was constructed by local workmen without any design drawings. The small windows were

retained, because in the heat of the summer it is important to keep the house as cool as possible, and picture windows would have spoilt it. The windows are set in deep embrasures, showing the immense thickness of the walls, and these natural sills provide ledges for ornaments.

Joyce Wreford decided against curtains and opted for shutters which are fixed on the outside and can be closed during the heat of the day. Because the house is usually cool, she chose to avoid the usual hot-climate colours of blues and greens. Instead she has used yellows, pinks and oranges for the soft furnishings. These colours look fresh against the walls, which are painted throughout with the local brand of whitewash. Whitewashing of the country houses is a yearly ritual, carried out by the daily woman, who slops it on the walls, ceilings, beams and all, inside

and out. The old quarry tiles on the floors in the ground floor rooms have been matched in the new rooms upstairs. In places these are covered with rush mats and tumble twist rugs, which look well and are practical.

The garden consisted of a potato field with a large terrace near the house, and a small walled garden outside the kitchen. The beautiful garden walls, built with the local stone, act as wind breaks and are a typical feature of this area. Garden designer John Brooks drew up a plan to convert the rough ground into a disciplined garden full of typical Mediterranean plants like grapefruit, lemon, almond bougainvillaea, oleander, mimosa and palm trees. Unfortunately, cruel winter winds and the absence of regular water in summer have caused it to look rather more random than planned.

The best of old and new

No amount of conversion will turn a small house into a big one, but a simple extension built on to an old house can provide all the extra accommodation required, at reasonable cost.

Michael and Carol Nicol bought a two-up, two-down cottage in Hertfordshire. Parts of it were 17th century, with odd bits added later. Various ramshackle buildings were attached—shed, conservatory, lean-to kitchen, outside lavatory, and an outhouse with a corrugated iron roof. Once used for storing hay, the outhouse still had a manger and milk churns.

The cottage was once occupied by a man who dealt in rustic garden furniture, which he made and sold on the premises. Little had been done to the house since he left, although the fabric was sound. The Nicols felt that, although many of the outbuildings were unusable in their present state, once converted they could be incorporated with the cottage to make a comfortable family house. Architect Anthony Page

was asked to convert the house for them, as he lived nearby, and appreciated the rare qualities of that part of the old town that has become a conservation area. He realized, however, that the outbuildings would have to be demolished, although their basic shape could be retained in the design of the extension.

The architect was limited to some extent by various problems inherent in the site. One was the problem of ground levels. The site sloped up from the road, making the back garden considerably higher than the street level. The other major worry was one of light; the open side of the house faced almost due north, and the large house attached to it on the other side blocked much of the afternoon sun.

As the original cottage was structurally sound, it was left much as it was. The living room now acts as a study, with a dining room off it. An old

Right. The door at the front of the old part of the house is now sealed for safety, and access is through the gate at the side.

spiral staircase leads out of the study to the first floor, housing the main bedroom, two tiny bedrooms for the children, and a bathroom. The only alterations made to this part of the house were where the extension was added on; glazed doors have been used throughout to create a feeling of light and space. A minor problem was that the front door opened straight out from the

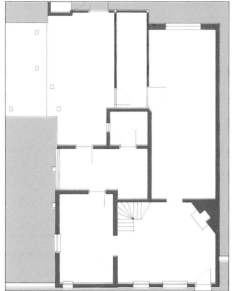

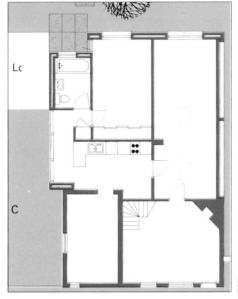

Top left and right. *The main entrance is now at the side of the house, where sliding glazed doors open into the corridor kitchen, which leads to both the living room and the old dining room. Painted whitewood units are complemented by ceramic tiles.*

Above left and right. *Floor plans showing the ground floor of the house before and after conversion. The single-storey extension to the house is of simple design, and follows the general lines of the old outbuildings, which were pulled down completely.*

living room on to the pavement, which was not only unsafe for small children, but also made the living room both draughty and noisy. This was solved simply by sealing the front door and extending floor-to-ceiling heavy silk curtains across the whole front wall, providing noise and draught protection. The main entrance is now through the sliding glazed doors leading into the corridor kitchen at the side of the house.

All the outbuildings were carefully pulled down, and the new living room constructed to follow both the roof slope and the rear line of the old outhouse, running back from the study. A spare bedroom, bathroom, and fitted kitchen were built alongside. The problem of sloping ground was solved by having the maximum amount of window area possible high in the walls at the back of the house, where the floor level was well below the ground outside. A vertical damp proof course was laid to protect the extension.

The living room has a flat ceiling, and an extra light source was provided here by two large

cone-shaped rooflights built in the space between the ceiling and the sloping outside roof. These rooflights have the clever effect of funnelling the daylight and diffusing it softly all over the living room. The roof space also houses the water tank.

It was important that the garden should be accessible from the entrance at the side of the house, so the rear wall of the extension was returned to leave room for a narrow path, which continues up the garden. The timber-framed glass screen entrance doors tie up well with the loggia in the drive at the side of the house, which was retained in its original state.

Right. *View from the new living room into the study in the old part of the house. The windows give directly on to the street, with the sealed-off front door alongside. The photograph above it shows the view from the study, with its old ceiling and wall timbers, looking back into the living room. The modern decor tones well with the old materials.*

Above. *The old back living room before it was converted into a playroom. The lean-to conservatory was removed, and a terrace now runs along the back of the house.* **Top.** *The open-plan area at the back, with sliding windows opening on to the terrace. The kitchen is round the corner on the right; the door on the left leads to the playroom.* **Left.** *Looking back down the hall towards the front door. The open wooden staircase has closely-spaced banisters for safety.* **Right.** *Detail view under the staircase.*

Child-proofed for safety

A household full of young children can revolve around their activities. This is seldom taken into account in planning, but sometimes in a large house it is possible to provide play areas for them, rather than give all the priorities to facilities for adults.

Architects David and Miriam Howitt were asked to modernize a large late Victorian house in West Hampstead, London, for a family with four children, and provide a self-contained flat above. The emphasis was to be on family life, with adult activities playing a distinctly minor role.

The house had previously been owned by an elderly woman who rented out the upstairs rooms as bed-sitters, each with a gas fire and sink, and minimal furniture. Her own living quarters on the ground floor were particularly run-down, with an antiquated kitchen.

The double-fronted house had five bedrooms (one of which now acts as a study) and a bathroom on the first floor. This floor has been modernized, but the layout retained much as it was originally. There were three reception rooms on the ground floor, a kitchen with three ancillary rooms off it, and a conservatory at the back. The conservatory, larder and scullery were knocked down to make room for a terrace to run along the back of the house, and the kitchen was incorporated with the rear of the hall to provide an open-plan kitchen/dining area.

Part of one of the two reception rooms at the front of the house was divided off for a cloakroom, and the remaining area is now used as a hobby room. The other room is now a comfortable living room for the parents. The large living room at the back was converted into a playroom.

One important aspect of the brief was that everything should be super-safe. The double-glazed picture windows on to the terrace at the back of the playroom are protected by a crash barrier which also serves as a bench. It consists of a wooden rail fixed firmly into the floor with steel dowels, and permits the children to career up to it on their tricycles, and even topple over it, without crashing through the glass. Floor to ceiling unlined curtains in robust striped hessian cover the whole wall, and the curtain track extends round to the side wall to let in the maximum amount of daylight. A cupboard unit running along one wall incorporates a recess for parking tricycles. A modular cupboard unit has doors which interchange to vary the display of toys on the shelves. The walls are covered in hessian, for pinning things on.

To give the children plenty of space for riding around the hall on their tricycles, the existing ugly staircase was removed and replaced with an open flight up to the first floor. The banisters were closely spaced, like the dowels on the sides of babies' cots.

The original oak parquet floor in the playroom was sanded and polyurethane sealed to withstand the ravages of children's games. The hall is covered with a brown sisal carpet, which is hardwearing and a practical colour. The floor in the kitchen is factory-sealed beech.

The chimney breast on the side wall of the kitchen has been camouflaged by fitting the deeper units, such as cooker and refrigerator, at each side, with the shallower sink unit in front of the protruding section. In this way the equipment runs flush at the front. The cupboards above the sink have aluminium rods instead of shelves for draining saucepans, so that the water drips down into the sink. Since the dining area is part of the kitchen, a Venetian blind fitted behind the sink pulls down to conceal the ugly washing up equipment and mops when not in use. An extractor fan above the cooker has been fitted with controls for recirculating the air.

A small door to the left of the cooker hides a food mixer fitted on filing cabinet runners, which extends right out on to the counter for working. The window at the side of the kitchen was blocked in, and replaced by a large window overlooking the back garden.

A ramp running up the side of the house enables prams to be pushed up to the back door; it also conceals all the meters, which can now be read from outside. The only alteration to the front elevation was a new double front door, wide enough to wheel prams through, which opens into a draught lobby.

The old stairwell has been used to provide access from the separate entrance at the side of the house to the flat on the second floor.

DAVID AND MIRIAM HOWITT

The house in the hill

Inverting the conventional layout of a house by putting the living areas on top of the bedrooms may seem revolutionary, but in this way you can take advantage of a pleasant view.

When architect Philip Pank was commissioned to design a house to be built on an attractive London site, he was given a fairly open brief. The clients wanted a spacious house with a large living room and combined kitchen and dining room nearby. There were to be two double bedrooms, two bathrooms, a music room, self-contained staff flat and a double garage.

It was to be built on a site of just over half an acre (0.2 ha), overlooking the east side of Hampstead Heath. Instead of breaking up the plot by building the house near the road with gardens in front and behind, Philip Pank decided to set it 'dug' into the hill at the back of the site. This would not only give a feeling of privacy, but also take full advantage of the large and

Natural materials have been used and left exposed over much of this house, with fine detailing throughout. **Opposite page, top.** *The large first-floor living room has sliding glazed doors leading on to the terrace at the front.* **Far left.** *Teak cupboards and black tiles give a rich appearance to the kitchen, which is separated from the dining room (**centre**) by double-sided china cupboards.* **Right.** *The pine boarded ceilings are open joisted, and the floors are maple strip.*

This page, above. *The bedrooms are on the ground floor, with French windows leading on to the garden.* **Left.** *The first-floor terrace runs the full length of the house.*

attractive garden, which slopes away in front of the house towards the Heath.

The site has been exploited by building the ground floor—housing bedrooms, bathrooms, music and utility rooms—into the slope, with a paved area in front and only high level windows at the back. The living floor has been constructed above, set back from the ground floor, with a terrace running along the front, partly sheltered by a canopy. A staff flat was built on top of a double garage behind the house.

By reversing the conventional method of building the bedrooms above the living floor, the architect has managed to give the living rooms a pleasant view of the Heath from high up. Double glazed sliding doors open from the 20ft x 30ft (6 x 9m) living room on to the tiled terrace. Instead of an ugly safety rail, a flower trough was constructed along the front of the terrace. The inside ledge, paved with precast concrete slabs, was made wide enough to sit on. This would also prevent anyone who might trip from falling into the garden below. The beams carrying the cantilevered canopy which covers part of the terrace span the front and back walls of the house and jut out behind.

The glazed French doors on the ground floor rooms open out on to the garden. Continental vertical slatted wood shutters can be pulled down at night so that the windows are secure while still open. Natural materials have been used and left exposed over much of the house, but the ground floor rooms were plastered and carpeted throughout.

The first floor is covered throughout in maple strip, and a corridor leads from the living room to the dining room. The kitchen and dining room are separated by a room divider constructed of double-sided cupboards with sliding pine doors on the dining room side and glass doors in the kitchen. A door at the end completes the partition, so that the rooms can be closed off from each other.

Rescue on the river

The Thames sailing barge has suffered a sad demise in recent years. At the beginning of the century it was a common, and magnificent, sight on the East Coast of England and River Thames estuary. Now, most Thames barges have been broken up, or are rotting in derelict wharves.

When artist-designer Allan Chidgey bought a disused barge to use as a studio he took on more than he expected, because he decided not only to convert it into a home but also to restore the hull. The result is an elegant sailing barge, fully rigged, which serves as a permanent home and studio. Its Thames-side mooring in front of a distinctive Georgian church makes it an idyllic retreat.

The Raven was built in 1904 as a traditional Thames sailing barge. It was used for carrying wheat and general cargo from the East Coast to London up to 1965. Long before that (in about 1948) the mast had been cut down and it had been converted to a motor barge.

The raw material the designer had to work on was a wooden hull 80ft by 18ft, two open holds surrounded by decks, an engine room in the stern, and a forecabin. The barge leaked badly, and the hull was in very bad condition.

The transformation involved a great deal of forethought and hard work, and a solution to the problems inherent in such a venture demanded a certain amount of ingenuity.

First, the whole existing structure had to be made good, which involved stripping it down completely and burning off all the paint and tar. All internal steel was treated with rust sealer.

The longest and most arduous task was the recaulking of the decks (filling between the planks with waterproof jointing) to prevent leakage. This involved stripping out nearly a mile of 3in. seams and refilling them with oakum, tar and pitch. The decks were then rebolted to strengthen them.

A temporary wooden roof was erected over the exposed area to protect the interior while work was in progress. Even at this stage it was important to allow adequate ventilation to prevent rot.

One of the worst problems was the damage that had been caused by steel plates which were fixed to the exposed woodwork to protect it from the steel grabs used for unloading cargo. These had corroded and eaten into the wood, leaving severe gashes and rents when they were removed. This was overcome by putting a $\frac{1}{4}$in. layer of a plastic-based filler over the wood. This gives it a smooth surface while retaining its texture and appearance.

The floor had also suffered considerable damage. A new floor was laid directly on to the old one, using old floorboards bought from demolition sites. Once they were cleaned and

ALAN DUNS

ALLAN CHIDGEY

scraped and the nails had been knocked out, they provided a good, solid floor at minimal expense. They were sanded down with an industrial sander, then polished and coated with a polyurethane varnish to give extra durability.

Electricity on a houseboat is essential, as gas or oil lights are not bright enough for working or reading. However, a connection from the nearest power source involves a considerable voltage drop, so that only lighting, a refrigerator and 'light' appliances such as record players can be run off electricity.

Cooking is done with bottled gas, which is economical and convenient, as the containers are delivered by van. Water, which comes from the mains, is run off a large tank and pumped to a header tank to give adequate pressure to the kitchen and bathroom supply. The basin and sink had to be raised higher than is usual to allow outlets above the water line.

The layout of the interior was determined by the need to use the low areas (maximum height 5ft 6in.) under the sailing beams. This was done by building a cabin on one side and a bathroom on the other, and placing the ends of both the bed and the bath under the lowest beam in each case.

Tongued and grooved planking was used for the partition walls. To allow for the flexing of the vessel ($\frac{1}{2}$in.-1in.) with the movement of the tide, these walls had either to be hung from the ceiling and left clear of the floor, or fixed to the floor and left clear of the ceiling. The remaining gaps at the top or bottom were then disguised with beading.

The space between this area and the existing forecabin—11ft x 18ft—was made into a kitchen/dining room. Cupboards and shelves were built on the partition walls and a bench seat was fixed against the side walls of the dining area. The floor beam running along the centre of the boat creates a natural division between the kitchen and the dining area.

The forecabin is used as the main bedroom, and the remaining space (32ft x 18ft) in the rear of the boat is the sitting room/studio.

The walls were painted white, and the woodwork was treated with varnish to give colour. Skylights in the roof give a generous amount of daylight, and a skyline view of a church. These skylights were recovered from other boats which were being broken up.

When the new roof was built, the old curved hatch covers were forced down over a centre beam, leaving maximum headroom and giving a more pronounced and attractive curve to the ceiling. To give sufficient circulation of air, two hatches were built into the roof, one at each end. These also give access to the interior via ladders. Portholes were fitted into the sides of the roof to provide additional ventilation. This does not spoil the boat's exterior appearance or affect its sailing qualities.

Heating is provided by slow-burning anthracite fires, which are both elegant and efficient. They heat the water and also help prevent condensation. A gas water heater is used in hot weather.

Cupboards and bookshelves are built in, and free-standing furniture has been kept to a minimum. This is because the sloping floor makes it stand at a slight angle.

'The Raven' was built in Rochester in 1904, as a traditional Thames sailing barge.
Opposite, above. *The outside of the barge was scarcely altered by the conversion, but the interior, below, was transformed.*
This page, top. *The sitting room/studio in the rear of the barge was left its original size (32ft x 18ft). Skylights in the roof let in plenty of light.*
Above. *The ladder leads to a hatch which is used for access. Another hatch was built in the roof above the kitchen/dining room.*
Right. *A cabin under the sailing beam on one side. The maximum height is 5ft 6in., so the bed is fitted underneath the lowest part, with the water tank underneath it.*

ALAN DUNS

Flexible living for the future

In this housing scheme in Velp, Holland, the houses are built in circular groups instead of the usual straight streets or blocks. They have been specially designed so that they give the most flexible use of space possible, to create highly individual and convenient homes. Their design overcomes one of the main objections levelled at modern housing—that it looks regimental and offers few opportunities for imaginative treatment inside.

A generous landscaped garden goes with each house, and communal grounds help to boost a 'family' atmosphere. The scheme was designed by architects Schouten and De Jonge of Lievelde, and was landscaped by A. Gerts of Meteren. But even without the benefit of

specialist advice, you can adapt many of their design ideas into your home, or your neighbourhood. Many housing estates now operate 'Good neighbour schemes' where groups of householders can establish their own communal amenities and take a pride in the neighbourhood.

Though the whole idea is to make life more pleasant for the community, the individual houses themselves are built with privacy in mind. Each house has one blank outside wall with no windows in it, which is ideal if the owners want to add an extension later. Another side wall slopes to enclose a private terrace at the back of each house.

All the walls—both the inside and outside surfaces—are of natural light-coloured brick, with which the dark brown wood framing makes a striking contrast. Exposed brickwork in interior walls is fashionable, and its natural rough texture

makes a room seem more welcoming. Pine boards, unpainted oak beams, and hessian hangings are other examples of such natural materials. They provide plenty of interest to the eye, making most ornaments unnecessary, and so leaving the room spacious and uncluttered.

This Dutch house is remarkable for its flexibility. There is enough room to re-arrange the space as the family grows up and its needs change. The interior combines both open and closed-plan features; you can leave it as one open area or divide it up according to your requirements. There is a covered area at the entrance which can serve as a carport or a sheltered play area, or even as a studio for messy jobs.

The upper floor can be left as it is or split into one large or two small rooms, and the space under the sloping roof can be used as bathroom,

AVENUE—DAILY TELEGRAPH SYNDICATION

Left. *The interior is split into three levels—the lower floor being sub-divided into eating and lounging areas. The upper floor is reached via a 'ladder' staircase, and the two lower areas are distinguished by their individual floor coverings.*

Above, left. *Warm tones for the sleeping area upstairs. The orange and white storage unit harmonizes well with the sharp green of the bedspread and yellow cushions.*

Above, right. *Another corner of the upper floor that is reserved for sleeping. Here the storage unit acts as room divider, and an ultra-modern daybed provides an elegant focal point. The wall-to-wall carpet helps to create an illusion of greater space.*

Right. *A communal patio for several families who live in this housing scheme.*

bedroom and storage space, or as two fair-sized bedrooms and a small shower area instead. Obviously not every home provides such good opportunities for rearranging the interior, but nevertheless many homes keep too rigidly to the conventional use of space when they could be remodelled without much difficulty.

The appearance of the interior is as unconventional as its plan. In the living-room, attention is drawn to the ceiling by arched strips fixed between the beams in the flat part. Where the ceiling slopes, the beams have been left exposed to give a natural appearance that goes well with the unpainted brick walls.

It is always a good idea to plan your decor round the tones of the building materials. Here, very plain but subtle colours have been chosen to create a relaxed appearance. The sitting well, which is three steps lower then the dining area, has been carpeted in dark brown. This emphasizes the cosiness of the low area with its open fire, and harmonizes with the brown and white of the loose furniture. There is a brown leather sofa, two matching easy chairs and six white plastic tables scattered around the area.

A round white dining table and four elegant chairs upholstered in brown fabric fit neatly into the dining area. Green and white checked curtains covering the window wall add a cheerful note.

The predominance of white in the overall colour scheme is a deliberate move to add freshness to the interior. White brings a clarity to a decorative scheme that no other colour can match, and also reflects light to make any room seem bright and spacious.

Setting up an unobtrusive kitchen in an open-plan scheme is always a problem. Here it is overcome by tucking in a compact kitchen beside the dining area, with the units arranged into a wall that divides off a corridor running down the middle of the flat. Sheer beige curtains close off the kitchen when it is not in use, blending in well with the overall decor. Beige, oatmeal, grey, mushroom and other muted or neutral colours do not stand out from the background, and so are excellent colours for camouflage. Equal *tones* will camouflage, even where the *colours* are different whereas a blatant contrast in tone will highlight.

The upper floor is an open space above the living area and is reached by an open staircase from the dining section. This space could easily be divided off with a conventional brick wall, thus separating it from the ground floor, if more privacy was required at a later date.

The large upper area is split in two by a room divider constructed from double-sided cupboards. One section is used for hobbies, and the other is a spare bedroom. A flap-down bed is incorporated into this side of the room divider—this is a particularly good idea for rooms where space is cramped, for example in a playroom that doubles as bedroom.

A small shower room completely tiled in white leads off the spare room. In the bedroom itself, a sunny effect has been achieved through the use of yellow and green, which is set off well by the white walls and units. The cupboard doors are painted yellow, a warming colour to contrast with the cool green of the fabric on the pouffe and bedspread. Both colours combine in the flower motif of the curtain material, and are echoed in the cushion covers. Two-tone colour schemes benefit from meeting in a focal point where the eye can quickly appreciate the contrasting or complementary colours.

The main bedroom has been fitted into the space under the sloping roof at the back of the house, with a bathroom next to it. A completely glazed wall leads on to the terrace, making the bedroom very sunny.

Pink and purple provide the bold colour scheme. The double bed is enclosed by sheer purple curtains hung on a circular brass track. The chairs are covered in pink fabric, and a pink and purple floral pattern is used for the bedspread, backdrop and curtains.

This house is an experiment with space—its keynote is flexibility and convenience for the family who will grow up with it. It is an ideal example of how to mould your house to suit the needs of your family instead of letting it dictate to you.

A fresh look at a large house

A large house with a lot of rooms—many intercommunicating—can be converted in a number of different ways with equal success. But in replanning a house to suit a particular family, everyone's personal needs and activities must be taken into consideration. It is well worthwhile to bear in mind that a conversion on this scale is a long-term project—so you must try to anticipate the future variations in the space allocation requirements of a growing family. Remember that the space your children will need for hobbies when they are young must be easy to adapt as they get older.

Interior designers Peter and Juliet Glynn Smith outgrew their last house when their family increased in size. They then needed somewhere large enough to house them (plus three children and a nanny), with space for them both to work as well. The idea of a family room was a must, and this had to be considered as well as the usual kitchen, living and dining rooms. The lack of a garage and a garden in their last house had aggravated them into putting these needs well at the top of the list of essentials in any new house they looked at.

When they finally found the house that—in size, at least—fitted their requirements, they nearly gave up at the prospect of the mammoth task of converting it into a habitable dwelling. The situation was delightful: close to the River Thames, with well-wooded communal grounds behind the house and their own ample front and back gardens. The rural river setting with its feeling of tranquillity and the safe open places around made it a perfect base for bringing up a young family.

The house had been well built in about 1860, but was nonetheless in an extremely sad condition. It had last been redecorated about 20 years before, and then allowed to go to seed. Most of the washbasins were cracked, and the bath had a hole right through it. The previous occupants—obviously mostly teenagers—had decorated their rooms with silver spray paint and gaudy posters. The playroom had been used as a motor cycle workshop, and so it went on throughout the house, each problem appearing more daunting than the last.

When the Glynn Smiths bought the two-storey double-fronted house, it was not planned for modern living. There were several fairly major structural alterations that needed doing: central heating had been installed (rather badly) but it was old-fashioned and needed replanning; the house also had to be rewired. There was masses of space, but it had not been put to the best use. The first job was to assign a function to each of the rooms and then proceed with the conversion.

There were four main rooms on the ground floor; one of them, at the back, was more like a corridor with doors on all sides, and no blank walls to stand furniture against. This became the family room, and was brought back into circulation by blocking up two of its doors, thus allowing at least one wall for some furniture. A frieze painted above the fitted dresser cupboard unit now disguises the very high ceiling, and makes the room look less box-like.

Off the family room, there was a long narrow kitchen with cupboards on both sides, narrowing it even more, and one high-level window allowing views of only the tops of the trees. A butler's pantry also led off the family room; it was like the black hole of Calcutta, with washing dripping onto the old floor. Thick pipes ran along the walls in all directions, and an old sink stood in one corner. A Victorian outbuilding running along the side of the kitchen housed a lavatory and the oil tank which fed the large black boiler in the cellar.

The Glynn Smiths planned the ground floor round the kitchen, which was completely altered. First they had it gutted, then removed the wall dividing the original kitchen and pantry, moved the door to leave enough room for a good run of units, and replaced the high-level window with a full height french window leading to the back garden. Half the outhouse was knocked down so as to let more light into the kitchen, which had been dark and dingy; the

lavatory and laundry room were retained. A door was knocked through to the old main room at the front, which logically became the dining room.

The dining room had been the old playroom. It had a very badly pitted cork floor, walls covered with posters and built-in desks, a window seat over the antiquated radiator in the square bay at the front overlooking the front garden, and the walls and doors badly marked by darts and drawing pins. Paper-backed felt was used to camouflage the damaged walls, and white vinyl tiles give the floor a fresh, smooth appearance.

The other large room at the front looked like a furniture store, with heavy curtains and a pelmet. Its good points were that it was a particularly light and airy room and led through two french windows into a huge conservatory at the side of the house. It was an obvious decision to make this room into the studio, where the two designers could work in attractive surroundings. The conservatory alongside, once heaped high with bicycles and painted (glass and all) in orange, purple and

Below. *In the family room, a decorating trick to lower a high ceiling: a wide band of colour painted at the top of the wall, banded with yellow and red striped ribbon.*

Above left. A coat of white paint restored the outside of the house to its former glory. The window blinds combine with the flowers to add splashes of colour. Above right. In the main bathroom, the areas surrounding the basin and bath are faced in plastic-laminated cork tiles, which water does not mark, with natural cork tiles on the walls above.
Left. The welcoming hall is painted yellow. The curving banisters were painted white, and the attractive herringbone-patterned boards in the hall were repaired, sanded and sealed.

black, is now a bright garden room, lined with vines and colourful pot plants.

The living room at the back retained its former function because of its size and attractive view over the back garden. Once a drab, grey room, it has now been transformed into a cool, inviting, comfortable retreat by the addition of cream paper-backed hessian on the walls, a luxurious off-white carpet, and natural wool curtains and upholstery.

The ugly mantelpiece was ripped out, and the open fireplace simply edged with a chrome frame. A white plastic piano and exotic plants in

enormous earthenware storage pots catch the eye, but the focal point is definitely the appliqué picture with ziggurat chequerboard pattern which hangs on one wall. It was designed specially by Juliet Glynn Smith, and made by Debbie Burnham, who sewed together the pieces of cream and white fabric with silver lurex thread.

The planning of the first floor and who slept where was dictated by the plumbing. The main bedroom was originally at the front above the studio—a dark room with a fitted wardrobe. The two rooms at the back with a view over the

garden were both more suitable for the main bedroom, but a choice had to be made between the added advantage of either a balcony or a bathroom. They finally decided that the opportunity of having a small dressing room and bathroom leading off the bedroom was too good to miss, so the back room with the balcony became the spare bedroom. The two large front rooms became children's bedrooms with the nanny's room (formerly a dressing room with a washbasin) connecting with the younger children's room.

The main bathroom off the small dressing room was completely refitted, with a false ceiling put in, and a new bath and vanity unit built. The second bathroom was converted out of what was originally a combination of a high, narrow corridor, a lavatory and a linen cupboard. By knocking them all into one, swapping the doors about, and adding a false ceiling and a new bath and washbasin, it became the children's bathroom.

Raising the roof

Adding another storey to a house need not be difficult or expensive. This floor was built in eight weeks by the architect and his friends.

When architect Peter Bell bought a terraced house in North London, it was divided into three flats whose inhabitants had been far from house-proud. In order to accommodate himself, his wife and their four children, and also provide office space for his small firm of architects, he decided to build an extra floor on top.

The basement area, once occupied by six people, was converted into office space. The front room on the ground floor is now a dining room, with a kitchen behind; an old bedroom at the back now houses a small workshop. The partition walls in the three-roomed flat on the first floor were knocked down to make one large living room with study area at one end. On the second floor there are three bedrooms and a bathroom for the children, and the new floor on top of the house comprises the main bedroom and bathroom.

To make the ground floor area more light and spacious, part of the wall separating the dining room from the hall was knocked down. This area doubles as a playroom for the children, where they can be supervised by their mother while she is working in the kitchen behind. Much of the furniture was designed and made by Peter Bell. In the kitchen, which was converted very quickly and cheaply, fitted cupboard units combine with the cooker, refrigerator and washing machine to form a U-shaped working area.

The dining room is simply furnished, with solid-looking furniture and alcove bookshelves. The colour scheme is orange—sheer curtains, hessian on the walls, dome lamp—creating a warm glow in the room, particularly at night. The lighting has been designed so that dinner guests cannot catch a premature glimpse of the laid dining table as they walk down the hall.

The stairs lead straight into the large living room, which occupies the entire first floor space (30ft. x 16ft.). The ceiling joists are supported by two steel beams slung from party wall to party wall. A seating area has been built into the front half of this room, separating

Below. This view of the terrace shows how the roofline was altered by the extra floor, set back to comply with planning regulations.

Above left. In the hall, a 'corridor' effect was avoided by a knocking down a section of the partition wall, to incorporate it with the dining room and **(above right)** kitchen. The floor of this area is covered throughout with 2ft (0.6m) square plywood panels.

Right. The dining room at the front doubles as a playroom for the children, who can be supervised by their mother while she is working in the kitchen. The orange curtains and lampshade combine to create a warm glow.

Below left. The stairs lead straight into the living room, which occupies the entire first floor, with a study area at the back. Adjustable spotlights fixed to a track can be directed so as to give the most effective lighting arrangement. **Below right.** The built-in seating area at the front of the room is constructed to form a practical 'perimeter development'. Shelves cover the upper part of one wall, with alcoves below.

PETER BELL

Left. French windows lead from the main bedroom on the top floor to a small paved terrace. The cantilevered dressing table shelf is supported by L-shaped uprights.
Below. Alcove bookshelves and pinboard panels make this an ideal boy's bedroom-cum-study. Bold colours and durable materials are used in all the children's bedrooms.

it from the study area at the back, where Peter Bell and his wife can work. A further delineation between the living and study areas is made by different floor coverings. The donkey brown wool carpet in the hall and up the stairs continues into the study area and throughout the circulation areas.

The built-in 'perimeter development' in the living room forms a square conversation area of a most practical design. It can seat up to 30 people, where no-one is ever more than nine feet away from anyone else. In this way it is possible for anyone in a group to talk to the others without raising his voice. The banquette-type seating is constructed in blockboard, providing ample storage space underneath. Heavy oatmeal fabric was used to upholster the boxed foam rubber cushions, the sloping backs being softer than the seats. By building in the furniture, a saving was made on the floor area left to be carpeted. The shaggy oatmeal carpet turns up under the skirting below the seating units. Lime green silk scatter cushions add a splash of colour to this neutral scheme, and match the hessian covering the walls. On one side of the seating area a cantilevered wooden surface acts as a table.

Fitted bookshelves were built all along the upper part of one wall in the living room, and reach right up to the ceiling. Naturally those books which are referred to least often are kept on the top shelves. Two large speakers for the sophisticated record player have been incorporated into this shelf unit. Lower shelves along this wall and the one opposite enclose bays faced with hessian-covered pinboard for

displays of photographs and knick knacks.

A 30ft. long plywood beam spanning the ceiling from front to back carries a lighting track with adjustable spotlights fixed to it. A handsome grandfather clock without its case hangs on the wall between the two windows, flattered by a spotlight. Sheer curtains in oatmeal and white cover the enormous sash windows most of the time, with natural linings behind which can be drawn at night.

The three bedrooms for the children on the second floor each have a definite colour scheme based round one strong colour: coffee in one, maroon in another, and yellow in the other. Otherwise they are furnished in the same cheap and practical materials: hessian-covered pinboard panels on the walls, for sticking up pictures and maps, and plywood on the floor. The bright little half-tiled bathroom is lime green and white, with an enormous mirror along one wall creating a sense of extra space.

A large window in the wall above lets in lots of light over the stairs and landings. The walls throughout the circulation areas are papered in anaglypta painted with white gloss, making them scrubbable. The uneven surface of this wallpaper hides most of the imperfections of the old walls.

Most of the new floor built on top of the house is given up to the main bedroom, with fitted wardrobes along one side and a dressing table unit opposite. A bathroom has been tucked in behind, with a tank room off it. French windows at the front open on to a terrace paved with light asbestos tiles.

Peter Bell has constructed all the furniture in

this room from Baltic pine-veneered blockboard, treated with clear lacquer to retain its light colour. The cantilevered dressing table has mirrors in each of the four bays with shelves above; hidden tungsten tube lights cast light down. The fitted wardrobes have simple doors on hidden catches, with the same concealed lighting above, throwing light on to the ceiling. The bedhead with flap-down doors is made to match. This natural finish is echoed by the exposed ceiling joists and softwood frames on the French windows.

Some form of sub-floor was needed on the old floors to even off any irregularities in the boards, and prevent dirt from rising through the cracks. During the conversion work, therefore, $\frac{1}{4}$in. thick 2ft. square lacquered plywood panels were laid on the old floors. These have the advantage of being able to be laid like a carpet, and are also a most practical floor covering. In the living room they have been retained, acting as a sub-floor for the carpet, which was laid directly on top. In places, however, these plywood squares remain as the only floor covering. In the dining room and kitchen they provide an attractive floor which can easily be washed clean, and in the children's bedrooms they supply the necessary practical and hardwearing surface.

The central heating system chosen by Peter Bell takes advantage of the structure of the old house. Using ducted warm air, it is both cheap and flexible. The ducts run up the recesses between the chimneys, and grilles have been placed strategically in all the rooms, avoiding the bulk of unsightly radiators.

A Regency conversion

A strategic conversion makes the most of the intrinsic nature of a house. Too often people buy a house for converting with a preconceived notion of how the finished product should emerge. This attitude can create 'blind spots' to unique features which already exist. In converting the Regency home here, full advantage was taken of its original shape and character.

Below. A basement dining/kitchen room set off in bold black and white. Modern acrylic chairs add to a spacious, streamlined look while an adjustable lamp gives a splash of colour to the subdued medley of creams.

Built in 1810 as a private residence in North London, this terraced house eventually became a shop—its location on a main road made it an ideal spot for business. About seven years ago it was bought by an industrial designer who had two objectives in mind when purchasing.

Firstly, there was an antique shop at the front which the buyer wanted to take over and perpetuate and, secondly, the rest of the house lent itself to a potentially successful conversion—the inherent grace in the structural lines created a natural charm.

The house is long and narrow with a gently curved brick wall at the back which runs through all three floors. This curve adds an unusual note to the decor in the basement dining/kitchen room, the ground floor drawing room and the first floor bedroom. It adds an immediate note of distinction and elegance to the house.

Another appealing feature is the unpredictable floor levels. Originally there was a small garden between the front of the house and the street. In about 1880 it was converted into a single-floor shop. From there one flight of stairs leads down to the basement and spacious back garden beyond. A second set of stairs—about four or five steps—takes you up to the drawing room and study. This irregularity in floor levels adds personality to the house.

If you want your conversion to have originality, you've got a head start if the house you buy has features like the curved wall here or the variety in floor levels. When house hunting, keep an eye out for aspects which could be highlighted to give your home a different look. 'Givens' are often neglected because the eye glosses over them too quickly. Look very carefully at the visual endowments or impediments a house has to offer before making it yours.

Conversion work in this Regency house began in the basement which consisted of two rather dreary, dark rooms. The windows on the curved wall were made into wide French doors, allowing more welcome light to filter into the room. The partitioning wall was pulled down and replaced with a steel joist which spans the 15ft width of the room.

Another wall was erected farther back to allow enough space for kitchen appliances to be fitted in without encroaching on the original space definition of the room. A false ceiling, built out from the steel joist, and floor tiles differing from those in the main body of the room, help to define this small 'kitchen' area.

The effect achieved was one of greater spaciousness and light. All the furniture and decoration was then scaled to the room. A round dining table, complemented by perspex and chromium chairs, echoes the curve in the wall. The transparent and light texture of the perspex was an excellent choice for this small room; it allows the flow of space to continue. A heavy wooden or upholstered chair might have hindered the visual fluidity.

It's very important to select furniture according to the size of the room it's going into. Light, delicate pieces can look lost and insignificant in a large room with a high ceiling, whereas heavy or bulky items can overwhelm a small room by completely dominating it. In general, furniture should follow the size dictates of a room. If you've already invested in a certain style of furniture and are moving, make certain it will fit in with the sense of space in your new home.

The adjustable Italian lamp over the dining table is in keeping with the light, non-bulky feeling of the room. Especially small spot lights were put on the low ceiling—consideration was given to their size so they would not seem too large in comparison to the room. A potted palm plant on the floor fits gracefully into the curve in the wall.

One of the most eye-catching visual accents in the room is the floor which is covered in black and white marble squares, arranged in a checkered design. The marble was bought second-hand, is easy to clean and adds to the period flavour of the house. The walls and ceiling were painted a neutral shade of off-white.

Behind the wall housing the compact kitchen units, an efficient bathroom was built. An advantage to this layout was that the plumbing systems of both the kitchen and bathroom could be made together. This also meant that there were no ugly pipes on the two floors above. The same colouring in subtle shades of soft browns and creams were used here.

Full advantage was taken of the area under the stairs which often becomes an untidy catchall for miscellaneous items in other homes. The area was broken down into three sections: a broom cupboard at the highest point, followed by an area for the dustbin, and finishing off with a section for kitty litter. The complete area was then covered with blockboard with the appropriate doors. This is a superb example of how often wasted space under the stairs can be utilized for many purposes.

The flight of stairs leads up to the 'shop' which has now been converted into a studio so the industrial designer can work at home. It's ideal because light pours in through both a slanted skylight above and the entire side of the house front, made from floor-to-ceiling panels of rough-cast glass. This unusual choice of material was made because it was relatively inexpensive to purchase and install the glass, it helped to keep the former 'shop' character of the room, and also provided natural light for working. Durable studded rubber was put down on the floor which is very practical in that the studio also doubles up as a visually arresting entrance room.

The window, which was once part of the outside wall when the garden existed, was opened out to let more light into the study. It creates a lovely link between the studio and study—between the street level and the ground floor, several feet higher.

The two ground floor rooms were basically left as they had been. The door between the smaller study and drawing room was widened to create a greater movement of space and light, while still giving the impression of two separate and distinct rooms.

The drawing room colour scheme is a restful combination of beige, eggshell and cream with splashes of brilliant colour scattered around in the decorative touches. The theme of 'variations on an off-white colour' is a consistent background throughout the house. This neutral colouring gives plenty of opportunity for experimenting with more dramatic colours on a smaller scale elsewhere.

Two bright patchwork cushions, for instance, set off the small chesterfield, covered in a deep brown suede. Similar vivid colours are seen in a 19th century tapestry, hanging in a gold frame above the chesterfield. Both the tapestry and the sofa are framed by a lovely—and original—shallow arch which is another example of how an intrinsic aspect of a house can be used for maximum visual impact.

Another original feature which still holds a great deal of fascination today, is the deep alcove built into the recess created by the chimney breast. Its decorative treatment is very effective. Rather than trying to fill in the high space, all the knick-knacks on the shelf are low, leaving an expansive arch above where light from a 1930's lamp casts an eye-catching interplay of light and shadow. The absence of overpowering decorations and the use of light create a strong visual impact.

Other furniture includes a modern leather swivel chair, a period armchair, covered in rich green velvet, a black cast iron fireplace and a luxurious coffee table. The marble slab serving as the table top was once a washstand top—it was bought from the Salvation Army in Switzerland. Its colours are a magnificent mixture of soft beiges, browns, reds and pinks.

Another feature worth noting in this room is the mahogany side table originally used in Victorian times for holding a chamber pot. Its cylinder shape repeats the curve in the wall which, as in the dining/kitchen room below and the master bedroom above, creates an appealing focal point.

The bedroom upstairs is sparsely furnished with a number of handsome pieces including a rich walnut bureau, enhanced by old French church candelabras in brass. Two wooden framed mirrors over the bed give extra depth to the room. The Indian bedspread is a subtle shade of soft green, accented with grey floral stitchwork. The satin beige curtains are lined with felt for extra protection from strong sunlight.

The grace and attractiveness of this home largely results from taking full advantage of the inherent features which were available. It's a good example of a conversion where the most was made of a basic structure.

An illusion of space

It's never easy working within the confines of a small flat, yet there are many techniques which can create a feeling of openness and space. One of the most effective is the use of mirrors. The dimensions of any room seem to expand through cleverly placed mirrors. This ninth floor flat mirrors the world outside and makes you totally unaware of its actual limited size.

Hat maker George Malyard designed this flat —his twenty-first. His main objective was to get away from the pressures of the chaotic world. He succeeded in finding a flat in central London which was far enough away from noise and car fumes; it was nine floors above the congestion and commotion of the street.

The main consideration was how to eliminate the feeling of being cooped up in two little garret rooms. The answer to this problem was solved with ceiling to floor mirrors on the walls.

The effect is miraculous—the illusion of space in the flat continues as far as the eye can travel looking out of the window. There seems to be no division between the world without and the world within. There is an added dimension.

Mirrors are invaluable if you want to 'open up' a room. Give careful consideration to where you put them. They should pick up the maximum amount of light available in the room, and also reflect an interesting view or objects. Before choosing the spot for your mirror, try sitting in different parts of the room and see where the mirror can have the greatest impact. Try placing the mirror on different levels and at various angles. It is worth experimenting in this way as mirrors can appear as ugly holes in the wall when their function is misused.

As Mr. Malyard looked out the flat windows, the colours he saw were the greys and silvers of concrete buildings and the reds of tiled roof tops. His colour scheme was decided. He would bring the colours from the immediate outside

world into his own flat. Grey, silver, terracotta and white are the dominant colours. The designer didn't want to live with a view, but *in* a view.

The entrance lobby leads into the sitting room, which measures approximately sixteen feet by twelve feet. Hues of terracotta emerge from the Italian leather button-backed chairs and the Spanish floor tiles. The unusual curves in the tiles echo the curve over the door. The settee is a dark brick colour, made from coating fabric with central insets of Persian rug. The Persian motif is repeated in the floor rug which has similar patterns and colour tones.

The remaining objects in the room do not have a fabric or leather finish, but a hard metallic one —just like the chrome and concrete in the world seen outside. The transparent tables are solid perspex; the dining chairs are perspex and steel. The sliding windows are framed by part-polished and part-lacquered aluminium. During the day, the drab, fog-coloured blinds—again an echo from the outside—can be used to give a

Below. *A small room with a big look. Floor to ceiling mirrors capture the panoramic view, making the room seem far more expansive and open. Beluchi rugs serve as couch insets.*

The refrigerator neatly fits under the oven. The cupboard surfaces are covered with dark blue melamine.

Silver-grey colours also dominate in the bathroom in the tiles and vinyl floor. The design has been kept simple to eliminate the cluttered look.

The flat has been designed for labour saving. All surfaces can be cleaned with a cloth except for the Persian rugs and the suede-like bedroom wall covering, which can be vacuumed with a small cleaner. Leather cream is used on the terracotta chairs, and the perspex tables are rubbed down with anti-static polish.

Another feature worth noting is the lighting. Most of the lights are spots and have dimmers to save on the electricity bills. Dimmers are practical and can have a dramatic effect. They can be adjusted according to the time of day and your mood. They are useful in a room where study is done some evenings and television watched on others. HOME DESIGNER 59 gives ideas for various methods of making the most of lighting in the living room.

From one small flat, George Malyard has created a spacious looking home through the miracle of mirror and design. If you are confined with rooms that make you feel closed in, remember that clever placement of mirrors can make all the difference to enchancing the room as well as making it look larger.

Below. *A striking silver sculpture and two ultra modern lamps overlooking the city set a streamlined urbane tone to the room. Mirrors again reflect the night lights outside.*

Above. *Looking out of the ninth floor window. Steel and chrome outside echo the aluminium window frames and perspex table and chairs. Another mirror serves as a drinks table top.*

restful green colour in the room. At night, blinds aren't needed. In fact, there is enough light from the city to sit and relax in the room without any indoor lighting. George Malyard finds looking at the panorama around him far more interesting than television.

The ornamentation is in keeping with the metallic look. The picture frames are solid white gold leaf. The silver sculpture on the window sill is a polished aluminium alloy. One modern Italian lamp has a silver finish and the other, an watched on others, putting into practical use some of the various ways of making the most of lighting in the living room.

Mirrors are used again in the bedroom. It consists of a double bed set into an alcove, surrounded by mirrors, and two big walk-in wardrobes with mirrored sliding doors. The walls are covered with a mushroom brown imitation suede which is actually waterproof raincoating. The delicate print of the continental quilt cover contrasts well with the more subdued brown-champagne colours. The trim around the alcove and the wardrobes is nail-studded chrome and steel. There is a surprise colour—a butterfly blue—carpeting the wardrobe floor. The teak shelves in the wardrobe are set against printed silver foil in terracotta and grey.

The compact kitchen repeats the metallic and white motif. It is well fitted with a built-in eye-level oven and grill and a waste disposal unit.

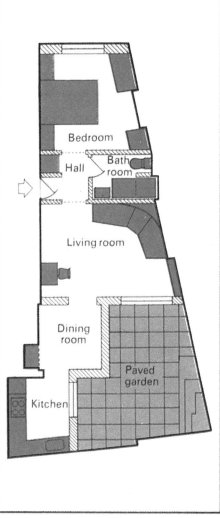

Making every inch count

A small flat can easily appear poky and it is not always possible—or desirable—to make it more spacious by open planning. But the effect of open planning can be achieved by a few simple ideas which still allow the rooms to keep their separate identities.

When Urban Projects Ltd. bought a two-storey house in Fulham, London, the front part of the ground floor was an off-licence, with living quarters behind and above it. They decided to keep a shop at the front, occupying part of the ground floor and basement, and convert the rest of the house into self-contained flats.

Interior Projects Ltd. was called in to supervise the conversion of one of these flats and plan an interior design scheme for it. The two rooms and small kitchen which were to become a comfortable bachelor flat on the ground floor had served as part of the living quarters behind the off-licence. Because it was on a corner site, there were awkward shapes and curious angles everywhere.

The first job was to plan the basic layout of rooms and find space for a bathroom. Various factors governed the final layout, such as the plumbing and room sizes. A new kitchen was built on at the back, because the existing one was inadequate. As there was a small garden behind the house, it was obvious that the living room should be at the back, despite the southern aspect of the front of the house. The bathroom had to be internal, because there were windows only at the front and back of this 'long black strip'.

The only way to lighten the flat was to make it as open plan as possible, and to streamline the layout so that a long view of it was possible from either end. Breaking up the area would have made it appear even smaller, so the doors leading from the hall to the bedroom and living room are glazed with opaque glass and slide away into the wall. This allows all the light that pours in the large window at the front to shine through the whole length of the flat.

The centre part of the load-bearing wall separating the two original main rooms was removed, and parts of the rooms on either side were used to make a tiny bathroom, which was tucked in the middle of the flat. Steel beams were slung in above for support, and the piers that remain on each side both have a useful function. One frames the shower at the head of the bath and also screens the lavatory ; the other is used to form a coat cupboard in the hall.

The high ceilings which normally enhance the proportions of large rooms in Victorian houses only added to the problems in this tiny space. So the ceiling in the entrance hall and bathroom in the middle of the flat was lowered, providing stacks of storage space above the false ceiling. It is accessible from both the bedroom and living room.

Ugly angles in the bedroom at the front have been concealed by a built-in wardrobe in the alcove at one side of the chimney breast, and a specially made chest of drawers in the other. These are linked by a curved white laminated dressing table top, providing a knee hole below. The specially made bed, built on a plinth, tilts at the head end for extra comfort while sitting up. The foot end can be raised to get at the storage space in the base. A simple bedhead unit provides a shelf on each side.

In what is now the living room at the back of the flat, an ugly fireplace with bookshelves around it was removed. As part of this room was 'stolen' for the bathroom, one wall now lines up

with the edge of the chimney breast. A timber frame was built into this corner to house a curved seating unit, which nestles well out of the way. This leaves the maximum amount of open space, which is important in this room, as it leads to both the dining room and the garden.

A sloping section of the ceiling below the stairwell was straightened off to provide more storage space and house two spotlights directed down to give additional light. Since space was at a premium, a small black laminated cantilevered desk was fitted to the wall under the low part of the ceiling. Fitted corner shelves also take advantage of this alcove.

The window at the back of the living room was replaced by large sliding doors which lead on to the paved garden. The garden is fitted with a barbecue and non-corrosive furniture. The optical illusion gained by taking the living space 'into' the garden by means of a large window area makes the living room appear much bigger.

The old kitchen at the back has been transformed into a dramatically-lit dining room, with the emphasis on night-time entertaining. As the room was so small the designers wanted to give it some extra height, and they were allowed to 'steal' the area directly above this room and so make it double-height. The window overlooking the garden was blocked in and replaced by a high-level window opposite.

Because this room will be used mostly at night, a feature has been made of the lighting. Four spotlights—red, gold, green and white—controlled by dimmer switches, create the right mood. White Holland blinds cover the window to reduce this room to a tall white funnel, with an eye-catching mural on the ceiling. Above the dimmer switches a smoked perspex 'control panel' conceals the meters, whose red pilot lights shine softly through at night. Next to it a double oven is recessed into the wall, within easy reach of the hostess while she is still sitting at the dining table. This arrangement also leaves more room in the kitchen.

The new single-storey kitchen was built on to this room at the back, making the dining room another through room. There are, however, no inter-connecting doors to get in the way—only arches with rounded sides. Wooden units were built round the walls, incorporating a double stainless steel sink and refrigerator. The fitted hob has a hood above leading fumes to an extractor fan. Lemon laminated worktops and white Holland blinds on the door leading to the garden give the kitchen a fresh look.

A stunning feature of the dining room and kitchen are the stainless steel floor tiles, which reflect everything and lighten the whole area. Throughout the flat the design has been kept as simple as possible, with one theme being carried through to help create a sense of continuity. The walls

Opposite page, left. In the living room a curved seating unit fits neatly into a corner. The glass and chrome tables appear less bulky than wooden ones of the same size.
***Right.** The floor plan of the flat. The kitchen was built on and the bathroom was made by removing part of the wall between the two main rooms and taking space from both.*
***This page, left.** The original tiny kitchen was transformed into an unusual dining room. The designers made it extra high by 'stealing' the area above and made a feature of the lighting for night-time entertaining. Stainless steel tiles are also used in the kitchen (beyond). Some borrowed light is given to the dining room by the French door in the kitchen which opens on to the paved garden.*
***Right.** The awkward shape of the bedroom has been disguised by built-in furniture. The only strong colour used is the carpet which links the rooms.*

are painted white throughout, and the purple carpet links the living areas, with bright stainless steel tiles in the dining room and kitchen. Even accessories like door-knobs are the same throughout. The open-plan layout takes advantage of all the available light and disperses it throughout the flat. The result is a compact flat where the limited space has been used to best advantage in practical terms and at low cost.

A flat full of ideas

Living in a small flat can present problems—too little storage space and a feeling of being confined and cramped. These problems can be overcome by making the most of the space available. In converting this flat, every inch of space has been used to its fullest advantage.

When designer Alf Martensson and his wife moved into their two-room flat, he applied various design and building techniques to 'gain' space. Wherever possible, he built structures, such as the bed unit, which could serve more than one function. Secondly, he used plants and screens as room dividers which, unlike a solid wall, allowed interplay of space between different areas. Finally, he built upwards, taking advantage of the high ceilings.

The first technique of building structures with multi-functions is used in the construction of both the bed and couch/work area. The

Martenssons needed lots of space for storing items, large and small. Their solution to the problem was to build a platform bed with a storage area underneath. The bed is about five feet high with a grouping of large, irregular steps leading down to the floor. The headboard for the bed is also the back wall of a clothes closet. The 'bed' closet has many functions. It helps to create a separate entry area into the flat, stabilizes the bed, and serves as a back rest as well as counter space for a television and plants. It's also used for clothes!

At the other end of the bed there are two doors which open out into a wardrobe. Beyond this, neatly tucked away under the platform, is a huge storage area which houses anything from trunks to paint brushes. Having a large area in which to put various or unattractive objects out of sight, is particularly useful in a flat without attic or basement space.

The deep steps leading up to the bed are covered with cord carpeting in a bold purple

which contrasts well with an apple green bed cover. A colourful grouping of cushions in reds, yellows, pinks and oranges adds a touch of style and comfort.

The construction of the platform bed was not complicated and the materials were not expensive. A platform bed not only uses space to advantage—it also economises on heating. The top part of any room is always warmer than the lower part, so a bed situated at a high level will be that much warmer to sleep in.

A second platform construction which utilizes space is the couch/work area in the living room. A platform was built out from the wall just large enough to accommodate a small desk. Again, the area under the platform serves as valuable storage space. The side of the platform then became the back of the couch—another example of using materials for more than one purpose. The materials that went into making the couch were inexpensive: discarded packing crates, foam rubber and carpeting.

The brown carpeting covers the platform and then has been carried down to cover the couch; the visual line is unbroken in both colour and texture. The brown sets off the cool turquoises and blues in the cushions, creating an effective contrast.

Opposite page. A sitting room designed for space-saving. A platform behind the couch houses a desk and chair and, above, a perspex drawing board suspends from the wooden frame. Above, top. Not an inch of space is lost in this kitchen. Colourful pots and pans conveniently hang from the timber frame which also supports a hang-up unit on the wall, a workbench underneath and a draining board.

Over the couch there is a suspended perspex drawing board which utilizes otherwise lost space. It is well situated—light comes in from the window behind; and the building material well chosen—the perspex doesn't prevent the light from filtering into the room.

The placement of the drawing board has made use of the space resulting from high ceilings. The couch supports have been extended upwards to hold up the drawing board, and outward to support hanging flower pots, drawing instruments and lights. The construction was neither complicated nor expensive, but lends itself to many uses.

The colours used in the living room have subtle variation. The 'sunshine' colours have been used, but only in limited areas. The skirting board and dining chairs are painted fire

Above, left. This small colourful bathroom has handy shelves for storage and a useful wooden bench which serves as an effective room divider along with the potted hanging plant. Above. A platform bed with ample room underneath for storing many items. A wardrobe at the other end doubles up as headboard and shelf space. Bold colours accent the unusual steps leading up to the bed.

engine red; the backing to the bookshelves is canary yellow, and the trim on the shelves is bright orange. Similar colours are repeated in the shaggy rug in front of the fireplace.

In the kitchen there is a timber frame which serves more than one function. Free-standing posts hold up the frame from which a large number of colourful pots and pans can be hung. The same posts also support the kitchen hang-up unit (an imaginative and practical idea which is also quick and straightforward to construct) as well as the workbench and draining board. The same materials have been used for more than one purpose and space has been 'gained' by utilising the upper half of the room.

The technique of using room dividers, other than solid walls, is particularly effective in the bathroom. There are three areas : bathing, dress-

ing and washing. The wooden bench not only serves as a divider, but also as a towel rack and a support for the linen shelves. The hanging potted plant also helps to break up the room. The wooden slats on the floor next to the bath are easily picked up for cleaning.

Plants are used as room dividers throughout the flat. Potted, hanging or sprawling, they have been strategically placed to help create different areas of living. Plants can be both decorative and functional and are flexible in that they can be moved around without much effort.

Lovely natural wood can be seen in many places in the flat. The original floors have been sanded down and polished, leaving an elegant look. Plain construction grade timber, sanded and finished with polyurethane, has been used for building. None of the joints were complicated and carriage bolts were frequently used for easy assembly.

The work involved in converting this flat was not overwhelming and the materials were not expensive. A great deal of imagination and originality was applied, however. If you are in the process of re-doing a home, bear in mind that all parts can work together to the benefit of the whole. The bed unit in this flat is a perfect example.

Big impact on a small budget

Hannerle Dehn's first venture into design was the conversion of a ramshackle Hampshire cottage into a comfortable weekend house. A professional model, she is now also an established interior decorator. This conversion proves that with a little money and lots of ideas, a tiny cottage can be transformed into a delightful retreat.

When she and her husband Robin Sligh bought the two-up and two-down cottage, it had been empty for about 40 years. Built around 1800, it was once a gamekeeper's lodge in the grounds of a grand house. There were two tiny bedrooms, a small living room, and a stone-floored dining room with an area outside where the game was hung, drawn and cooked on a range. The cottage was damp, there was no mains electricity, and the only water came from a pump in the garden.

The two-gabled cottage looked rather like a box, so in order to improve its proportions and make it large enough, it was extended on both sides. There is now a sitting room with dining area, a family room and a kitchen on the ground floor, with three bedrooms and a bathroom upstairs.

Local builders in the country are renowned for having a 'feel' for traditional house styles and the materials they work with. An added advantage in this case was that the builder chosen to supervize the structural work was born in the cottage, and so had a particular interest in its conversion. As it was structurally sound, the old house was left much as it was, with its original gables and casement windows. A generator was built outside to provide electricity, and mains water was brought in. The rambling parkland garden was bulldozed into shape and planted with shrubs which thrive unattended. An artificial pond with a waterfall was constructed, complete with rockery, bog plants and goldfish.

According to the unwritten rules of interior design, the colour scheme in one room should harmonize with that in the next room. In this cottage, however, practically every room is finished in a totally different, unrelated colour. But it works—and the total effect is stunning.

Hannerle Dehn has achieved a continuity throughout the house by using the same materials in nearly all the rooms. The walls are covered with bookcloth—less expensive and less 'cottagy' than hessian, and with the advantage that it is scrubbable—and sisal carpeting covers the floor throughout, except in the bedrooms and bathroom, where it would be a little hard on the feet. All the curtains and bedcovers are made up in cheap curtain lining fabric, in colours chosen to match or tone with the walls. The result is an 'earthy', easy to live in cottage, finished in natural materials. The furniture, mostly chunky pieces in either oak or

ROBERT BELTON

natural pine, blends in well with the rural background.

One of the ground floor rooms was extended to form the main living room with a dining area at one end. The handsome old mantelpiece was retained, and cupboards built in the alcoves at either side. These pine units were designed and constructed in traditional style by a local carpenter. Although the quarry tiles in the dining area were in good condition, sisal carpeting was laid on top of them for warmth. The other original room is now a cosy family room, finished in warm amber tones. As no English country cottage is complete without an enormous open fire, a marble fireplace was fitted in this room, where the family gathers on cold winter evenings.

Grey slate tiles were specially chosen for the kitchen, which is built on next to the family room. Here oak cupboards look well against the mid-brown bookcloth walls and pine panelling.

Hannerle Dehn is a collector of antiques and objets d'art. Her great love is *chinoiserie*—particularly pictures and ornaments. As she hates shutting ornaments behind glass in cabinets, she designed shelves and special alcoves where they could be displayed to advantage. Another interesting feature of her design work is that she likes to hide ugly modern appliances like television sets and record players. So these are always housed either in an old piece of furniture with doors that flap up or out accordingly, or hidden in a cupboard, so as not to offend the eye and spoil the overall appearance of a room. In this cottage the televison is concealed in a cupboard beside the fireplace in the living room.

One of Hannerle Dehn's more economical hobbies is treating and restoring wood. She stripped a carved oak wall-mounted clock, which she bought for a few shillings, to reveal its attractive grain. The coffee table in the living room was a pig bench, which she bought cheaply from a local farmer. She removed the swill, cleaned it up, and now this solid hunk of wood is a handsome piece of furniture. What was once a plain deal table is now, after stripping, a fine rustic dining table. In the kitchen she stained pine units with a mixture of linseed oil and brown shoe polish to achieve the desired colour. The medicine chest in the bathroom was an old chemists' cupboard, which she stripped, painted white, and faced with mirrors.

All this natural wood is complemented by converted brass oil lamps and brass door furniture, which Hannerle Dehn has collected over the years to add the final touches to her cosy country cottage.

Opposite page, top. *Proud in peacock blue! The antique-looking prints are taken from an old art book and the furniture is skilfully restored to look both simple and impressive.*
Opposite page, bottom. *A welcoming sitting-room in warm tones of apricot and browns. The fireplace is the original marble.*
This page, top. *The mood of the whole house carries into the kitchen, where natural woods and modern appliances mix and match.*
This page, bottom. *One end of the living-dining room, with its warm-toned cupboards boasting Ming and Delft plates.*

ROBERT BELTON

Above. *An elegant Adam fireplace is the eye-catching focal centre of the drawing room. The circular table was bought in two parts— first the top at one shop and then, later, the base at another shop. It's clever shopping.*

The tall and narrow

Like many nineteenth century town houses in all parts of the world, this London house is tall and narrow. Adapting houses of this type for modern living is not always easy. Usually there are one or two rooms on each floor and the houses are often designed with facilities for the children on the top floor and the cooking in the basement. Here the design is both practical and attractive.

The owners of this house knew it had potential as a comfortable home, but found their main problem was to re-organize it so there was room for the children near the kitchen during the daytime. Their aim when converting it was to make it structurally sound with all the practical conveniences of modern living, without losing the period feeling. The conversion was devised by Carolinda Tait, the owner's wife, who is an interior designer.

First step in the renovation campaign was to repair old and rotten floorboards, joists, and other important structural parts combined with total re-plumbing and re-wiring. By doing this work, they made the house sound for the future, knowing that if the work was done before the situation became too bad, they would be saving money in the long run. And in fact they discovered, during the course of the renovations, that one of the main beams supporting the front of the house was almost totally infected with rot and would need immediate replacement. They found the rot just in time—if they had not its likely that the whole house front would have collapsed.

Other unexpected problems arose which meant prolonging the estimated time for converting. It's important when moving house to allow ample time for the often chaotic business of renovation and structural work. Particularly with older houses, unseen snags may crop up which increase the work time and often can delay moving-in dates seriously. It is pointless to start re-decorating until this type of work is complete.

Starting from the basement and working upwards, the owners re-planned many of the rooms to make the house more practical. The basement entrance was made more welcoming with new stone steps and a new area for the dustbins.

It was a major job to re-plan the basement so there could be a playroom for the children. The owners decided to turn the original kitchen into a playroom and then to build a new kitchen by combining a dark and dreary scullery with a boiler room and airing cupboard. To help them re-design, kitchen consultant Katie Dyson was called in.

One of the first problems was how to make as much space as possible for the new kitchen, First step was to re-position the large central heating boiler. This was moved to an outside coal hole at the back of the house. More space was gained by removing the back door and making a pleasant French door from the new playroom into the garden behind the house. This meant there would be as much wall space as possible for building in kitchen units. All major structural alterations like this needed planning permission first.

Above top. Soft cornflower blue and olive green make a restful setting for the bedroom.
Above bottom. The other end of the bedroom suite houses 'twin' marble sinks and a bidet.

Above. This modern compact kitchen emerged from a dreary scullery and boiler room. An asbestos lining is fitted above the rich pine ceiling which has built-in spotlights.

Another problem was that the new kitchen was a low room. Because of this, lighting needed careful planning. Spotlights were set into an attractive new pine-clad ceiling. This is a practical idea for lighting in any low room because the spotlights don't hang down and encroach on the height of the room. The powerful spotlights, combined with the heat of cooking, made the ceiling in this small room hot —hot enough to make built-in floor heating in the study above. For added fire safety and heat-proofing, an asbestos lining was fitting above the pine ceiling.

The owners wanted split-level cooking and as much cupboard space as possible, together with a sensibly sized sink and dishwasher, to fit into this small kitchen. There was just enough room to accommodate all this efficiently, working to a tight plan which made maximum use of the limited kitchen space available. It was important to have a ventilator to extract cooking smells and stop them from spreading throughout the house, so one was fitted above the cooking hob.

To save more space, a sliding door was sensibly fitted to divide the kitchen from the playroom. Most of the wall between what is now the playroom and the passage was demolished, and replaced by a beam. This increased the playspace and made the basement seem much more airy. The new French door gave the playroom the appearance of being lighter and was further brightened with cheerful green and white colours.

In one corner is a fitted bench and table for the children's meals and games, or homework, when they're older. Fitted cupboards were put in along one wall to make plenty of space for storing toys. One of the most practical ideas is the way the chair covers have been made in sensible pvc-coated fabric. The idea of a pvc coated chair cover is well worth noting, because it makes such a sensible yet attractive surface in a room where children with sticky fingers or dirty feet may be playing.

While the playroom is both cheerful and practical, the adjoining dining room is quietly elegant in a pale green colour scheme with a rust-coloured carpet and antique furniture, the chair seats are upholstered in a soft-coloured

tweed. Like so many of the other 'soft' furnishings in the house, this material is extremely smart, yet practical, because a tweed, being a thick heavy-duty material, will last far longer than a lighter fabric like cotton. In the large window bay is an unusual flower trough. This is an old tin bath which the owner's wife found in a junk shop. It was smartened up with a coat of paint and mounted on legs, now making an ideal display point for greenery and potted plants.

Leading off the turn in the stairway up to the ground floor is the owner's study. The colour scheme of deep blue and white is worth noting, because it makes the room peaceful, yet extremely smart with a definite masculine air. Detail is excellent, the long curtains have pinch pleat headings and each group of pleats is accentuated with a neat white covered button. This effect could be copied quite easily by people who sew at home. The curtain fabric, a heavy deep blue linen, is an exact match with the wallcovering, a linen-type fabric normally used for book-binding. New fitted cupboards and bookshelves are painted white and have their Adam-style moulding and edges picked out effectively in a dark blue to match the colour scheme—an unusual treatment that needs to be carried out by a painter with an extremely steady hand. For this kind of work it

TUBBY

TUBBY

is best to use the dense gel-like thixotropic paint and sable brushes if possible.

The large drawing room takes up the whole of the ground floor. This had originally been two rooms, and there was a low beam and pillars where the old wall had been. The owner's wife wanted to unify the room and to get rid of the 'two-into-one' feeling. To give it a greater feeling of width, one pillar was removed, together with the low beam, which was replaced by a new high reinforced steel joist which effectively got over the two-room feeling. A false-angled wall was built to conceal the other pillar and in front of this went new fitted cupboards with an antique finish and attractive glass display shelves above.

The ceiling was re-plastered and a new piece of lead cornice made as an exact match for the cornice in the rest of the room. Colours in the drawing room are a subtle mixture of oatmeal and browns, with pale chocolate covers, patterned with turquoise blue birds, and blue lampshades. This makes a cool and smart colour scheme that effectively sets off the antique furniture to its best advantage.

On the turn of the stairs up to the first floor was a bathroom. This now is a spare bedroom-cum-studio for the owner's wife. The bathroom has been moved up to the former spare bedroom on the first floor where it became part of the main bedroom suite.

Above. A playroom with couch and chairs covered in practical pvc. Handy cupboards fitted along one wall provide ample space for storing toys. Beyond the door is a garden with swings and games for the children to play with on warm sunny days.

The first floor was originally two bedrooms. But the owners decided to convert the whole of it into a suite, so there would be no need to walk out into the landing and down the stairs when they wanted to take a bath. A wide arch was knocked out between the main bedroom and old spare room, and the door from the passage to the spare room removed and blocked up. The big glassfibre bath was moved up from the old bathroom and put in under the window. Two fitted wash basins with marble tops mean there is never any need for a squabble about who's to wash first in the early morning.

A new lavatory and a bidet were installed, and large fitted cupboards put in both the bathroom and the bedroom end of the suite. This means the owner has what almost amounts to a neatly fitted dressing room for his clothes and no shortage of storage space. There's plenty of mirror space in the bathroom, cleverly made by fitting an old long mirror sideways up above the two basins. Attractive Edwardian lights are a feature in the bathroom, as are the door knobs, which are a feature throughout the house.

Colours are a peaceful combination of cornflower blue and olive green. There's an attractive border on the curtains and dressing table skirts. The large bedspread is attractively decorated with Italian quilting. A soft patterned wallpaper on the wall behind the bed moulds the colour scheme together. The cane bedhead and matching bedside tables were designed by the owner's wife. These make a pleasing touch. The carpet is a luxurious white deep shaggy pile.

Upstairs again is a second bathroom; this one for the children. The hot water storage tank was moved up from the basement and a useful airing cupboard built around it. The washing machine is also housed in this bathroom. Both of these have been sited upstairs so as to help make more room in the small basement kitchen. A sink has also been installed in the bathroom, where it is useful for hand washing clothes and for washing up if the children have breakfast upstairs in their small kitchenette on the top landing. The whole of the top floor can be effectively shut off from the rest of the house by a useful stable door at the top of the stairs. The newly made kitchenette makes a bright and useful eating corner for breakfasts and snacks with a small table and stools, plus storage unit and mini-cooker.

Imaginative interior design ideas, clever colour schemes, and interesting soft furnishings have combined to make this house a totally comfortable living unit.

Preserving that natural look

Above. Some of the exterior panels of this Swiss half-timbered farmhouse were replaced by windows during the conversion. This view of the house shows how the glazed areas sit comfortably with the original lath and plaster panels.

When Herr and Frau Werner Maurer bought a big half-timbered farmhouse near Berne, Switzerland, it was perfectly habitable, but with no 20th century conveniences. They decided to have it converted to incorporate modern living facilities and a studio for Herr Maurer, an illustrator.

Apart from their three children, the family consisted of a big dog, four cats and 48 birds, all of whom had to be accommodated somewhere in the house. Room also had to be found for Herr Maurer's collections of hats, old toys, and musical instruments—preferably displayed to advantage.

The farmhouse, built in 1846, is situated in a small village with only eight houses. The other inhabitants are farmers, most of whom have lived there all their lives. Theo Kuentz, an architect from nearby Flamatt, was called in to deal with the construction side of the conversion, and interior designer Hans Eichenberger took over with the detail designing.

In places the outer walls of the house had to be

115

renovated, some of the exterior panels were replaced by windows to make the rooms lighter, and the facade was newly painted. The structural alterations mainly involved converting stables and barns into habitable rooms.

The living quarters, up one end, comprising living room and hall with three bedrooms above, remain much as they were. Part of the old farmhouse kitchen with its large fireplace was converted into a smaller modern kitchen equipped with dish-washing machine, refrigerator and electric cooker; the other part is now a dining room. The small stable in the middle of the house became a smart ground-floor bathroom, tucked under the stairs.

The upper section of a barn where hay was once stored became Herr Maurer's studio, running the full depth of the house, with a dark room next to it. As the studio was very high, a suspended ceiling was installed to improve its proportions.

The area below the studio on the ground floor now houses the master bedroom and a workshop at the front, with a utility room at the back. This holds a water heater and equipment for the oil fired central heating, which was installed throughout.

The big lean-to stable at one end of the house was turned into a garage, with an aviary behind for the 48 birds.

The internal panelling and structural timber was in excellent repair and largely retained. A few old panels, however, needed replacing, and in the old smoky kitchen the walls had to be washed down. Some rooms were enlarged by removing sections of bricks and panelling between the structural timbers, leaving just the vertical columns. The dining area is separated from the living room in this way, and in the playroom a swing fixed to one of the exposed ceiling joints hangs between two uprights.

Throughout the inside of the house the joists are exposed, the timber panelling left in its natural state, and all brickwork painted white, with black radiators. In order to brighten up this neutral background scheme, all the doors—whether old or new—have been painted in bright colours. This has the added benefit of camouflaging the imperfections on the old ones. Additional splashes of colour have been introduced into the decoration by Herr Maurer's collections of ornaments, toys and musical instruments, displayed to great advantage throughout the house.

Above. *The children's playroom houses their vast selection of toys and playthings, such as the swing, which is hung from an exposed ceiling joist. Bright colours were used here to relieve the neutral background of the natural wood.*

Opposite page, top. *The main bedroom houses Herr Maurer's own collection of 'toys', such as his train sets, displayed with ornaments in a glass-fronted wall cabinet. The domed perspex bedhead unit with sliding doors is attractive and capacious, and the natural wood panelled walls are an effective setting for the pictures above the bed.*

Right. *The dining area is separated from the living room by a 'screen' of vertical timbers. The simple modern furniture makes a contrast, yet combines well, with the old timbers on the walls and ceiling.*

Far right. *The dark blue tiles in the bathroom had to be collected in ones and twos from all over Switzerland because the colour had been discontinued. The shelves in the alcove are made from perspex.*

JOHN MYERS

Above. *Two rooms on the first floor were knocked into one to form this elegant drawing room. New Georgian-style sash windows which reach to the floor were fitted at the front.*

Flats-into-house conversion

It can be very rewarding to 'rescue' an old house which has been divided into flats, and convert it back into a comfortable family house.

Architect Anthony Perry, of Heber-Percy Parker Perry Associates, was called in to do just this to a five-storey Georgian house in London which had been badly damaged during the Second World War and subsequently divided into flats in an unimaginative conver-

sion scheme. Ugly metal windows had been fitted where the original sash windows had been blown out, and a two-storey addition had been built at the back.

As the house was full of dry rot, much structural work was necessary to restore the fabric to good condition. The block at the back was built up to the full height of the house, and now incorporates a cloakroom, laundry and other service rooms. All the window openings at the back of the house were re-proportioned and

fitted with new Georgian-type sash windows. Most of the partition walls that had been built during the previous conversion were knocked down to open up the large well-proportioned rooms.

The basement was fitted out as a self-contained staff flat, with a quarry-tiled kitchen alcove in the sitting room which can be closed off with louvred doors. The rest of the house has a conventional layout, with the kitchen and dining room on the ground floor, the drawing room on the first floor, and bedrooms on the two floors above.

A hatch links the dining room at the front with the kitchen, where the window sill was lowered to take advantage of the view over the back garden. Cork tiles faced in clear vinyl with a matt finish provide a practical floor covering in the kitchen, which even hot fat will not mark. Copper-coloured laminated cupboards, combined with white vitreous ceramic tiling and ivory paintwork, give a rich appearance. All the lighting is provided by hidden tungsten tubes.

Two rooms were knocked into one to make a large first floor drawing room which runs the full width of the house at the front. Here the new tall sash windows reach right down to floor level, and a matching window was fitted at the back. The original Adam pine mantelpiece was retained, and finished in white matt paint. The marble hearth and cast iron basket grate

Top left. *White-painted louvred doors seal off the kitchen alcove in the sitting room of the self-contained flat in the basement.*
Above left. *Copper-coloured laminate finishes on the cupboards in the kitchen combine with the ivory paintwork and white tiles to give it a rich appearance.*

are new.

What were once two second floor bedsitting rooms have been transformed into a handsome main bedroom with bathroom en suite, where the colour scheme is sage green and white. Fitted wardrobes were built in the alcoves on each side of the bed, and a row of cupboards runs along one wall of the bathroom, where the door to the landing once was. Folding doors fitted between the two rooms can be either fixed

Top right. *In the bathroom off the main bedroom (above right), all the appliances were fitted along one wall, with a row of cupboards opposite. Both rooms are framed with English ash and panelled with sage green hessian. The thick white wool carpet and white curtains complete the elegant scene.*

back to open up the whole area, or closed to seal off the bathroom. Both rooms are framed with English ash and panelled with sage green hessian. Over the bath a canopy framed in ash improves the proportions of the room, while providing space above for the hidden tungsten tube lighting.

The top floor houses three guest bedrooms, and an internal bathroom, lit and ventilated by a rooflight.

Open plan upstairs — privacy below

There is a need for both community and privacy in a house, so often the best solution when designing one from scratch is a combination of open and closed plans.

When Mr and Mrs John Garrett decided to have a house built on a site in South East London, they automatically chose an old friend, architect Edward Cullinan, to design it. They knew and admired his work, he understood their needs and way of life, and was therefore in a good position to produce a satisfactory design for their new home.

The areas which need the most sound and visual protection—bedrooms, bathroom, and garage—were put on the ground floor, the bedrooms being the usual self-contained type separated from each other and from the more

Top. The staircase that leads into the first floor living room is framed by the curved white-painted brick wall. The sloping windows above the long built-in shelf and cupboard unit slide open on plastic track.
Left. The exterior is stained hemlock, and a wooden ramp leads down to the back garden from the first floor living area.

noisy living areas. Reversing the usual building plan in this way has given those parts of the house which are used mostly by day the maximum amount of light, air and view. Bedrooms need walls, so they are on the ground floor, forming a construction which easily supports the first floor structure. The living, dining, cooking and circulation areas are open plan, as they need practically no dividing walls, and resemble a huge attic. The roof was steeply pitched to let the sun pour into the upper part of the house from the side, and the pitch was designed to follow the roofline of the adjacent houses.

The site was well suited to having the living quarters on the top of the house, because the back garden sloped up away from the house. A ramp connecting the first floor areas with the garden at the back falls only about half a storey before meeting the ground.

The garage, bathroom and bedroom cupboards have only a 6ft 9in. (2.06m) ceiling. However, as the bedrooms are at the side and can use some of the roof space, their ceilings are higher and therefore comply with regulations. In this way the height of this two-storey house is comparable with a one-and-a-half storey house of normal design.

A narrow path at the side of the house leads to the entrance door, which has a canopy over it. The door opens into an area that doubles as a circulation area for the ground floor bedrooms, and a hall leading to the stairs and living area above. The eye is led to the curved staircase winding up to the first (living) floor.

The ground floor bathroom doubles as a laundry, housing a washing machine, ironing facilities and a linen cupboard. As there is a wash basin in each of the bedrooms and a separate lavatory, this does not present problems of congestion on washing day.

An advantage of building the bedrooms at ground floor level is that the water tanks—which in a conventional layout are housed in the roof—can be on the first floor level. The kitchen runs off the mains water supply, so the tanks are needed only for the ground floor wash basins and bath.

The first floor houses living rooms, dining area and kitchen, but these areas flow into one another and are only divided by an island unit with double-sided cupboards accessible from both the dining area and the kitchen.

A 35ft (10.7m) built-in unit runs the full length of the house, serving both the kitchen and the living room. Cupboards at one end hold kitchen utensils, and open shelves hold books, ornaments and a television set in the living area. Above this unit, sliding windows protected from the rain by the sloping roof are fixed in plastic cupboard track, a cheaper substitute for aluminium.

Except in the bedrooms, all the interior walls are of white-painted sand-lime bricks. These are made in a press, not baked, and so take emulsion paint better. They are also cheaper for interior use. Brown linoleum was used throughout the ground floor, covered in places with rush matting.

In the kitchen the joists of the exposed roof

Above left. The built-in unit, with cupboards instead of shelves, extends into the kitchen, fitted at one side of the staircase. Above right. The dining area is separated from the kitchen by an island unit with cupboards accessible from both sides. The timber double doors open on to the ramp which leads down to the back garden.

structure provide a support for shelves. An electric oven and a refrigerator are fitted in the wall behind the stairwell with a cantilevered concrete shelf sealed with clear polyurethane varnish fixed below them for resting dishes on. Three heavy cast iron gas rings on enamel trays (bought for very little) provide stable hobs which can be moved around on the black laminate worktops. Thus split-level cooking facilities have been achieved at less cost than a conventional cooker, with the added advantage of the combination of an electric oven and gas hobs.

Edward Cullinan's interior design theory for a cosy and inviting house is to have rich dark surfaces—here the blockboard cupboards have been stained in warm oranges and yellows—with lots of light all round. In this way the furniture absorbs the light, which should come in from at least two directions so as to eliminate glare, creating a calm atmosphere. In this house, all the opening panels are opaque, mostly timber, and the fixed sections are glazed. This construction, apart from being fairly cheap, makes the house dark and cosy in winter and light and airy in summer.

Simplicity in stone

This old farmhouse was built in 1815 deep in the state of New Jersey, U.S.A. The present owners bought it as they wanted quiet and privacy, the rural charm of an early-American home, combined with modern comforts and ease of running.

Early north American farmhouses were simple rectangular stone structures, usually without porches or terraces. Here, ugly cement porches had been added on both sides of the simple house, with a bathroom built as an extension to one of them. These were removed, and a flagstone terrace was built along one side of the house. It harmonizes with the simple lines of the house and provides a welcome outdoor eating area. A semi-basement below houses a cellar which served as the kitchen in the 19th century.

As is often the case in old farmhouses, the kitchen was by far the largest room. The rest of the ground floor was occupied by a front parlour, a back parlour, a bedroom adjoining each, and a hall running between. Above these four rooms was an enormous loft, with two more small bedrooms over the kitchen. A separate 'carriage house' with a chicken roost above the garage stood not far from the house, with a barn nearby.

The large kitchen was retained, and now serves as a kitchen/dining room. One long side of this room houses stove, cupboards, work surface, refrigerator, dish-washer etc. On the other side stools and rocking chairs have been grouped in front of a wide fireplace, which was discovered intact under the cement with which the previous owner had covered it. The house is just as attractive under snow as in the summer, and this is a particularly cheerful room on dark and miserable winter evenings.

The front parlour now serves as a dressing room-cum-study, and its adjoining bedroom has been converted into a bathroom and large wardrobe. The partition wall between the back parlour and adjoining bedroom, also the wall separating them both from the hall, were demolished to make one large living room. Steel uprights were installed in the cellar to take the extra weight. A large open fireplace has replaced the two small ones which, back to back, served the two original rooms.

Although central heating has now been installed, the other open fireplaces were also retained and are still used throughout the house. The considerable thickness of the walls makes the house as easy to keep warm in winter as it is to keep cool in summer.

Of all the rooms in this house, the loft has the most charm, and retains the traditional character of the old farmhouse. It has been transformed into a delightful master bedroom,

Above. *The dining area in the large old farmhouse kitchen, which combines cooking and eating activities, is traditionally furnished. A Dutch door leads to the garden beyond.*

Below. *Two partition walls were knocked down to make this spacious living room. The large open fireplace has replaced two small ones which once stood back to back.*

Above. *The traditional character of this house is retained in the main bedroom, with its pitched ceiling and exposed rafters. The painting and rugs provide splashes of colour.*

with the pitched ceiling and exposed rafters retained. An open wooden staircase leads directly into it, and a small bathroom and walk-in wardrobe have been built at one end. Beyond, the two original bedrooms over the kitchen have been knocked into one, which now serves both as a study and spare bedroom.

A two-room flat has been built in the area above the garage where chickens once roosted. This provides useful self-contained guest accommodation within easy reach of the main house.

Throughout this farmhouse, traditional furniture and furnishings have been carefully chosen to complement the natural materials and rough finishes used in its construction. In this way, the charm and character of the old house have been retained, while providing for its owners a comfortable retreat in a secluded situation. As a result of this conversion, the exterior of the house now resembles the original more than it did when the present owners bought it.

L-shaped success

A small, box-shaped flat can be confined and dull, but with some planning—both structural and decorative—it can be made spacious looking and easy-to-live-in. The actual size of the flat may not change, but the sense of size can.

When the Guerras moved into their flat it was conveniently placed in the middle of London, but in a sorry state—the walls and floors were rotting; the kitchen taps were falling off. These faults were corrected, but major changes were not made. After the arrival of their two children, the flat simply wasn't large enough for comfortable living. The Guerras looked for houses in the suburbs, but the thought of tedious commuting didn't appeal. The price of other London flats was beyond their means. The situation seemed hopeless—until they contacted Michael Blampied and he applied his skill and imagination as an architect.

The original layout consisted of four rooms—two smallish bedrooms, a living room and a kitchen. The kitchen wasn't large enough to eat in, which meant carrying the food to the other side of the flat for dining. Ugly gas fires were installed in the bedrooms, taking up much needed space.

The architect succeeded in creating a sense of open space by changing the rooms around. The living, dining and kitchen areas were cleverly made into one L-shaped room. The flow of space carries from the farthest corners of the kitchen, through the dining area, to the far end of the sitting room—no walls stop the movement. The two bedrooms were put at one end of the house. The narrow and dingy hall was miraculously converted into a cheerful and welcoming foyer.

On entering the flat, the eye immediately focuses on the attractive storage units ahead. The rich looking mahogany doors with brass handles create an effective frame. The eye-catching wallpaper looks like mosaic tiles in a bold yellow—an unusual and inexpensive idea. The yellow complements both the dark rich mahogany and the gold trimmings.

There is wall-to-wall carpeting throughout the flat. The colour beige was a very good choice. It's neutral—easy to tie in with other colours—practical in that dirt doesn't show, and visually appealing because the light colour makes the rooms look bigger. When choosing a carpet, colour—its effect and practicality—should be kept in mind.

The L-shaped room has a great deal of character. The main ingredients working together to get this effect are the colours which

are bright, the textures which are rough and woven, and—most of all—the delightful arch which breaks up the space between the kitchen and dining areas.

The walls are covered with a warm yellow hessian. The yellow is then picked up in the heavy weave of the brown, black, yellow and white upholstery of the chairs and couch. The striped covers give a very smart look and are enhanced by the button backs. There is a shaggy brown rug under the mirrored-topped coffee table—another variation in texture. The blacks, whites and browns in the Turkish throw rug under the dining table echo the stripes in the couch weave.

There are some lovely touches in this room. The Thai prints—bought at a shop round the corner—have been framed and create an unusual and modern design on the expanse of yellow. The arrangement of pictures is important to a room; it's often the focal centre. An original grouping of pictures on a wall can set the tone for the overall motif. The white wrought-iron strip that runs from the floor to ceiling adds a delicate touch and also helps to set off the dining area.

The ceilings in the L-shaped room have been given careful consideration. In the living area, the ceiling was peeling and cracked. To combat

this, the ceiling was covered with woodchip paper, which isn't expensive, and then painted white. Woodchip paper is an excellent idea if you want to cover a surface which has cracks, and if you can't afford replastering. It gives a slightly rough surface and covers up noticeable breaks in the plaster. Any colour can be painted over it.

The dining area is set off by the ceiling. Plywood cut into large squares, is pinned to the ceiling and covered with varnish. The lowering of the ceiling is another clever touch—it shows off the wood and also hides unsightly beams.

The spotlights on the ceilings in the dining and living areas give a soft and dramatic effect. Mr. Guerra likes watching television with a light and Mrs. Guerra without. They compromised by buying spotlights—they could be turned in different directions, thereby giving off varied amounts of light. Now the Guerras both feel the lighting is right for them. Spotlights are versatile and decorative and can enhance any room, giving a strong clear light where needed for reading or paper work.

One of the most functional—and attractive—features in the room are the wall storage units. In a small flat, storage is at a premium. These cabinets are visually appealing; the brown and white colour contrast ties in well with the yellows in the rest of the room. They also serve as a very practical item for storing a stereo, books, china and ornaments—all things that need to be either visible or easily accessible rather than hidden out of sight in drawers or stored in cupboards.

Probably one of the most striking and unique

aspects to the room is the arch leading to the kitchen. Its beautiful, graceful lines serve as a superb room divider. The high walls provide counter space, and have been strategically designed to hide what you're doing in the kitchen. No one likes to see dirty dishes stacked up beside the sink, and most cooks prefer to have some privacy when preparing a dish.

Mrs. Guerra says serving is so easy now— she wondered how she ever managed to run back and forth between the old living room and kitchen.

Arches can be made in a fairly straightforward method—the method you choose will depend mainly on the size of curve needed—and add an elegant tone to a room. Any break in normal flat surfaces and common right angles gives a pleasant relief to the eye.

The cool blue and white colours of the compact kitchen contrast with the bright colours in the rest of the L-shaped room. The blue tiles are German and easy to clean. The white trim on the doors tie in with the other decor. There is plenty of working surface—a washing-up machine and refrigerator, covered with white laminated shelves, create the working surface. The central heating unit is hidden by a louvred door and takes the eye to the blue and white linoleum floor.

Outside of the L-shaped room there are other interesting touches. The bathroom has a bidet, and a wardrobe with a difference has been fitted into the master bedroom. Originally there was a fireplace which the landlord wouldn't allow to be moved. It wasted valuable wall space and didn't look appropriate in a bedroom.

Opposite page. View from the spacious sitting area into the dining and kitchen areas. A lowered plywood ceiling hides ugly beams and helps set off the dining area.
Above left. The graceful lines of the arch make a superb room divider and allow the flow of space to continue into the kitchen.
Above top. Looking out from a compact kitchen. Counter spaces from the arch makes serving easier and keeps dirty dishes and cooking out of sight from guests.
Above bottom. The entrance hall looks onto attractive storage units in the L-shaped room. Eyecatching wallpaper patterned like mosaic tiles contrasts well with the mahogany doors.

The chimney breast is now covered with plaster and floor to ceiling folding doors have been erected along the full length of the wall. Shelves have been put up in the narrow part of the wardrobe covering the old fireplace, and items like shoes and hats are stored there.

The architect was practical, and in the deeper part of the wardrobe he has put up two rails for clothes. The rail on top is for clothes that are not worn often, and the one on the bottom is for everyday clothes. This technique creates extra space for hanging clothes and is particularly appropriate in homes with children—the clothes are short enough to be stored this way!

What was once an unimaginative and difficult flat to live in is now a comfortable and attractive home. One of the major keys to its success is the L-shaped room which gives the feeling of spaciousness and makes everyday living easy.

JOHN BETHELL

Above. The white-painted cornice makes the living room appear taller. Slim black-painted industrial shelving takes up very little space.

Colour in a small flat

In a small flat it is often a good idea to link all the circulation areas such as the halls and corridors with one colour, and co-ordinate the living and dining spaces with it. A different colour scheme can be used in the main bedroom, and also in the kitchen and bathroom, to prevent the arrangement from becoming monotonous.

A three-room flat built round the light well at the top of a six-storey building, and with sloping walls under the eaves in some rooms, can be a daunting conversion prospect. This is why actor Jeremy Clyde decided to hand over the re-decoration of his London flat to designer Paul White, who came up with a most satisfactory scheme.

Jeremy Clyde wanted the flat to be as flexible as possible, combining a pleasant working environment for him in the mornings with a welcoming retreat when he returned home from the theatre at night. He needed an effective background for his large and varied collection of pictures, ornaments, porcelain and antique furniture. At the same time, he wanted the conversion to be carried out on a budget.

The drawbacks, although not insuperable, were many. The narrow hall was further restricted by a sloping section of wall; the bathroom was entirely baby pink—both the tiles and the paint; and the ugly gas fire in the living room was made worse by a pale blue tiled fireplace surrounding it. The entire flat was decorated in sickly pastel shades of green, blue, pink and grey, set off by awkward radiators at odd intervals.

What space there was obviously had to be exploited and made to appear bigger wherever possible. The flat was in good structural condition, but a lot of making good was necessary before it could be decorated.

In the hall, everything has now been finished in matt brown paint; the sloping parts of the walls were ignored, and, together with the cornices and skirting boards, were 'painted out' to make the hall appear bigger. Only the soffit of the archway leading to the other rooms has been highlighted in white. White Holland blinds cover all the windows, as curtains would get in the way.

A solid wooden butcher's block, which Vanessa Clyde restored, stained and sealed, now stands on two trestles and acts as a handsome hall table. The dark brown carpet carries on throughout the living and circulation areas; this is most important in a small flat, as then all the areas are linked and the total space appears larger.

The 17ft square living room is entirely yellow ochre, which is a good background colour for the furniture and paintings. There is ochre felt on the walls and matching paint on the ceiling. Again, the skirting board has been 'painted out' in the predominant colour, but here the cornice has been picked out in white to make the room seem taller. Even the radiators are painted ochre, so as to camouflage them. The pale blue tiled fireplace was given a coat of diluted pva adhesive to form a key, then painted matt black; the gas fire was removed and replaced by an open grate.

Most of Jeremy Clyde's books are housed in black-painted shelves fitted in the alcoves on each side of the chimney breast. An open bookcase built from industrial metal shelving bolted together and painted black holds the rest of his books; this has a lighter appearance than a fitted wooden unit.

There was not enough room for a conventional sofa and easy chairs, and so two enormous red floor cushions provide the main seating accommodation. They back up against a pair of library steps, on which two converted brass oil lamps stand. Their jade green glass shades combine with the red cushion covers to relieve the predominantly brown colour scheme. When the lamps are lit in the evening, with a log fire in the grate, a distinctly Victorian atmosphere prevails. Spotlights fixed to the ceiling and walls and directed on to particular paintings and pieces of furniture supplement these table lamps.

The small bedroom was painted terracotta, and became a studio where Jeremy Clyde could work in peace. The larger room at the back was fitted out as the main bedroom, with a straw colour scheme.

The only cheap solution for the baby pink bathroom was to make positive use of the colour rather than try to alter or conceal it. Rampant pot plants now cover much of the bath tile surround, which has been restored, and the rest

Above left. *The narrow hall is all brown, with a few important details picked out in white.* **Above right.** *The tiled fireplace in the living room was transformed by a coat of black paint—a cheap disguise for an ugly feature.* **Below right.** *The pink tiling in the bathroom was retained, and the walls and ceiling painted glossy brown. Mirrors, pictures and plants cover the whole room.*

of the room has been finished in glossy brown paint, which acts as an effective background for more light-hearted pictures.

The only colour not in the brown spectrum is saxe blue. This is used with red in the tiny kitchen. Walls and ceiling, skirting board and cornice are again all painted alike, with odd contrasting splashes relieving the plain background. A gold-painted carved wooden fish hangs decoratively above the red and white gingham-covered table, and red plastic letters spelling the name Jeremy are fixed to the wall.

In this small flat, the maximum feeling of space has been retained by the clever decoration scheme. All the colours flow into one another, with no harsh contrasts in the main living areas. The dark brown carpet fitted throughout links it all, toning with all the various colours, and the brownish scheme is relieved occasionally by a few important white details.

Improvement through planning and patience

Sometimes a whole house has to be 'rethought' and simplified in order to make the most of its potential. If you have the money this can be done in one massive operation, almost 'overnight'. But few people can afford to tackle a whole house at once. It is often best to spend time and energy on the early planning stages before beginning to improve your home little by little.

The owners of this Edwardian house in South London took their time over re-designing and decorating their home—in between children, in fact. It took patience to achieve their ingenious but simple improvements to their home—they started on the ground floor and worked up-wards, doing rooms as they could afford it.

The icing on the cake is their latest conversion of a draughty passage and two pokey attic rooms into a master bedroom suite. With two young children and two student paying guests, the owners needed privacy. Turning things round in this way was the best way of getting it. The main front bedroom on the first floor is now a spacious bed-sitter for the students. They share a bathroom with the children, whose bedroom is on the first floor landing at the back of the house.

Having done all the hard work of stripping,

Below. An elegant through-room, partially joined by sliding doors. The colour scheme flatters the traditional style furniture.

painting and putting up cupboards throughout the house themselves, the owners decided they would complete their work the professional way. So they asked Alan Gaskell, a student architect, to convert the attic into a self-contained bedroom and bathroom with masses of cupboard space. Leading off the attic is a loft for water tanks and storage, so Mr. Gaskell's plan had to include a boxroom entrance.

He started by re-organizing the walls. A new door leads into the bedroom, through which the bathroom is reached. The dividing wall between the bedroom and bathroom has been moved to enlarge the bedroom. In the bedroom, the dominant feature is a complete wall of cupboards. A floor-to-ceiling feature like this gives extra height and length to a room and here it has been cleverly designed not to break up the limited space. The cupboard doors were made out of blockboard and painted matt white.

A chimney breast is now a shallow cupboard with shelves, and there are generous hanging cupboards on either side. With all this storage space, there is no need to clutter the room with other furniture to hold clothes, so the whole room seems much larger than it actually is.

Recessed 'eyeball' spotlights were fixed in the ceiling. These are directed towards the white cupboard doors, giving a feeling of width. The rest of the room, with its attractive sloping ceiling, is decorated in blue flowered wallpaper. Rather than break up the pattern on the window wall by using plain curtains, the owners chose a matching thick cotton. Again the effect is to add more size to the room. Furnishings are kept to a minimum, which always makes a room seem more spacious.

Rather than clutter up the bedroom with a dressing table, the owner's wife chose to have hers in the bathroom. A white laminated vanity unit with drawers underneath and an inset basin gives a look of length and brightness to the room. A wall of mirrors behind it makes the room seem much larger. They are lit by a fluorescent strip concealed behind a false wall. The lavatory cistern is hidden behind a cupboard on the other side of the bathroom. This has mirror doors and doubles as a lock-up medicine chest.

Two of the mirrors behind the washbasin are also doors, being in fact the entrance to the box room—a clever camouflage trick. The built-in bath is surrounded by deep blue-green tiles with a useful shaving mirror let into the tiles at its foot. The bathroom is decorated in the same soft flowered wallpaper as the bedroom and the whole suite is richly covered with a deep pile carpet in a restful pale beige.

To make a large kitchen and dining room, the owners knocked the two rooms, larder and wc into one. The floor was levelled and most of the dividing wall was knocked out between the old kitchen and scullery, leaving a low bar on the dining side, so that kitchen units could back on to it. A steel joist was put in to support the ceiling; it was faced with pine panelling on the dining side and useful cupboards on the kitchen side. The whole room was given a feeling of space and light by the addition of a new window taking up almost the whole of the end wall behind the sink, and by converting an existing double window into full-length french windows.

The plaster on one of the kitchen walls was in a bad state, so this was masked with pine panelling—always an effective treatment that brings warmth to a room. The owners bought kit cupboards which they fitted in the kitchen end. These they painted with seven coats of orange gloss, ending up with clear polyurethane varnish. This meticulous treatment was well worthwhile, because it makes the cheap units look as if they came from an expensive manufacturer. The surface is beautifully smooth and shiny, but extremely tough. Matching orange and white tiles were chosen to go behind the cooker and sink. The kitchen flooring is practical—vinyl tiles with a white marbled effect, and there is a beige fitted carpet in the dining end of the room.

In one corner of the room there was an old fitted dresser painted bright blue. It was this dresser that actually sold the house to its present owners; they could visualize the pine underneath all the blue, so one of their first jobs was to restore the dresser to its natural beauty by stripping off all the layers of paint.

The dining table is also of stripped pine—it is kept against the wall for everyday use. For parties, it is pulled out into the centre of the room and adorned with a floor-length cloth in a rich cornflower blue, which sets off the blue and white china.

In the hall, an old glass door was taken out and layers of wallpaper stripped. The original brown and white ceramic floor tiles were kept, and their colours are echoed in the new paisley patterned wallpaper above the white dado. There is a new Regency-style front door of stripped pine, and a sage green stair carpet. A table carved by the owner's grandmother is a much-loved piece of furniture.

The effect is completed by the lights. In the hall itself, there is an expensive-looking 'period' chandelier, which surprisingly turns out to be plastic—a real budget buy from a chain store. On the first floor landing at the head of the stairs is an old marble washstand topped with a brass lamp made by the owner from a 40mm Bofors gun shell. The Tiffany shade is bright orange and yellow cotton, and was made by the owner's wife.

The long drawing room has its original sliding door as an occasional room divider in the middle. A great deal of hard work was needed to give this room a new look. The owners started by removing two large fireplaces, blocking up one and replacing the other with a new marble grate and fireplace topped by a pine Adam type mantlepiece.

The alcoves on either side were lined with apricot silk and fitted with shelves to make an attractive background for ornaments. The existing radiators in these alcoves were cleverly disguised with brass grilles. Two antique mirrors were junk shop finds, re-gilded by the owner's wife.

Colours are white with a gold fitted carpet and floor-length curtains in soft moss green, gold and blue tapestry. The owner's wife made both these, as well as the silk drum lampshades. The lamps are old candlesticks. These were found in an attic and the white paint stripped to reveal brass, which was polished and lacquered to great effect.

Above. *The welcoming Edwardian hall. The expensive-looking chandelier is in fact from a chain store. The shades of brown in the floor tiles tone with the furniture.*

Below, left. *The vanity unit is built in to enhance the clean lines of the bathroom.*
Below, right. *The kitchen was given an imaginative open-plan treatment.*

NELSON HARGREAVES

Above. *This timber-framed house built on jackstuds—'stilts' below floor level— served as a comfortable temporary home.*

Makeshift garden home

Converting an old house or building a new one can be most rewarding once the work is completed, but there is always the problem of where to live while the work is going on. Architect Walter Segal found a solution while having a new house built on the site of his old one in London, by constructing a temporary home at the bottom of his garden. He has since designed many permanent houses built in the same way, using a simple and cheap method of construction.

The basis of his design is the use of standardized and mass-produced building materials which are easily available. These are assembled simply by a carpenter, producing a cheap but sound structure which can be dismantled or altered without damaging or wasting any of its components.

First a modular timber frame was built on jackstuds—'stilts' below floor level—using a nail construction, each stilt supported on paving slabs. Raising a lightweight structure such as this above ground level has many advantages. The foundations need not be so elaborate, sloping sites are not difficult to deal with, and as the floor is naturally ventilated there is no need to protect it against rising damp. A major benefit is one of ease of planning; it is not necessary to site the kitchen and bathroom together and use a vertical service duct as in conventional house building, as the underneath of the house serves as an easily accessible servicing grid.

The cheapest and most practical material Walter Segal could find for constructing the walls were woodwool slabs. The size of these slabs governs the module on which the plan of the house is based. These are placed vertically on the timber frame, and clad inside and out. The layers are held in position only by pressure and friction, making assembly very easy.

The exterior cladding is mineralized felt, and laminate sheets provide a light and practical finish for the interior. The roof is constructed of woodwool slabs and plasterboard laid in between and on top of the beams, spaced to provide ventilation. Roofing felt lying loosely on

Plasterboard, laminates and glazed asbestos sheeting fixed on both sides of the woodwool slabs were used for the interior cladding. **Top.** *The bedrooms were constructed to minimal proportions.* **Above.** *The structure also housed furniture and books to advantage.* **Right.** *The kitchen leads off the spacious dining room with its view over the garden. The floor was constructed from pine boards.*

top of the woodwool slabs, to allow seasonal movement without damage, is held down by a layer of coarse gravel.

The supporting frame and roof are built first so that construction can proceed in bad weather conditions. This house took six weeks to build for £853—£1 per square foot or £10 per sq m. and cost a relatively small amount to construct. construction can be done by an unskilled person, and leaves few areas for error. The result is a building that is cheap, lightweight, easy to erect and flexible.

ROBERT BELTON

The Georgian home revitalized

New houses built in the Georgian style—while being fair copies—seldom have the feeling of the real thing. However, a clever conversion and design scheme can recreate a traditional atmosphere.

Interior decorator David Mlinaric was asked to replan a two-storey house in Chelsea for a bachelor. The house was in good order, but not attractively decorated. The two reception rooms, separated by frosted glass double doors, were too small, and were badly proportioned. The owner wanted a design scheme that would last, both in its quality and its effect. He did not want a 'way-out' design that would intrigue people for a year and then become boring, but one that was rather more classic.

In his 'tidying up' operations, David Mlinaric used several tricks for improving the proportions of the house. The first step was to knock the two small ground floor rooms into one to make a large living room. The Adam-style wooden mantelpiece was replaced by a handsome grey marble fireplace, and a cornice was fitted round the top of the plain walls. New panelled double doors were fitted, and brass cabin door handles take the place of the old glass knobs.

Burnt orange paint and cinnamon upholstery create a relaxed atmosphere in the living room, where a combination of old and new furniture works very well. Paper borders have been used on the walls to define particular areas and attract attention to the chimney breast and corners.

Roller blinds have been fitted to all the windows in addition to curtains. These are useful in summer, when they allow the light in, but protect furniture from being bleached by the strong sun. They also provide privacy while avoiding the closed-in feeling created by heavy curtains drawn at night.

ROBERT BELTON

The main bedroom was made from two smaller rooms, and now runs the full length of the house from front to back, with a bathroom off it. The unusual colour scheme of blackcurrant and white gives a certain elegance to this bedroom, which also serves as a second living room, where the owner can relax and entertain. A Victorian patchwork bedspread combines all the colours through the spectrum of pinks and purples, and a small sofa is upholstered in linen to match the blackcurrant carpet. The white linen curtains are backed up by white roller blinds printed with a small pink design.

A white painted cupboard unit was built all along one wall of this bedroom, and houses everything its owner might need: television, hi-fi equipment, drinks cabinet, refrigerator, wardrobe for clothes, and bookshelves. The

Opposite page. The combination of old and new furniture in the living room looks well against burnt orange paint and cinnamon upholstery. **Top left.** Paper borders frame the walls to good effect. **Above left.** Continuity is achieved in the tiny spare bedroom by using matching fabric throughout.

doors are lined with blackcurrant felt so that the unit coordinates with the scheme of the room whether the doors are open or closed.

The main bathroom is completely tiled in a design chosen to tone with the carpet, which is the same as in the bedroom. As this bathroom is so small, one whole wall behind the bath was mirrored to double its apparent size, and the glass was fixed flush with the tiles so that no joins show. The original white fitments were left,

Top right. Every amenity for entertaining has been provided in a long fitted cupboard in the main bedroom. The doors are lined with blackcurrant felt which matches the carpet and the sofa. **Above right.** The bathroom off the main bedroom. A full-size mirror makes it appear twice as large.

and a white roller blind completes the scheme.

The spare bedroom furniture consists of a 19th century bed, a bedside chest and a chair; there is no room for anything else. As it is such a small room, David Mlinaric had the bed covered in the same heavy cotton as the walls, so as to create one single effect as you enter the room. To ensure that the effect is total, the curtains and roller blind were also made up in the same old-rose chintz fabric.

Back-to-front for the sun

When architect Alexander Hamilton-Fletcher, partner in the Richmond firm of Manning-Clamp & Partners, was called in to convert a late 19th century house in Surrey, his brief was a common one. His clients wanted a practical family house that was easy to run without help. He did this by turning the house 'back to front'.

The clients had three school-age children; a boy who was to have his own bedroom, and two girls who were happy to share a bedroom so long as they had a playroom as well. This would later become a sitting room where they could entertain their friends. A studio-cum-hobby room solved the problem of somewhere for any member of the family to do dirty jobs, practical activities and homework. A large living room was needed, with a dining area near the kitchen rather than an individual room. A separate laundry, however small, was a must.

The architect decided to put the main living quarters at the back of the house, to get away from a dull road with a northern aspect, and to take advantage of the view over the 50ft south-facing garden at the back. Therefore the ground floor of the house was completely replanned, and the large room at the front,

Below. *The extension added at the back of the house has made this living room a better size. Glazed doors slide right away to link the house with the terrace in summer.*

Above. *The wooden mantel was replaced by this tiled hearth unit. The pictures above are grouped on a panel of hessian-covered pinboard, to avoid marking the wall.*

MICHAEL DUNNE

usually used as the main living room in houses like this one, became the hobby room.

The large room at the back became the living room, and was enlarged and made L-shaped by the addition of a sloping-roofed single-storey extension. This runs almost all the way across the back of the house in place of a lean-to porch and kitchen, both of which were removed. With the greater depth that the extension gave the living room came the problem of insufficient light, so the architect designed cone-shaped rooflights to throw the daylight back as far as possible into the room. The deep shafts, topped with two sheets of clear glass with matt fibreglass between, diffuse the light without causing glare.

The dining area, tucked round the corner in the extension, has the maximum amount of window area, with a large double-glazed door at the back which slides right over to open on to the terrace outside in hot weather. A side-hung door provides access to the garden at other times. The living area is delineated by a carpet, laid for safety at the same level as the black pressed clay tiles used in the dining area, kitchen and hall. As the ground floor had a suspended wood floor, this had to be specially prepared for the tiles. This was done by removing the boards, cutting them up and laying them as a base on battens between the joists, which were then topped with expanded metal; all this was covered with a concrete screed on which the tiles were laid.

In the living room an ugly wooden mantel was the first thing to go. This was replaced by a combined hearth and seat unit with a shelf above, faced in black tiles, running along one side of the room. The working fireplace was reshaped, with a skirting radiator fixed below, so that the hearth is now about 1ft above the floor level.

A major feature of Alexander Hamilton-Fletcher's domestic design work is his concern that the circulation areas should be strategically planned for maximum accessibility with minimum inconvenience. He believes that every family house should have a passage running through, giving access to kitchen, living and dining areas, but without conflicting with the cooking activities or going through the living room. In this way the mother can supervize her children while she is working in the kitchen, without running the risk of colliding with a small member of her family while she is carrying a hot saucepan.

In this house the old dining room was gutted and completely refitted as a practical modern kitchen, with the 'throughway' alongside it, running from the hall to the dining area at the back. An 'administration centre', housing telephone, directories, cookery books, first aid and a notice board, is strategically placed in this passage, within easy reach of everyone. The kitchen units were made of birch-faced blockboard with pine frames and lips, simply treated with a polyurethane varnish. The electric hobs were set in a specially made slab of cast terrazzo.

Upstairs, two rooms were knocked into one to form the main bedroom, now the full width of the house and overlooking the back garden. Fitted wardrobes built all along one wall were

Above. Looking into the living room from the extension at the back, which houses the dining area. Cone-shaped rooflights throw light into the room without causing glare.

Below. The fitted kitchen is connected to the dining area by a hatch. A passageway runs from front to back, giving access to all the rooms without going through the kitchen.

MICHAEL DUNNE

designed to enclose two old chests of drawers to form 'his' and 'her' dressing table units with a mirror at the back of each recess. Painted dark turquoise to match the walls, they sink well into the background. A study area up one end is similarly fitted, with a shelf unit with hinged flap-down front supported on chains. A pin-up panel on the wall displays pictures effectively. Two small windows were knocked into one and the sill lowered, making a picture window overlooking the garden. The entire back wall is curtained in gold silk.

The focal point in this bedroom is a late 17th century Portuguese travelling bed which dismantles completely for transporting. Made of Brazilian rosewood, its four posts resemble barleysugar columns, and the bedhead is a screen of stalagmites and stalactites. The wall behind is plain, as a patterned wallpaper would obviously compete with the ornate bed; instead an attractive patterned wallpaper has been used on the ceiling.

The ceiling in the main bathroom was lowered by 18in. to improve the proportions, and the false ceiling, the wall above and below the basin, and the bath are all panelled in hemlock. The area round the basin and at the head of the bath is faced with Italian glass mosaic tiles, with a large mirror in the recess adding to the apparent size of the room.

In this conversion the clients were given just what they asked for. The decorations are as simple as possible, and designed to make cleaning easier. The clay tiles in the hall just need wiping over, and the sisal stair carpet lasts practically for ever. The bedrooms are close carpeted, the units in the bathrooms are tiled in, and the kitchen is planned for ease of running.

Above right. *The focal point of the main bedroom is this Portuguese travelling bed. The patterned wallpaper on the ceiling acts as a perfect foil for the plain walls.*

Below left. *A study area was provided at the other end of the main bedroom. The dark turquoise paint is an attractive background for the collection of pictures.*

Below. *The main bathroom, where the false ceiling and cupboards are panelled in hemlock. The areas round the bath and basin are faced with honey-coloured glass mosaic tiles.*

Above. *A colourful kitchen-cum-playroom tailored for easy, modern living. While children play in the spacious foreground, meals can be cooked in the adjoining kitchen area, handsomely fitted out in rich oak.*

Transforming the past

A successful home conversion does more than transform the old into the new. It takes into account the individual features and existing structure, unique to that house, and maximizes on these characteristics. When converting this late-Victorian house in South London, every inch of space was utilized by putting careful and clever forethought into the reshaping of the house.

Built in 1890, near Wandsworth Common, this house had evolved into a collection of dreary bedsitters, each with its own drab decor and gas fire. A family on the look-out for a large house, within convenient commuting distance of central London, bought it, realising that the possibilities for an effective conversion were plentiful.

In spite of its shabby state, the house had a flexible layout and a large back garden—ideal for summer parties and children's play. Three spacious floors, with two rooms leading off the half-landings on the stairs, provided ample area for the family, as well as spare rooms for lodgers.

Renovation began on the ground floor. Unlike so many houses where two small parlours are converted into a through living room, the parlour here was left structurally as it had been. The floors were treated for woodworm and the garish orange mouldings painted white. Advantage was taken of the southern exposure by installing double-glazed sliding doors along one wall where there had been a pokey door and two narrow windows.

The glass had the effect of opening out the room into the expanse of the patio and garden beyond. The extra light filtering into the room highlights the colour motif—a soft combination of mushroom and golds with accents of luxurious rich green seen in a small velvet chair, settee and curtain trim.

A focal centre, the fireplace, was 'a find'. When converting a house in the City of London into an office, the builders concerned had to dispose of a handsome green and black marble fireplace which, fortunately, was snapped up by the owners—at no cost—for this room. The antique gold mirror above sets off the elegant tone of the living room.

The patio beyond was built by the owners who had to raise the level of the ground using the builder's left-over rubble. Then crazy paving was put down, leaving an attractive surface for summer entertaining. A well constructed and carefully sited patio makes a comfortable and secluded outdoor living area which can enhance a garden and provide a hard, level surface for recreation which, in this case, is conveniently visible from the house.

A foot-high wall surrounding the patio was erected, mainly for a functional purpose. More seating was needed for a large party so a wall, made from low brick pillars with oblong stone slabs laid horizontally on top, became a convenient surface area where a number of guests could be comfortably seated. The wall also adds a decorative finishing touch.

The patio gracefully spans the width of the house so it can be easily reached from both the living room and the spacious kitchen-cum-playroom. This room was tailored for easy living, effectively combining a modern kitchen with an adjoining area for children to play. Any mother can appreciate the difficulties of keeping an eye on young children when cooking and a superb way of overcoming this problem is to create a play area as part of the kitchen.

Originally this room had been an unimaginative lean-to, crowded with a lavatory, bath, stove, sink and old range. These were pulled

Above. The mauve bathroom. Design began with the bath—bought at a sale—followed by striking wallpaper and a luxurious carpet.

Above. The blue bathroom, featuring double sinks and a bidet. Soft colouring creates a restful and elegant atmosphere.

down and several girders set into the ceiling to support the new room where expansive double-glazed windows again maximize on the southern aspect. On warm summer days, the children can go directly from the playroom to the patio and garden while still being surveyed from the kitchen area.

The modern fitments are in a U-shape and have a rich oak finish which adds a note of warmth to the room. The stove has four burners : two gas and two electric. It's been designed for people who want immediate heat for boiling as well as controlled heat for more complex cooking ; it's also highly advantageous in case of a gas or electricity failure. Easy-to-clean vinyl tiles in neutral shades of grey were the wise choice in a room where meals are eaten and children are at play. Spotlights were built into the ceiling for a soft and dramatic effect at night.

Modern living means adapting to the changing times. This house was built during a period when servants and nannies were expected to look after the children. With fewer servants and more chores for mother in the 1970's, this kitchen-cum-playroom design is a great help in replacing the amenities from the past. It allows for cooking and children's play in one room, giving more freedom to both mother and children.

Before converting rooms, give careful consideration to their functional demands as well as to their decorative requirements. Thorough forethought in planning a room will save you time and energy in the long run. A first conversion often suffers from too little practical thought and too much emphasis on visual impact. Both considerations are important, but convenience tends to outweigh the decorative aspects over a long period of time. In general, decoration should follow functional dictates.

A marble chopping board in the kitchen came from the same source as the marble on the entrance hall floor. Bought at a sale, these marble slabs turned out to be less expensive than ceramic tiling. The study, as well as the living room, kitchen and dining room, leads off the entrance hall and has a masculine look with its handsome purple carpeting.

Across the hall, the dining room is characterized by a generous bay window, vibrant rosy red walls and contrasting white trim. A heavy oak table and chairs add the necessary weight to this rather large room. It's always important to balance furniture with the size of a room, taking height and floor dimensions into account. Delicate antique furniture, for instance, would tend to look insignificant in a room of this size.

Three corner cupboards add a period flavour, while a brass and glass lantern makes an unusual 'chandelier' over the table. Grey floral curtains create a cool contrast with the warm red walls. Wooden parquet tiles, covering the floor, tie in well with the rest of the decor.

The final room on the ground floor is a bath-

room which emerged from the original passage to the old kitchen and cellar and a small larder. All space on this floor was utilized to the full, where best advantage was taken of every aspect.

The stairs and hallway were given a distinctive air through boldly patterned wallpaper in vivid shades of purple, blue and red and thick red carpeting. A patch of royal blue in the lodger's room at the half-landing arrests the eye where there is a clever accent in chequered blue and white dress material in the form of a strip around the ceiling border and in the curtains. A small decorative touch like this can be inexpensive and go a long way to giving a room an individual look.

Moving up to the first floor, there are two bedroom suites, each with its private bathroom. The two bathrooms are back to back and were made from one large room. In one bathroom, design began with a purple bath, bought in a sale, and from there the rest of the decor followed, with a brown carpet accented with a eye-catching wallpaper in subtle shades of mauve, beige and purple. The floor-length curtains in the attached bedroom are the same pattern, which helps to co-ordinate the two rooms.

The master bedroom, in contrast, was conceived in a soft skyblue seen in the fitted

Above right. A dining room rich in colour and atmosphere. Corner cupboards, a brass lantern lamp and an oak dresser add to the period flavour. Grey floral curtains create a cool contrast to the vibrant red walls.
Below right. View from the garden looking at the patio, smartened up with crazy paving. A surrounding wall was built so guests could be comfortably seated for entertaining on warm summer days.

carpeting and wall-length wardrobe which has delicate white beading on each of its six doors. The blue motif is carried into the bathroom suite which is luxurious and spacious, and fitted with double sinks, bidet and bath— all in the same shade of blue.

Like the kitchen-cum-playroom downstairs, this bedroom suite was tailored for easy living. No dashing downstairs on a cold evening to get from the bedroom to the bathroom—all is self-contained for the maximum ease of movement, resulting from imaginative planning.

On the second floor there is the children's and au pair's room with a handy utility room on the half-landing, attached to the children's bathroom. The utility room includes a sink, washing and drying machine and airing cupboard—a good means of avoiding long trudges up and down stairs when washing the children's clothes.

This Victorian house was brought up-to-date, aiming at easy and convenient modern living as well as attractive and striking decor.

Take your time for the best solution

Sometimes a house has to be added on to gradually instead of in a single operation. Whatever the reason, this gives the owners a chance to co-operate more fully with the architect and the builders because decisions don't have to be taken in a rush. And taking time brings the advantage that advice can be sought about problems that do not have a quick and obvious solution.

The extensions to this house in Gerrard's Cross, Buckinghamshire, were undertaken in two stages, because the owner is an American executive who is never very sure how long he will be staying in one place. He had first to be certain he would be in that house for long enough to make any major extensions worthwhile. Once the decision was taken to add on,

the work progressed remarkably quickly under the guidance of architect Pamela Morris. She was given separate briefs for the two extensions which were carried out two years apart, and details of the whole operation were built up by the owners and the architect as the job progressed.

The first requirement was a family room to be added to the existing kitchen so that the owner's wife could watch her four children play and continue with her chores at the same time. 'Family rooms'—originally an American idea—have spread to other countries and are excellent ways of creating a social centre in the home where each member can enjoy his own area of activity.

An additional reason for the extension was that the existing kitchen was too narrow to take a table large enough for the family to eat

together—and the owner wanted somewhere to set up a bar for parties. After considering the various alternative schemes, Miss Morris and the owners decided on a most economical plan which meant no alteration at all to the existing kitchen and the minimum of disruption to the household.

The external wall of the kitchen was partially removed, and a strengthening steel girder incorporated over the opening when the window was taken out. Fire resistant timber panelling was used on all the walls of the extension except one, which was left unplastered.

Timbered walls give a cosy appearance to a room, because the tones of the natural wood add a warm glow to the furnishings. They are also long-wearing and need minimal care.

The old window position made an excellent serving hatch for the bar in the centre of the kitchen; a strip light was incorporated in the old window head detailing and the bar itself was covered in easily-cleaned plastic laminate. Wherever possible throughout the alterations, Miss Morris used what was there already rather than create new, and unnecessarily expensive features. The old back door was removed and the opening was panelled round. Louvred doors have been fitted in the opening and a shutter over the bar so that the whole room can be shut off completely if required.

The existing waste pipes which had been on the external wall were now within the actual 'den', behind removable panels for easy access, and a trap door was made in the new timber floor for access to a manhole.

When the owner realized they would be staying in Britain for a further two years they planned a second stage of making additions to the house. The brief was for an extra bedroom, bathroom and some additional living-area—also space for the newly acquired deep-freeze! The owners particularly liked the idea of extending the existing living room but also being able to close it off as a separate area if needed.

Here they came up against a major problem: adding anything on to the existing living room would cut most of the ground floor off from natural light. In fact, the previous occupants had moved because they thought adding on impossible. The owners didn't want a whole glass roof, because the back of the house faced south, and it would be unbearably hot in summer. And the height of any new roof would be restricted as it would have to fit under the bedroom windows. The owners realised that they could build a large room but it would have a low roof.

The light problem was discussed with a con-

LEONARDO FERRANTE

Left. *The new 'family room' with its fair-face brick wall, and unique roof lights. Furniture is restricted for added space.*

140

sultant engineer who pointed out that in order
to get daylight back into the depth of such a
room, most of the light should come from the
very top of the window. If the window is extended
up into the roof the light will fall still further back
into the room. The answer was to adapt for
domestic use the sort of roof lights used
extensively in factories—an ingenious solution
to a tricky problem. The exact calculations over
size and so on were provided by the advisory
service of a large glass manufacturing firm.
Such firms are often happy to give advice to
people contemplating major rebuilding schemes.

Many people when faced with a problem in
adding-on give up if they can't see an easy way
out—in this case the previous owners simply
moved. In fact, once owners and architect had
put their heads together, and called in other
experts' advice the answer was fairly simple.
With the lighting problem solved, this second
extension—the conservatory—could be added
along the back of the house linking the
previously-built family room with the living
room, and providing complete circulation
through three different living areas. The adapted
factory lights both gave illumination and added
an interesting line to the roof, producing a feeling of height and spaciousness.

The new window high in the wall was fitted
with glass louvres and a lighting trough was
incorporated into the ceiling so that the
artificial lighting would come from the same
place as the natural lighting. The flat roof light
had a strip light fitted into the opening and non-
reflective transparent plastic was used to cover
the opening level with the surface of the ceiling.
This has the same effect as double-glazing.
Leaving the strip light on allows light to filter
into the hall at night so that the youngest child
(who sleeps in the bedroom at the top of the
stairs) has a feeling of 'being with the family'.

The extra bedroom and bathroom were built
over the flat roof of the first extension and were
planned to look like part of the original design.
It is always important to blend extensions in with
the rest of a building, otherwise they look out
of harmony and garish. You can do this by
building your extension in the same (or similar)
design to the original house, or by building it in
the same materials. If you can manage both, the
extension can be a perfect match to the rest of
the house with the new part blending in
smoothly with the original structure.

With both extensions, minor touches which
anyone could adopt made a major difference to
the final effect. One example of this kind of
touch was that wherever a window was removed
during the extensions the opening was finished
internally with mirror tiles. This was done in the
original bathroom, the upstairs toilet and the
downstairs cloakroom. Mirrors add enormously
to the effect of any decor, and mirror tiles are an
inexpensive way of flattering your home. They
are very much cheaper than one-piece glass
mirrors, and easier to apply.

A second was that, because rooms without
windows can get unbearably stuffy, mechanical
air extractors were fitted in the bathroom and
other windowless rooms. These work automatically through holes in the original window
and are ducted by pipes to the exterior. They
start whenever the light is switched on and
work for a further 15 minutes. This is a particularly good idea for internal bathrooms which
will tend to get hot and steamy and where you
will naturally switch on the light and conse-
quently start the extractor working.

A third idea—which could make a difference
to any home—was that a cupboard was fitted
wherever there was a space. So the house has a
vast number of unobtrusive built-in cupboards.

The owners had liked the house so much that
they were willing to take a gamble with a tricky
adding-on operation. It worked and as a result
the house is easier to run and more attractive.

LEONARDO FERRANTE

Open-plan designing

Open-plan living is ideal for some people. It means ease of movement, convenience, and greater spaciousness because of fewer walls and doors. This Italian apartment is based on an open-plan scheme, and its colourful decor is designed to complement this type of modern living.

Certain ingredients are necessary for successful open-planning. A co-ordinating element—such as colour or texture—is needed to unify the various areas. Effective techniques for dividing one living area from another are also required. And, finally, a great deal of forethought is a must in planning the layout to facilitate practical and fluid movement in the home.

This streamlined flat is basically built on an open-plan scheme; the bedroom and bathroom being the only rooms which are partitioned off. The front door leads into a small entrance hall which opens out into the main living area. There are two sections to the lounging area—the 'sunken' part, spruced up with brilliant colours,

and the 'fireside' part which suggests warmth and casualness. Beyond this is the dining area, originally a second bedroom, which leads into a small, but efficient, kitchen.

The flat is designed for comfortable living. There are no long journeys between the kitchen and dining room. If you're relaxing in one of the chairs or couches, you can easily keep track of anything brewing on the stove. It's compact living which still allows for a maximum amount of movement.

It's also tailored for easy cleaning. No laborious bouts with the hoover; the elegant, red tiled floor simply needs a wipe down, and no old-fashioned skirting boards or picture railings to collect dust. The absence of lampshades and curtains also eliminates the need for a tedious annual cleaning. If you're looking for ways to cut down on housework, this flat has some good

Opposite page. Spaciousness of a home built on an open-plan scheme, viewed from the 'sunken' area, looking through the cozy 'fireside' section into the dining area— originally a partitioned-off second bedroom.
Above top. *Colourful cushions and an unusual white and red brick wall give the 'sunken' area a look of modern comfort.*
Above. *Bold stripes set the tone for this fresh looking bedroom. The blues and greens are repeated in the dream-like wooden figure which replaces a more conventional bedhead.*
Right. *A bathroom accented with a sharp green mirror. A single spotlight adjusts for detailed work or soft, flattering lighting.*

ideas for keeping it to a minimum.

The dominating greens and blues subtly co-ordinate the decor from one part of the room to the next. These colours are found in the cushions, apple-green dining table, bathroom mirror and bedspread. The choice of colours is a good one —it's both warm and soft and the eye isn't likely to tire of them quickly.

If you're trying to get an overall feeling of harmony in a small flat, it pays to put energy into finding a colour scheme that can be effectively applied in any room, from the living room to the bathroom. Variations in tones and in combinations of colour can be made for interest, but the ultimate effect should be one of unity.

Continuity in this flat also results from the techniques used for dividing the different areas. The divisions emerge in various ways. First, there is a sunken floor, offset by two steps

spanning the width of the room. Second, there is a free-standing shelf unit which suggests a change in space definition for the kitchen/dining area and lastly, there is a variation in wall texture from a smooth plaster to a rough finish and finally into brick.

The lowered ceiling also helps to offset the main sunken sitting area. All these features work together to subtly alter the feeling of space without breaking up the sense of fluidity. The use of red and white wall bricks is inexpensive, modern and attractive. It's an easy technique to employ and the only thing to keep in mind is that it should blend in with the rest of the furnishings. A wall with a geometric pattern like here, for instance, would only be antagonistic in a room with curved period chairs and ornate tables.

The straight clean lines of the wall are repeated elsewhere in the square cushions, the

low white table and simple canary yellow vase on top. The yellow motif is picked up in the drawers in the desk opposite the couch and in the cheerful 'kite' bird which gracefully hangs over the dining table.

The beauty of this room is the ease with which it can be re-arranged. The four velvet cushions on top of the steps can be removed altogether to make room for a large party. These cushions can also double up as a bed for an overnight guest. All the other pieces of furniture are light enough to be moved about with no trouble at all.

Versatile furniture is an excellent idea. Out of necessity or mood, most people like changes in home decor and to have the facility for simply interchanging various items is a convenience. Floor cushions can be economic and, as here, a luxurious addition to a room, as well as being flexible.

Moving up from the sunken area is the fireside section, smartened up with black and white fur skins found in the rug and modern slung chair. A strip around the fireplace, like one of the walls, is roughly rendered plaster—a small but effective touch in that it creates different wall textures and saves the room from a sterile white-wall look so commonly seen in modern buildings.

The niches over the fireplace add delightful variety and again help to break up what would otherwise be a featureless expanse of white wall. The low white floor light was an appropriate selection for the modern decor, and the slung chair adds to the feeling of coziness.

The bedroom offers another splash of colour, mainly seen in the striped cotton chenille bedspread and simple window curtains. Rather than having a conventional bedhead, space was saved by putting a wooden figure directly on the

Above. *Vibrant colouring in the wall decoration gives dramatic impact to the dining area. The free-standing shelf unit breaks the flow of space, setting this area apart from the living area. An elegant red tiled floor is designed for easy care and cleaning.*

wall. It was a good choice in that it has a dream-like quality and also picks up the colours already decorating the room.

A built-in wardrobe with sliding doors runs along one wall. Inside there is a colourful chest of drawers which is neatly hidden from sight when the doors are pulled shut. Another space-saving idea was to take the same material as the curtains and make wall 'pockets' for storing items like newspapers and hair brushes.

It's worth taking note of the superb method of making 'extra' room for storage, as seen in the

high long shelf over the bed here and in the main room. The shelf is sufficiently near to the ceiling not to distract from the central design of the room. It's ideal for displays, books or stereo speakers and could also be made a focal point by featuring hanging plants—if you have the time and patience to attend to plants at such a height !

Moving finally into the bathroom, there is a repeat of the blue/green motif with a rich tone of gold which adds warmth. The single spotlight on the wall is useful for close work like shaving or putting on make-up. If softer lighting is desired, the spot can be adjusted to reflect off the walls or ceiling.

The decor in this flat was not particularly expensive, but through careful planning and expertise in selecting compatible colours and furnishings, it has emerged as a comfortable home with a great deal of visual appeal.

JOHN MYERS

Adding living space

Above. *Careful colour scheming and the creation of horizontal lines, by installing bookshelves, can visually unite a two-into-one conversion of stylistically different rooms.*

Adapting to changing needs in the home requires a versatile imagination. A totally suitable home can suddenly become inadequate if a major change occurs. When this small Victorian cottage was originally converted, it was ideal for the couple living in it—until their first child was born. Then extra room was needed to accommodate the baby. An ingenious solution was found by building a cleverly conceived extension which fulfilled the demands brought about by the change in the family.

When teacher Julian Wolchover and his wife Janet, a textile designer, bought their London cottage in Parson's Green, it was just the right size for them. An artisan's dwelling, built over a hundred years ago, it consisted of two small downstairs rooms and two upstairs, with a more recent extension at the back—a ground floor kitchen and a bathroom above. An uninspiring concrete yard spread out at the back.

The Wolchovers were fortunate—before purchasing their house, a council grant had supplied it with a new roof, damp-proof course, bathroom and plumbing. A great deal of work

still was to be done. Throughout the house the wood was rotting, including the floorboards, joists, doors and skirting boards; the general tone of the place was gloomy.

Architect Stan Playford advised the Wolchovers on the structural changes to be made. The two pokey ground floor parlours were made into a single more gracious through room. A reinforced steel joist, supported by a pillar and wall buttress, replaced the original dividing wall. A new staircase was built which also had the effect of opening out the space in the room.

The room now has an elegant and comfortable

atmosphere. Soft, neutral colours—a co-ordinating link throughout the cottage—were chosen. Most of the walls were painted white and some, a subtle shade of cobweb brown. Rich brown wall-to-wall carpeting was put down, providing a flexible background for the rest of the decor. Two matching brown settees face one another from opposite ends of the room.

Splashes of contrasting colour are seen in straight-back chairs, upholstered in a stunning peacock blue, wall ornaments and a period fireplace, found in the country and brought back to town by the Wolchovers. The brightly decorated green tiles add a cheerful note and are effectively offset by the bold black tiles of the hearth.

The approach to colour in this home was practical; the end product is restful and visually appealing. Conservative and neutral background colours tend to be the best choice for home decor. It then gives you an opportunity for bold or inventive colour treatment in the decorative touches, like cushions, tiling or paintings. A mistake in colour scheme or a change in your taste is far less expensive to alter if you are simply dealing with small items. A complete repainting or new carpeting requires far more money, time and energy.

Contrasting with the period flavour of the room is the modern looking coffee table, designed and made by Mr. Wolchover. The supporting 'legs' are made from chromium tubing bent to gracefully curve from the ground upwards. A slab of smoked glass with bevelled

edges became the top and, for a relatively small amount of money, a handsome and unusual piece of furniture has been produced.

A strategic technique was used in this room to bring the two sections together. The pillar, buttress and two chimneys—both different sizes —stop the fluidity of space in the room. To overcome this segmented feeling, shelves were built along the 'chimney' wall, filling in all the irregular recesses and creating continuous horizontal lines which carry the eye from one end of the room to the other. The practical shelves also serve as a vehicle for visually co-ordinating the room.

Upstairs there were fewer structural changes; most of the alterations came about through applying imaginative decorative ideas and hard work. The motif in the master bedroom is Edwardian, with an intriguing Japanese accent, seen in the wall prints. The legs of the brass bedstead were shortened by about a foot to give more spaciousness to the room and to eliminate clambering up into a high bed every night. Louvred wardrobes were neatly fitted into existing recesses, created by the blocked-up chimney breast.

The Edwardian English oak bureau was in a sorry state when the Wolchovers bought it. The elaborate hand-carved facade was covered with a heavy black varnish, almost completely disguising its original beauty. The Wolchovers stripped it in a couple of hours, using caustic soda, heavy rubber gloves for protection, a floor scrubber and constant running water from a hose. They picked a day with a slight breeze to

Left. Techniques of effective conversion have been used to improve a bedroom.
Above. The bathroom was reduced in size to accommodate a new passage, but its new decor gives the illusion of space.
Right. The small area available for the dining room extension has been put to the most imaginative and effective use.

do the job to make certain the wood would dry out properly. If you're interested in enhancing your furniture by stripping and refinishing it, you will find that the job, although often tedious, has very rewarding results.

Clever wall decorations, costing very little, are the six Japanese prints—bought as post cards at a London museum, and framed with ordinary black and gold frames—picked up for a very

JOHN MYERS

nominal cost at a common chain store. The array of small pictures adds a distinctive note without costing a fortune.

The adjoining room was used as a necessary studio for Mrs. Wolchover, who works at home. When the baby finally arrived, it was the obvious place for him because the room was next to the parents' room and close to the bathroom. Additional space was then required for the family.

Already existing at the back of the house was the kitchen/bathroom extension. Building adjacent to this, Mr. Wolchover conceived of a further extension which would provide room on the first floor for a studio and additional area on the ground floor for a dining room which meant the 'two-into-one' room could be used exclusively for lounging. The concept was straight-

forward, logical and met all the Wolchovers' needs. One major hitch arose.

Building onto the back of the house meant covering up the outside wall of what was to become the baby's room. By law this wasn't permissible because there wouldn't be adequate light or ventilation. An ingenious solution was found. A two-floor extension was built with each floor being substantially lower than those of the original cottage. This meant the total height of the new extension would be a good eighteen inches lower than the main body of the house which allowed for a high window of regulation size to be fitted along the outside wall of the baby's room.

Initially it appeared that the Wolchovers would have to be content with only a one-floor extension. Through inventive thinking, though, they got around a very real obstacle and were able to make a two-floor extension. A good house conversion or extension begins at the drawing board. It doesn't always take an architect to solve difficult problems; ideas and solutions are often generated from the people who live with the problem—they're the most involved.

In creating a passageway into the new studio, the large bathroom was reduced in size. It is now decorated in a vivid buttercup yellow with contrasting cocoa brown tiles. The bath was spruced up by putting hard board, painted a bright yellow, around the sides and finishing off the corners with a chromium strip. The floor is carpeted with a speckled golden carpet which gives a feeling of luxury and warmth.

The ground floor extension became the dining room which has easy-to-clean ceramic tiles in a provençal pattern and French doors leading onto the patio beyond. The long trestle table is complemented with black pvc pedestal chairs with chromium bases.

The adjoining kitchen window was lowered and now is the serving hatch between the dining room and kitchen. The outside door became the passage between the two rooms. The compact and efficient kitchen is, perhaps, one of the most notable aspects of the house.

Faced with a kitchen measuring just over eleven feet by seven, the Wolchovers knew they would have to do a lot of careful planning to accommodate all the modern equipment they wanted. They sat down with a layout of the kitchen on graph paper and then tried different arrangements of fitments, juggling until they found the best combination.

The equipment they were using was modular, most pieces measuring 21in. in width. This meant that exactly four units could be slotted along the seven foot wall. Now the small kitchen has washing and drying machines, a dishwasher and an abundance of cupboard space and working surfaces. The tall fridge/freezer fits neatly into a recess, emerging from where the original kitchen door was blocked up.

The key to this successful conversion is the significant emphasis that went into the planning stage. All possible space was utilized to the full, taking advantage of every corner and recess; and complementing this clever planning, is the simple and attractive decor.

Do-it-yourself
with original ideas

Turn-of-the-century houses are a converter's ideal. They are generally spacious and solidly built, so major alterations are easier than in flimsier buildings, and offer endless possibilities to both architect and handyman. When the people who live in such a house take an architect's advice and then, as far as possible carry out the work themselves the results can be stunning—and inexpensive.

From the front, this house in South London, England, looks much like its neighbours, but the back is entirely different. The owners have built on a two-storey conservatory with a sloping roof and a complete wall of windows overlooking the garden. This integrates well with the back of the house and gives it a feeling of space and light. A conservatory can be an interesting way of linking house and garden: by bringing the garden into the house it extends both usable space within the house and enjoyment of the garden during the winter months.

Inside too, there has been a complete turnabout. The main living and kitchen areas now take up the whole of the first floor—a good idea for the type of house where the most spacious and adaptable rooms are at first floor level.

The owners originally lived in the top-floor flat, and later, when they bought the rest of the house, they chose to keep their bedrooms there, opening up the rooms lower-down as a playroom for the children, a workshop and a bedsitter for their student sister. The playroom and bedsitter are relatively cut off from the rest of the house, which gives the children and sister independence on the ground floor, and the owners peace upstairs.

As the owners began to plan the changes to their home, it became clear that the structural alteration to the house would be considerable, so they asked architects John Spence and Partners to draw up suitable plans that would fit in with their tight budget. The high conservatory was the first consideration; it was planned to cover an area that had not been used to its full potential. The architect's aim was to put in as much glass as possible—hence the high wall of windows overlooking the garden and the glass roof, which catches the sun. To avoid enclosing the second-floor windows, the conservatory roof was designed to finish just below them.

A doorway was knocked into the wall of the first floor leading from the conservatory through to the dining room. The house also has a back garden, which is reached from ground level through a gallery-cum-office that was created for the owner's wife, and down a spiral staircase from the conservatory; this can be seen silhouetted inside the high window.

Decor in the conservatory has been kept simple to flatter the plants and to harmonize with the rest of the house, where natural finishes are much in evidence. The conservatory wall has been left in plain brick and painted white. The exposed beams have been treated with sealer but not painted; the metalwork on the spiral staircase and the joist hangers are finished in black. Seen from inside at ground level, the conservatory might have seemed too long and narrow, but the cunning use of diagonally-laid white ceramic floor tiles gives it a much wider look. This is an idea worth copying for any long and narrow room.

Apart from knocking out walls and installing central heating, the owners have done all the work in the rest of the house themselves in their spare time. In the living room, for example, one of the main talking points is the new false ceiling made by the owners from tongued-and-grooved ramin boarding. This particular wood was chosen because of its attractive pale colour. Each plank is quite wide, but has bevelled cuts along it to make it look like three slim ones.

Installing the ceiling was a tricky operation. First, a frame was made, which had to be sunk into the outside and supporting walls. Then the cladding was slotted tightly together and fixed with concealed nails. The whole ceiling was sealed immediately to keep the wood from shrinking or darkening.

Although the house was altered extensively, the owners had to keep to a tight budget, and one of the most rewarding and money-saving ways they found was to make their own furniture. Anybody could follow their example in making simple pieces of furniture – many DIY magazines on the market can show you how. One of the things they made was a sofa, which fits snugly into a bay window. The frame is of stained and sealed pine, and is lined with comfortable foam cushions. Generous bolsters form arm-rests, and the cover is of rich-looking olive-green velvet. For a small outlay, the owners have made themselves a highly individual and comfortable piece of modern furniture. A similar sofa bought ready-made would have cost ten times as much.

A wall was demolished to make an extension to the living room. To give an attractive 'gallery' effect, it was only knocked down to just above waist level—a useful height that makes a good back for built-in seating. A beam with wooden props was put in to support the ceiling; this adds to the effect.

A small wooden staircase leads into the lower part of the room. This area has a sealed wood floor, and makes a good corner for dancing when there are parties. The owner removed an old fireplace and built in a row of shelves and cupboards to house drinks, stereo equipment (with four speakers) and ornaments. The cupboard-door fronts are finished with a practical white plastic laminate.

The kitchen was originally a bathroom and separate lavatory. It is now very much a cook's kitchen, efficiently planned with all the equipment close to hand. A cork-lined false ceiling was put in to disguise a row of ugly pipes. There are built-in units to save space, and the window over the sink has been enlarged to let in more light. All these are ideas which could make a major difference to any kitchen. The floor and window sill are covered in attractive blue-and-white ceramic tiles.

On one side of the cooker there is a mar slab which was once a washstand top, and the other side a worktop of polished aluminium.

A good space-saving idea was to fix a sliding louvred door between the kitchen and living room. Two refrigerators are stacked one on top of the other and well hidden behind another louvred door. A hatch was built through to the dining room, where an old fireplace was removed and cupboards built in with louvred doors and black laminate tops.

The floor was stripped and sealed with an unusual finish worth noting: the owner used six coats of a white primer, which turns clear when dry and gives a soft polished effect; it is not as glittery as the more common polyurethane sealers, but has a subtle sheen. He has used this primer to seal all wooden surfaces throughout the house.

Old pieces of furniture can often be adapted to suit new decor with great effect. Here, a large dining-room table has had its original top replaced by a new and larger one of blockboard; the legs have also been slightly modified. A new table of the required size would have been an expensive buy, but by 'doctoring' an old one, the owners were able to use its strong frame to support the new top.

The two-storey conservatory is the touch that makes this house original, but the whole house is an excellent example of imagination and hard DIY work that has paid off handsomely.

Below. *The kitchen is a small but compact 'island' between the dining room and the living room. It is arranged so that all the fitments are within easy reach. The walls and ceiling are clad in warm-toned T & G and the floor tiled in blue and white.*

LEONARDO FERRANTE

Above. A room with a view—to another room ! The separating wall has been partly knocked through, and the inner room is reached via a few steps at the side of the 'window'. The colour scheme is composed of subtle shades of green.

Below, left. The two-floor conservatory has a complete wall of windows overlooking the garden, making the interior feel light and spacious. The spiral staircase looks dramatic silhouetted against the sky outside, and gives access to the garden.

Below, right. The conservatory extension includes a first-floor gallery which is used as an office for the owner's wife. This is a good example of getting the most from every inch of space, and planning to fit in a room for all your needs.

Blending old with new

Successfully blending the old with the new requires skill and imagination—especially in a home conversion. The new materials should harmonize— visually and structurally—with the old. This converted Tudor cottage has effectively combined the past and present. It still retains its original character while benefiting at the same time from modern materials and conveniences.

When bio-chemist Frank Brown bought his small sixteenth century cottage tucked away in a quiet Oxfordshire village, the modest profit he had made on selling his semi-detached house had to go a long way. Much renovation and repair was needed, but Dr. Brown was determined that his conversion would not be at the cost of losing the old world aura of the cottage.

It originally consisted of four small rooms—two up and two down. Several centuries later, a ground-floor extension, which served as a primitive kitchen, was added at the back, form-ing the cottage into an L-shape. A couple of uninspiring outhouses stood beyond.

There was no bathroom or plumbed sanitation, no entrance hall or landing, and the rooms on each floor were interconnecting, giving a cramped and confined feeling. The roof timbers in the older part were in such a state of decay that the back wall awkwardly and dangerously bulged out.

Added to this, there was an out-of-doors space problem—no provision for car parking. Access to the land at the back of the cottage was impossible; it was inconveniently blocked by the house itself. Parking was forbidden on the green in front because of village bye-laws. This tedious problem was ingeniously overcome through a structural change, suggested by an architect called in for advice by Dr. Brown.

A first floor extension was built above the kitchen projection at the back, providing enough room for one large bedroom and a bathroom. A passage—wide enough for a car to pass through—was then created through the ground floor of the extension, with the upstairs bedroom section forming an archway above.

Although this reduced the amount of space downstairs, it still left room for a reasonably sized kitchen, with a small utility room on the other side of the passage. Now cars can easily drive through the archway into the back garden which provides more than ample parking space.

This clever solution to the car parking problem has benefited the cottage both visually and practically. The archway adds an unusual decorative note, while creating an intriguing entrance to the secluded land behind the cottage. The archway may also be used as a carport during stormy or menacing weather.

The foundation of the new 'archway' extension was not strong enough to support more than timber-frame walls. These were then clad with rich wood which not only complemented the exterior stucco, but also served as a relatively inexpensive and simple method of constructing the outer wall.

Next the roof was tackled. Some time during

the last century, the thatch on the older part of the house was replaced with tiles. Similar tiles had been used for the newer kitchen projection and, fortunately, these could be re-cycled for the roof on the 'archway' extension.

The choice of roof material was a good one. By using similar tiles on both the old and newer parts of the cottage, a visual continuity was achieved. The extension, rather than looking as a 'stuck-on' afterthought, seems to emerge as an integral part of the house.

Dr. Brown worked together with his friends on the replacement of tiles in the new section. Before attempting the job, however, he called in a professional builder to give guidance in re-doing the roof timbers on the older section. This combination of professional and amateur effort is often a good compromise if you're working on a slim budget. The professional specifies and guides, while the amateur does the main bulk of physical labour. It may cause slight backache, but you'll see greater results for your money.

Other changes, which helped to brighten up the cottage, evolved out of the new roof in the old part. The pokey front windows were heightened to make graceful dormer windows. Further light was allowed to spill into the up-stairs by building generous French windows, offset by a balcony, for the main bedroom.

Above. *Side view of the cottage showing the later extension. The unusual archway adds an interesting visual touch as well as allowing cars to drive into the back garden where there is ample parking space.*

Below. *The imposing fireplace, with its original cross beam, serves as a handsome focal point for the living room. The bricks retain warmth from the fire and act as a giant storage heater for the cottage.*

An effort was made to keep the character of the house wherever possible. The existing purlins in the old section, for instance, were left exposed, although they don't provide the true support which comes from the new purlins hidden behind. The other old roof timbers were replaced, but still put to good use elsewhere for internal construction. After being treated for woodworm, the old timber was used in one room, for example, as cross beams between the purlins to support the plaster board ceiling.

Early investigations in the old section showed that there were a number of beams in the walls and ceilings downstairs which had been plastered over during an earlier 'renovation'. This is quite common with houses of this period and, although uncovering them is a tedious and messy business, it is well worth the result of the added character they give.

Another discovered feature, uncovered by Dr. Brown, was the magnificent central fireplace. It had been bricked up in the past when smaller fireplaces were in vogue. Using a cold chisel, a wide stone fireplace with an imposing heavy beam above and a bread oven to one side was revealed.

The bread oven, which was in poor condition, was removed and then concentration centred on cleaning up and restoring the fireplace. Once this laborious task was finished and a fire lit, a new problem arose. Heavy, dark smoke poured into the room, creating an intolerable atmosphere. As an experiment, the pot was removed from the chimney and, fortunately, this eliminated the unwanted smoke. When the fire is used on a regular basis, the bricks in the wide chimney become warm and act as a giant storage heater for the house.

Once the large fireplace was exposed, it tended to dominate the small room which also formed the main thoroughfare of the house. Consideration was then given to opening out the room by knocking down the existing partition between the two downstairs rooms. Investigation showed that, although it was essentially load-bearing, by putting a large vertical beam in the middle under the heavy existing cross beam at ceiling level, the wall could be safely removed.

The new beam was 'treated' to make it blend with the other decor. First it was stained to make it look older and then the corners were chamferred. Now the 'new' beam not only serves as a functional item, but also as an attractive feature in the spacious room.

Below. A dining area rich in colour and atmosphere. The heavy Jacobean-style table and straight-back chairs in dark oak contrast with the white walls. The ceiling beams add to the period flavour, while the rich red gives a dramatic note and warmth to the decor.

Obviously the furniture in the room couldn't be modern in style if the period look was to be maintained. Instead, heavy and imposing Jacobean-style table and high-back chairs in dark oak were chosen. Further chests, tables and book cases also follow the Jacobean motif. If you're interested in getting old world style into your home, there are many interesting and exciting ways of introducing a period touch through imaginative interior design. A single piece of antique furniture, for instance, can add a great deal of charm to a room, giving it new character or style.

As a foil for the dark wood, the walls were painted in white emulsion, to which a small amount of brown was added to lessen the glare. An inexpensive and hard-wearing floor covering—carpet tiles—in a rich brown were put down. The tiles have the advantage of reducing waste when they are fitted wall-to-wall and they can be rotated to distribute the wear evenly. A bold splash of colour comes from a fireside rug and chair upholstery in rich red—a popular Jacobean colour.

The ultimate mood of the cottage is one of old world comfort and charm. The warmth of the fireplace and the richness of the beams and rafters add to the overall effect. It's a superb example of how modern materials can be used in a cottage conversion without losing the period flavour.

NELSON HARGREAVES

Above. *Casualness in a kitchen, once a dark, dreary and lifeless room. Terracotta tiles on the wall add a warm decorative touch.*

Total renovation

Converting a mere shell of a house has both positive and negative aspects. It gives you freedom in applying your individual ideas to interior design which often results in unique decor. It also requires more imagination and effort on your part—a simple skeleton of a house contributes little to the overall character which finally emerges after renovation. This conversion began with a bare structural minimum, but through inventive application, it was transformed into a home of comfort and style.

Choreographer Johnny Greenland bought his mid-nineteenth century house in Islington about eight years ago. It was in a state of complete disrepair—floors and ceilings were rotting, plaster was blistering and faded wallpaper was peeling off the walls. A total renovation was badly needed from top to bottom.

Major jobs were dealt with first. Central heating and plumbing were installed; re-plastering and re-wiring were done; and a bothersome water leakage repaired in the roof. Most of the decaying doors and broken windows had to be replaced.

Conversion work then began on the ground floor. Two small rooms were made into one long spacious drawing room-cum-study. The walls were covered in a rich brown hessian and the windows dramatically framed with raw silk curtains in a brilliant burnt orange. The wall covering and the floor-length curtains contrast well in colour—the sharp orange breaks up the large expanse of brown—and in texture—the fragile raw silk sets off the rough hessian. Contrast in texture can be as important to effective interior design as contrast in colour.

A further splash of colour comes from the antique gold velvet settee and armchairs. The sunshine colours of orange and gold are the 'warmth-givers' in this room. On either side of the settee are two magnificent, eye-catching lamps; the bases are converted plant holders with soft beige shades setting them off.

The side tables are interesting, mainly because they avoid an old-fashioned 'matching table' look. One table is long with a green and black marble top, bought at a reasonable price from tombstone makers. The other is a more conventional leather-topped table. If you're buying

furniture, try not to be limited by common fashion trends. The side tables here are a good example of the smart look that can arise from applying a little originality to design.

Most of the furniture here and throughout the house was bought at second-hand shops or auctions. The grey marble fireplace, for instance, was rescued from a house about to be demolished. The mantel of a second matching fireplace now serves as an attractive shelf camouflaging the central heating radiator in the entrance hall.

Another superb 'find' is the large, imposing gilt-framed mirror which helps to bring the two parts of the room together by creating a continuous visual flow. The frame—originally used for pictures—cost under ten pounds, the mirror itself a bit more. The visual impact is unforgettable; the magnificent mirror is the focal drawing point of the room. Often it's the well conceived item—rather than an expensive one—which becomes the most attractive feature.

Underneath is a handsome mahogany sideboard which balances the heaviness of the mirror above. As a general rule, a wall picture or mirror should be narrower than the object directly underneath it, such as a couch, mantel or chest of drawers. If the wall hanging is wider than the object below, it has a tendency to be

Above. *The Regency exterior, smartly set off by a rich wooden door, yellow-tinged bricks and contrasting sharp white.*
Above right. *Richness in a handsome bedroom. Velvet curtains and bedheads in luxurious burgundy complement the heavy weave of the attractive bedspreads. The lamp bases originally were brass firedogs.*
Right. *A living room bathed in warm antique gold and brilliant burnt orange. The elegant gilt-framed mirror over the mahogany sideboard tends to dominate, while porcelain plant holders serve as eye-catching lamp bases.*

NELSON HARGREAVES

overbearing, dwarfing or diminishing the item on the floor. A harmonious balance between wall decorations and furniture can improve any room.

Resting on top of the sideboard is a silver tantalus and graceful candelabras, which help to perpetuate the Victorian tone of the room. Other contributing pieces are a small Victorian chair covered in French blue velvet, a rich looking desk and a mock gas lamp. Bookshelves have been built into the recesses, created by the blocked-up chimney breast, to make an unbroken visual line in the wall.

Moving from the living room to the passageway, there is a new open riser staircase which provides two advantages over conventional stairs. Firstly, it doesn't hinder the flow of space and, secondly, it allows more light to filter in, a frequent need in a stairwell. If you're installing a new staircase in your house, a good DIY home carpentry manual will give you ideas and instructions for building simple and stylish open riser stairs.

The stairs lead up to the new extension at the back of the house, which includes a complete bathroom on the half-landing, with a smaller bathroom below. The main bathroom door was built by extending the original window on the half-landing. It's a rich looking room with pine-clad ceiling and walls, carpeting and boldly patterned shower curtains. The pine also partitions off the hot water tank with an airing cupboard above.

This bathroom has an exterior ceiling and

Above. *The dining area of the kitchen, highlighted by a bold black and white chequered floor and a wooden refectory table and chairs. The imposing oak dresser was stripped to give greater visual appeal.*

three walls which means it could be quite cold during the winter. The pine lining in the room helps to insulate it as well as adding a handsome decorative touch. There is a lovely wall hanging —a Roman god-like figure head—which was carted back by Johnny Greenland from a film set in Rome.

From the bathroom the stairs lead onto the first floor landing, with its grand mahogany tallboy, past a small Victorian bedroom, into the master bedroom. This room has a masculine look, featuring burgundy velvet curtains and bedheads with contrasting deep green walls and bedspreads.

On either side of the beds are beautifully inlaid Victorian side tables. Resting on these are eye-catching lamps—made from old ornate brass firedogs, topped off with beige lampshades. Like the 'pot planter' lamps downstairs, these 'firedog' lamps here are unusual, adding a note of individual elegance to the room.

Moving back down the open riser stairs, the basement begins with the utility room, fitted out with all the modern conveniences. Originally the basement had been dark and drab— two rooms with little life or light. The partitioning wall was knocked down to make one spacious room, and a decor was introduced which has a

casual look—totally different from the more formal look upstairs.

The motif in this dining/kitchen room is black, white, wooden and relaxed. To let in more light, the old door leading out to the coal cellars was made into spacious French doors. Light now spills into the dining area from the street above. The outside brick wall was whitewashed to reflect as much light as possible, adding a cheerful note.

A refectory dining table and oak chairs are set off by a large black and white chequered floor. The oak dresser, with its delicate carving was bought for very little. A great deal of time, however, was spent in stripping it, using polystripper, caustic soda and wire wool. It was a laborious task, but the results are well worth the visual appeal which has resulted.

Moving into the kitchen area, all the fitments are lined along one wall. Spanish-style floor tiles in terracotta were put on the wall which gives a slightly Mediterranean look to the room. The old dark door leading out to the 'jungle' garden, was opened out into French doors. Maximum light was brought into the room by putting glass doors and windows where there had once been light-robbing heavy doors.

The overall conversion in Johnny Greenland's house reflects individuality and creativity from the period look of the upstairs to the modern, casual atmosphere in the kitchen below. A mere shell of a house has been transformed into a most livable home through personal imagination and application.

155

Using money wisely

Setting up house when you have enough money to buy the furnishings you like might not seem to present many problems. But some houses — particularly older ones — need a special kind of treatment to prevent them becoming too austere and 'over-perfect'.

Making a house a home was the problem that confronted the owners of this Victorian terrace house in South London. They decided to approach the problem through an unusual use of colour and a careful choice of furniture, both old and modern, to suit the house and make it welcoming.

The house had been built in 1890, and when the present owners bought it three years ago, much of the original Victorian dinginess lingered on. There was dismal brown paint everywhere, and the wallpaper was peeling off the walls. The rooms seemed too small and the atmosphere was chilly and uninviting.

To make rooms seem larger, a good tip is to lay fitted carpet in a plain colour and continue it from room to room. This house has the ultimate luxury in this line, for every inch of floor—with the exception of bathroom, kitchen and playroom—is fitted with oatmeal-coloured wall-to-

wall carpet. The light tone serves to emphasize the extent of the floor area, and thus makes the house seem bigger and lighter. Any floor covering used on this scale will achieve a similar effect, especially when it reaches from wall to wall, as this takes the eye right to the edges of the room.

The once grim-looking sitting room has been transformed into a comfortable and original area for relaxation. Householders often stick rigidly to the idea that light colours automatically 'open up' a small or dingy room. This is usually true, but in the case of very high Edwardian or Victorian rooms too much white or cream, for example, would only make them seem higher and chilly. The owners 'warmed up' this room by papering it in a deep orange, black and grey Art Nouveau print. The sitting room, dining room and kitchen extension are all interconnected 'through rooms', and the paper is continued right through the two main rooms up to the kitchen door to give a feeling of unity to the whole ground floor. The sitting and dining rooms are separated by sliding doors painted white; when they are shut, these help to 'bounce' light back into the sitting room from the open fire and modern spotlight.

The fine marble fireplace came with the house, and holds an elegant French grate. Any room—

no matter how interesting—needs a focal point, and an open fire is still the ideal way of providing one.

Rooms as high as these need solid-looking furniture and fittings ; light, spindly pieces would be lost in them. Here, both alcoves on the side of the chimney breast are filled with sturdy beech shelves, which match the bench seating in the dining room and the cupboards in the sitting room. The beech originally looked too pale for its setting, so it was specially stained to match the greenish grey of the wallpaper and the framework of the dining chairs. These were designed by the Italian Magistretti, and have the advantage of being both very modern and easy to mix with older furniture.

Other furnishings in the sitting room include a William IV recliner chair, a squashy black leather sofa scattered with home-made patchwork cushions, and a square coffee table with a glass top revealing a dramatic print in green, gold and black. The furniture has been collected on grounds of personal taste, and not to follow one particular style.

Upstairs, the master bedroom suite is papered in an attractive floral print. In the bathroom, the bath and bidet are separated from the twin washbasins by a sliding door. This is a good idea where there are children—one person can now be washing while another bathes in complete privacy. It also cuts down condensation.

One effective way of protecting your treasured furniture is to provide children with a room of their own. Here, the children's room has been fitted out with robust, and very colourful,

Far left. The sitting room, dining room and kitchen form one through room. The same wallpaper is used in both the sitting room and the dining room to help unify the two rooms.
Above left. In the dining room the space saving bench seating is stained to match the

dark wallpaper and the frames of the Magistretti dining chairs.
Above right. The bathroom and masterbed-room are decorated in an attractive floral print. In the bathroom the twin washbasins and the bath and bidet are separated by a sliding door.

This reduces condensation—and queues.
Below. In the children's room the red storage unit forms an eye catching match with the striped bedspreads. The cork flooring is a sensible choice for children's rooms as it is both warm and durable.

furniture. Children love primary colours, and in this room red is the dominant theme.

A red floor-to-ceiling unit provides eye-catching storage, incorporating a pull-down worktop (at the right height for young children), slide-under toy boxes, and plentiful cupboard and shelf space. The centrepiece of this unit is a wide blackboard—an excellent 'wallcovering' for any children's room. This one is sensibly placed at the child's eye level and has a ledge for chalks and dusters. Reds, pinks and orange make a bright splash of colour in a tumble-rug, but the main area of flooring is covered in cork tiles for easy cleaning and toughness. The main danger in setting up a children's room lies in trying to impose too much adult taste on it, but here, a sympathetic choice of furnishings allows the children's own toys and posters to predominate.

Another bedroom makes a feature of a deep warm pink : the walls and ceiling are painted in one tone, and the fitted carpet is in another. The bedspreads are cream lace ; more pink would be too much of a good thing.

The house has emerged as a home, and a home to be proud of. The period of the house has been flattered, not fought, and the bold colour schemes have added the necessary warmth.

Colour planned for space and comfort

If you need a modernized kitchen with a playspace nearby so that you can keep a small child in view, a multi-purpose room made from an old kitchen and adjoining dining room is an ideal solution. Cooking, family meals and supervised play can all be catered for in this room.

This was just one of the adaptations carried out by the owners of a typical Victorian British 'semi' in Surrey which could be applied to many other houses. They chose the garden side of their house for the new family room because it had a pleasant outlook and caught the sun. Upstairs they needed an extra bathroom leading off the main bedroom, so that they could have their own self-contained suite. Rather than reduce living space by building the new bathroom inside an existing room, they chose to build on. Their extension fitted neatly behind the garage, giving them valuable extra space at ground-floor level for a utility room, larder and boiler room.

Originally they had planned their new bathroom to go over the garage, but this proved difficult because the garage foundations weren't strong enough to take the extra weight. The new extension is designed to give on to a pleasant small courtyard by the dining room window. It is built in the same bricks as the main house to complement it and form a complete unit, rather than a house and 'afterthought'.

Blending extensions with existing houses is always a tricky job, and here the owners designed the alterations they wanted themselves, knocking out walls and old fire-places to the layout of the new extension. Then they asked an architect to draw up plans and deal with the often difficult business of obtaining planning and building permission.

Once the 'go-ahead' was given, the owner was able to begin with the kitchen. Here, he knocked out a wall between the old dining room and kitchen, and moved another wall between the kitchen and breakfast room; this involved putting up steel joists to support the walls. An old tiled fireplace was removed from the dining room. The floors were on two levels with about 2in. difference, so the kitchen was re-screeded with concrete to take it up to the same level as the boards in the old dining room.

The back door was moved to make a better entrance through to the new extension, and a rickety old conservatory outside the former

TUBBY

dining room was demolished to let in more light.

Upstairs, there was a separate bathroom and lavatory to be modernized and an entrance to be cut through from the new main bedroom to the extension and its adjoining bathroom. The problem here was finding space for an airing cupboard, and 'creating' space in the new main bedroom, which was smaller than the original one.

The solution was deceptively simple. The wall between the bathroom and the lavatory came out. The new master bedroom wall was moved a few feet into the old bathroom, making enough room for a floor-to-ceiling fitted cupboard. The linen cupboard was built into the new bathroom with access doors on the landing outside rather than in the bathroom. These alterations meant a smaller, but still adequate bathroom.

Once the structural alterations were completed, the owners could begin on the decor. The house was treated as a whole unit, not just decorated haphazardly room by room, and the overall colour scheme was *planned*. Often fairly

Above. Planned colour co-ordination at its best—the browns of the striped chair cover are picked up in the curtain border.

small houses such as this 'semi' benefit from a 'top-to-toe' treatment; it makes the house seem larger and more comfortable, giving a feeling of harmony and unity as rooms 'flow' into each other creating an illusion of space.

The owners took the colours of the original Victorian floor tiles in the hall as their key. These are a mixture of browns with some blue and yellow. They added white, and began by using this for all the woodwork and for the walls above the dado in the hall. A brown geometric wallpaper was chosen to echo the floor pattern and emphasize the other brown shades.

The brown is re-emphasized in the drawing room and dining room. In the kitchen, the yellow and blue in the tiles are brought out to give a sunny effect. The brown is carried upstairs in the carpet and is mixed with yellow in the child's bedroom. Apricot—always a good foil for brown—is the predominant colour in the spare bedroom, together with pink and green.

In the main bedroom and the new bathroom, the colours are fresh green and white, which tone well with the browns outside on the landing.

The separate areas of the new kitchen and playroom are well defined. The kitchen is built in a U shape in one corner, and next to it is a built-in dining area with an upholstered bench seat. There is little furniture in the play space, except for a shelving unit with toy cupboards underneath. The area is near the french windows which lead out into the garden.

The kitchen units and dining corner are in an unusual deep blue, which is emphasized in the expanse of laminated worktop. Vivid colours can be used successfully in two ways: you can single out one small feature such as a cushion in a striking colour, to offer relief from an otherwise muted scheme, or you can use the dominant colour extensively for maximum eye-appeal.

The fitted 'eating-corner' backs on to one arm of the kitchen U. There are foam cushions on the bench seats, covered in blue tweed. This has been sprayed with a good dirt repellant, which protects the fabric from spills—a practical tip to note. The owners couldn't find a table to fit into this corner, so they had one made to measure—this turned out to be cheaper than many ready-made types. Purpose-built furniture can be made to almost any specification to suit your particular needs, and is always worth considering in cases like this.

Above the table, the blue motif is picked up again in the unusual spherical spotlights. They are directed on to the ceiling so that the light spills down softly. And the yellow is repeated in gloss-painted bentwood chairs.

Above. Rich browns predominate in the hall—the tones in the wallpaper are echoed in the staircarpet and the floor tiles.
Below, left. A multi-purpose room, used as kitchen, informal eating area and playroom. The colours look bright and sunny.
Below, right. The impressive dining room for formal occasions. The dresser is lit inside to flatter the crockery on display.

The owners planned to use the dining room for eating in the evenings and for entertaining. Here the accent was on 'atmosphere', so they used an eyecatching caramel and sharp white. The ceiling is papered in plain caramel, and there is an unusual geometric frieze in caramel and black round the top of the walls.

Blinds often 'dress up' a window more than traditional curtains. Here, there is a plain white holland blind, bordered in brown to complement the overall colour scheme.

The drawing room keeps to this room-by-room colour scheme, with its deep brown carpet and 'natural' coloured curtains with brown striped borders. One sofa is also in the 'natural'—or neutral—colour and has a striped skirt to add pattern. Another sofa is in soft apricot. All the shades are brought together by one large chair which is covered in boldly striped deckchair canvas. This is a good way of adding interest to an established colour plan, and is a focal point in itself. The deckchair canvas is repeated as a curtain border and in the sofa skirt.

An unattractive 1930's fireplace was removed. The owners scouted round demolished houses and eventually found a marble fireplace with a cast-iron grate which suited their house perfectly. Bargains are still around—if you look.

The final effect is one of a bright and friendly house, made more efficient by the new extension. It is smart yet full of inexpensive ideas, and is practical to run without looking clinical.

Above left. The fireplace is the main feature of this house. It was left as a load-bearing divider when the two downstairs rooms were knocked into one, and it is now an eye-catching background for the pictures. Above right. The other half of the room is the dining area, where an attractive feature is the genuine chandelier. An old linenpress stands against the back of the fireplace for cutlery and glass.

Simplicity in style

Simplicity of line can have a striking impact in house design. This Edwardian home has a streamline look—achieved through vivid imagination and an absence of fussy detail—without losing its sense of comfort.

It's difficult to imagine a home with practically no curtains, carpets or cushions to be anything but cold and sterile. But not with the house pictured here. It gets its warmth and attractiveness through simplicity of line, variety in texture and the use of colour.

When designer Michael Green and his family moved into their Edwardian house, no one had lived there for a year, and the state of the house was a depressing sight with rot and damp everywhere. The Greens decided on a plan of action: they all lived in one room and began working from the top of the house down. They knew that if they started on the ground floor, the renovating of the first floor might always be a project of the future!

The plumbing, fixtures and central heating were installed, and then the Greens set out to convert their home. No architect or builders were used; Michael Green did the designing himself, and he and his wife did all the work involved.

The most unusual feature of the house is the fireplace on the ground floor which has been left completely on its own, serving as a room divider. Originally there were two smallish rooms which the Greens thought of making into one large room. They discovered, however, that it would be far too expensive to completely remove the load-bearing wall and fireplace. It is difficulties like this that sometimes lead to ingenious solutions.

The Greens knocked down the walls on either side of the fireplace which was left free-standing in a large column-like fashion. It was covered with panels of cork which blend in well with the wood in the fireplace. Cork is a good material to work with; it's inexpensive, the texture is unusual, and pictures can be easily hung on it. The picture arrangement here is extremely eye-catching and creates an effective focal point.

The opening to the fireplace was raised and an aluminium strip put around the edge. A grating supports the logs, and underneath there is a removable basket which catches the falling ash and makes cleaning easy. The cornices and skirting boards around the fireplace column were rescued from the walls which had been removed—the Greens didn't want to run into problems of matching up. For other ideas on making a feature of your fireplace, consult a good DIY home manual.

The surround was made from a timber box, filled with cement and then covered with white easy-to-clean tiles. One of the nicest touches is the curve in the floor leading up to the white tiles. Mr. Green achieved this by putting moulding behind the curve to give it the necessary support. The same technique is used on the vinyl floor in the bathroom, which curves up to cover the complete side of the bath.

The ceilings and walls were in bad shape. The Greens used two techniques to combat this: embossed wallpaper and larger-than-life posters. The patterned embossed paper on the ceiling gives an Edwardian flavour to the room and effectively covers up cracks and peeling plaster with relatively little effort, using the correct materials and techniques.

The jumbo size posters are a great idea. They cover unsightly imperfections on the wall and cost the Greens exactly the amount it took to paste them to the wall. With two children, Mrs. Green wanted to keep wall cleaning to a minimum. The posters are easy to wipe down and add personality to any room. Another method for protecting walls from showing the dirt is to have a large grouping of pictures. On the wall going along the staircase, where fingermarks are likely to turn up, Mrs. Green has put pictures of various sizes and styles; they are a focal point with a practical purpose.

There are many interesting touches in the

Above left. *The staircase leads off the dining area and their slope gives useful extra space to the room. Beyond this is the breakfast room, where jumbo-sized posters have been used to good advantage to cover up poor walls.*
Above right. *The simple furnishings of the house are particularly apparent upstairs. The children's rooms are decorated in the clear bold colours they love, and the furniture is kept to a minimum.*

sitting room. The windows have been lowered to skirting board level, which gives a wonderful view out onto the patio and garden. The large expanse of window also makes the room look bigger. No fussy curtains impair the view; pull blinds are used, if privacy is needed. The Italian pendant lamp gives a splash of colour; the green contrasts well with the more subdued tones in the room.

Beyond the fireplace, at the other end of the room, is the simple and elegant dining room. The slope of the stairs in this room has not been ignored. The space underneath is used for storing the trolley and also houses a red chair. The red is then picked up in the warm reds and oranges of the throw rug. The circular rosewood dining table was bought for very little in a street market some years ago. Above the table is the only ornate piece in the room—a brass chandelier. This had been left by the previous owner. It was cleaned and the electrical wiring removed, and now is used with candles.

The Greens tried putting curtains in the windows which are set back and framed by an arch, but found that too much light was lost. The original lead window panes are in keeping with the Edwardian motif.

Discipline had to be exercised in this room. A natural tendancy is to keep adding to a room. Mr. Green considered putting up a large mirror on the wall behind the dining table, but decided not to because it would detract from the simple elegance of the room. One of the most effective —and difficult to achieve—looks is an uncluttered and streamline one. The secret is investing in pieces which have good lines and are essential to the room such as the table, chairs and lighting fixtures, and then resisting adding many more items. The most effective decor is often the simplest.

The floors are covered with cork tiles which the Greens put down themselves. They first laid hardboard over the floor boards to keep the tiles from cracking and the floor from warping. It was a difficult job, but they will not have to worry about repairs. The tiles are coated with a plastic seal varnish and don't have to be polished, just washed.

Leading off the dining room is the breakfast room, which successfully combines the new with the old. The large dresser against the wall was left by the original owner and displays the attractive china. The lead window panes still remain. The more modern items are the curved plain white chairs, and the spotlights. A louvred door covers the central heating unit which used to be the old coal boiler.

Two steps lead down into the cheerful kitchen. The ceiling is covered with pine panelling, and the brick walls are painted white—an effective contrast to the blue laminated tops. The original quarry tiles have been left on the floor. The window sill has been deliberately sloped, so that dishes and bottles won't impair the view of the garden. Again, the lines are clean and stream-

line. A shelf, the width of the room, cleverly suspends from the ceiling.

One of the nicest features of the house is the patio. Mr. Green was inspired by the simplicity of Japanese rock gardens. He built the patio using brick columns as a foundation. He then covered the foundation with long timbered Victorian beams which he bought from demolition people. Pine slats were then put on top of the beams and a finish was put on which gives a grey-green colour and blends in well with the colours of the garden. If you have the space, this is a delightful way of making the transition from indoor to outdoor living.

The four bedrooms upstairs continue the streamline motif of the ground floor. The master bedroom is a combination of olive green and white. One wardrobe is covered with a mirror and the other with beige hessian. The hessian covering is practical because it can be painted over if a change in colour scheme is desired.

The stark and bold look in one of the children's bedrooms is a perfect example of how effective an uncluttered look can be. The walls, ceiling, chest of drawers and toy chest are painted in a brilliant red. The curved chair, bedspread and vinyl floor are stark white. The only departures from the red and white are a cork strip used as a pin board and a massive poster which covers one wall.

One solution to a successful house design is keeping to simple, clean lines. The Victorians liked the cluttered, crowded look in houses, but today's home, like this one, can have a sense of beauty and style, without fussy detail and complex colour schemes and furniture groupings.

Space in a small flat

The term 'studio flat' is commonly used for something that is more than a bedsitter, but not quite as large as a flat, where every activity takes place in a different room. Quite often there is a single large living, dining and cooking space, with a separate bedroom and bathroom.

Attics in large old houses are ideal places to convert into studio flats, as the strange angles and sloping walls lend themselves to original design ideas, often producing fascinating results. The lighting problem caused by the lack of windows also provides an opportunity for ingenious solutions. When architect J P Campredon bought two rooms on the top floor of a decaying old building in the centre of Paris, he accepted the challenge of not being able to alter the basic structure (except by demolishing the interior partitions), but decided to create in it an open living space in which one could move from one area to another without interruption.

He was able to take advantage of some aspects of the existing, rigid structure, particularly the old open fireplace, which is now the focal point of the living area. To relate it to the bold decorations used elsewhere—unpainted wood is predominant throughout the flat—it was faced with pale grey lightweight concrete blocks.

Two enormous wooden flower troughs are a prominent feature just inside the door of the flat. They have been lined with a plastic film to make them watertight, with plants in pots inside. They wall off a tiny study, with just enough room for a desk and some bookshelves.

The triangular kitchen is tucked in one corner of the flat, where a long wedge-shaped built-in worktop disguises the acute angle. The refrigerator, oven and washing machine fit neatly underneath, leaving ample space for food preparation above. A fascinating feature here is the two earthenware basins that take the place of a conventional sink unit. Placed at different levels, they emphasize the downward-flowing movement of the water (which, however, is delivered by a conventional tap). In the tiny, wood-panelled bathroom, also triangular, the oval basin was intentionally *not* set in a frame, so as to emphasize its roundness and the swirling of the water in it. A round mirror on the wall above echoes the circular theme.

In his conversion of this flat, the architect was determined to make water, fire and light participate fully in the overall effect created, and these elements dominate the whole design scheme.

The lighting in the flat was designed to highlight the various functions already delineated by the use of different materials and finishes. The radiance of the open fire and the reflective quality of the light-coloured concrete slabs draw attention to the focal point of the living area. The dining table stands exactly below one of the deep, square rooflights which provide the only source of daylight in the flat. The downward movement of light gives this square area a vertical effect. The furniture is made of huge sheets of pine, the high backs of the chairs creating a semi-enclosed effect. A floor-to-ceiling pine china cupboard separates the dining space from the living area.

Opposite page. The geometric design of the dining room furniture is typical of the overall layout of the flat. There are no windows, but the various living areas have been located below the deep square rooflights to take advantage of all the available natural light. *Above.* Two large flower troughs are incorporated into the partition wall which encloses a study. *Below.* The open fire faced with concrete blocks is the focal point of the living area. *Below right.* The compact kitchen is fitted into a tiny triangular space.

Victorian into modern

A house exterior needn't be the tone setter for interior design. This Victorian house in Bristol has a surprise in store. The austere stone façade leads into a warm and modern interior, filled with bright colours and original and streamlined ideas.

When on the hunt for a house, Ron Ellis wanted a place with a great deal of space in the centre of town. He had two reasons: as architect and designer, he wanted, first, ample space to accommodate a working studio and, second, a house with potential for converting, where he could apply his own creative ideas. He found the answer in a century-old Bristol house, characterized by high ceilings and graceful bay windows.

There were three floors to work with. The ground floor, with its generous light from the bay windows at both the front and the back, was ideal for making into studios. The first floor then was designated for the living quarters and the second floor, used for additional rooms.

The conversion centred on the first floor, which had originally consisted of two large featureless rooms, a dreary and dark landing and a ten-year-old bathroom/kitchen extension. The aim was to get a feeling of free-flowing space and light, where the visual and physical movement from one area to the next would be unhindered.

The first step was to knock down walls—four in all— which were merely stud partitions rather than functional load-bearing walls. This changed the mood of the first floor from a collection of small confined rooms into an expansive and open living area which now includes a kitchen/living/dining area and two bedrooms.

If you're in the process of converting and cannot physically gain more space, try to increase the *sense* of space by keeping visual barriers to a minimum. A partitioning wall, for instance, totally arrests the eye. Wherever possible, use room dividers like screens or plants which help to define different areas but still allow freedom of visual flow. A feeling of space can be more effective than large amounts of actual space in a home.

Next a balcony, which serves as a private and secluded spot for sunbathing or dining as well as a practical carport, was built out from the house. The rich cedar finish of the balcony also offers an interesting contrast to the heavy grey stone of the house.

French doors lead from the balcony into the breakfast/kitchen area which had been the old bathroom. The main motif here, and throughout the first floor, is streamlined simplicity. The curves of the simple white Arkana table echo the curves in the chrome-framed chairs. Tiers of glass shelves along the wall create a dynamic focal point behind. The kitchen fitments beyond are in clear white plastic laminate.

White is the main background colour in this conversion and is used on ceilings, walls and floors. Mr. Ellis felt that white was the best foil for the brilliant colours he had used and for the varied and unusual furniture shapes and decorative objects in the rooms. The white floors are made from easy-to-clean vinyl sheets with a foam backing.

Making a good selection for your main background colour is an important decision which effects your entire decor. Usually, a light pastel shade is the easiest to work with because it

164

allows for colour variety in curtains, upholstery and decorative touches. If you decide on white, make certain you avoid a sterile clinical look by using vivid colours elsewhere. Or, if you select a bold background colour, then be prepared to limit your use of colour in the rest of your furnishings.

Rugs were used here as a technique for defining different areas. There's a rich redish yellow carpet in the breakfast area, a cool and elegant green and turquoise Spanish-style rug in the dining area and a luxurious shaggy white rug in the living area, made by lying nine goatskin rugs side by side. A small 'reception' area, which brings the other areas together and had once been a drab landing, is offset by a brilliant pink and orange rug.

Radiators are another feature which help to establish various areas, as well as adding a bold touch of colour. Rather than apologetically attempting to disguise the radiators, they were brought out into the open by painting them bright greens, reds or yellows to fit in suitably with the surrounding decor. They were specially made to fit the various wall lengths which makes them a colourful decorative accent as well as a functional object.

Don't neglect giving full consideration to items like rugs and radiators. It's too easy to expend all your energy in selecting the primary furnishings like a couch or wall-to-wall carpeting, while forgetting the secondary ones like cushions and wall decorations. The rugs and radiators in this house are instrumental in creating a visual impact.

The apple green radiator of the dining room is picked up in the cool hues of the handsome rug which sets off the light and delicate chrome and

Above left. *A cool and streamlined dining room simply done in stunning green and blue. A Spanish-style rug frames the light table and chairs. Above the colourful radiator on the right is an eye-catching grouping of pictures.*
Above right. *Night view of a living room glowing with warmth. Fascinating shadows, created from the modern mobile, bounce off the ceiling. The shaggy rug was made by lying nine goatskin rugs side by side. Brightly coloured cushions give a cheerful look to the otherwise undecorated windows.*

glass table, designed by Mr. Ellis. Decorative items include a potted floor plant and a cluster of pictures that cover an entire wall. Mr. Ellis made the frames from plywood, varying the thickness according to the picture size. He then screwed chrome mirror clips into the side which holds the picture, wood and glass securely in place. A feature such as this grouping of pictures can often make the difference between an average room and a visually outstanding one.

A further feature worth noting is found in the luxurious living area. Space was saved by building quadrant-shaped supports on the wall to house a hi-fi unit. The supports were made from blockboard, with curved hardboard fronts. Rather than looking for a spare corner to tuck away the hi-fi equipment, it's become an integral part of the decoration, adding to the appeal in the room. It is also an excellent way of keeping it out of reach from little children and eliminates annoying stains from party drinks. Another idea for making a feature of your hi-fi is to install it in a chimney breast that has been made obsolete by central heating.

Emulsion paint, applied directly to the wall,

was used for the bold cylinder wall graphic. The red in the wall design is then repeated in the smooth curves of the two perspex coffee tables which were unusually positioned in opposition to one another. More splashes of colour are seen on the window sill where there is an abundant display of cushions, made from old mattress foam, in the 'sunshine' colours of golds, reds and oranges. These bold and brilliant colours can be used effectively here because of the neutral and restful background colour.

The lighting throughout this first-floor conversion is strategic. Parabolic spotlights in vivid colours were positioned to maximize colour and shape, giving a dramatic and visually appealing mood to the rooms. Lighting is one of the most important elements for creating an atmosphere and warmth in interior design and careful thought should be given to selecting the most effective and useful method.

One original and eye-catching feature that benefits from lighting is a modern display unit which emerges from five cube-shaped boxes, stacked one on top of the other. Made from perspex and steel, it is ideal for displays in that it doesn't need a routine dusting, doesn't take up much wall or floor space and adds an individual touch.

The unit had first been used to hold literature at an exhibition. Designed by Mr. Ellis, he was able to bring it home from the exhibition for his own use. A good eye for adapting items, like this display complex, for new uses, goes a long way to enhancing an interior decor—and usually saves money.

From a featureless Victorian house, Mr. Ellis has created a home, characterized by vivid colour, bold design and imaginative ideas.

Old into new

Buying a house in the centre of a large city can be prohibitively expensive. But with enterprise you may be able to buy an older property and renovate it to make it feasible to live there.

Veronica and David Norburn found a house in Islington, London, which fitted the bill in all senses. At first, it was not everyone's idea of a bargain—the local authorities had taken out a closing order on the basement because of damp and the fact that it had insufficient daylight. The house itself had a leaking roof, decor untouched since the turn of the century, an outside wc, and a bulging back wall that needed rebuilding. However, it was inexpensive, in a quiet street close to the centre of London and it had six well-proportioned rooms arranged on three storeys.

The major building work, central heating installation and most of the electrical wiring were carried out by professionals, but David Norburn tackled all the other jobs himself, including a considerable amount of joinery.

The first job was to renovate the basement and to provide a bathroom. They decided to convert the previously unused area under the front steps into a bathroom instead of sacrificing one of the rooms in the house or adding an expensive extension on the back. This was easily done by building out about two feet into the front area, so that the room was wide enough to take a bath.

In Britain it is illegal for bathrooms to open directly off living areas (except bedrooms). So the Norburns took four feet off the front basement room to build a cupboard-lined corridor leading from the internal staircase to the new bathroom.

The cupboards house cleaning equipment, tools and family oddments. They cost almost nothing to fit up—except time—as they were made out of chipboard thrown out by a local builder. This is a useful tip for other budget-minded DIY enthusiasts, as builders' dumps often yield useful pieces of wood and old doors that can be utilized. Do ask permission to take anything, however, as otherwise removing even what looks like rubbish is illegal.

The remaining basement area was knocked

Above left. The dividing wall between two rooms on the ground floor has been removed to make a spacious living area and the back half is comfortably furnished as a study.
Above right. The fireplace has been bricked up to save space and the chimney breast has been painted white—the most reflective colour—to make the most of what is basically a very sunny room.

into one room and made habitable again by enlarging the front window, replacing the back door with a glazed one and laying a concrete screed with polyurethane damp-proofing membrane. The screed continues through the corridor and bathroom.

The front half of the room is now used as a kitchen and the back as a combined children's play and dining area. This arrangement works well, as small children usually prefer to play near their mother, and here they can do so without being underfoot. In the evening toys are stored away in a cupboard under the stairs and in the base of a built-in bench seat which transforms the place into a dining area. In such a dual purpose living area these cupboards are essential for easy storage and access.

The floor screed is covered with hardboard strip flooring. David Norburn found this time-consuming to lay, but it is inexpensive and easy to keep clean.

CAROL TABBERNOR

Above left. *The previously unused area under the front steps was extended by only 2ft to make it wide enough to take a bath. The house originally only had an outside wc so this adds to the value of the house.*

Above right. *The owner built this wall of cupboards himself out of packing cases. Some cupboards go back into the recesses so that every inch is made to count.*

The kitchen units, too, are his handiwork —made from old packing cases and painted orange and white. Blockboard could be used instead. The frames and drawer fronts are pine given a polyurethane coating and the worktops are sheets of plastic-laminate-covered block-board cut to size.

The ground floor was formerly two rooms, each with its own door and fireplace, but connected by folding doors. The folding doors and dividing wall have been removed to make a large through-room which is now the living room, and have been replaced by a reinforced steel joist which supports the ceiling. As a result, the door and fireplace in the front half of the room were unnecessary and have been bricked up to save space.

The living room storage units are made out of more packing cases (again, blockboard could be used instead). These are covered with hessian and edged with butt jointed pine, glued in place and screwed from the back. They have touch latches instead of handles. They look very effective and were so simple to make that their design was repeated for bedroom cupboards.

The living room and bedroom floorboards have been sanded and then sealed—a messy and noisy job, but well worth the effort. A large sander and a smaller one for the edges can be hired at a fraction of the cost of buying carpeting. In fact, the Norburns prefer their gleaming floorboards to carpet, as they are far less trouble to keep clean where there are small children around. They were also attracted by the natural colour and texture which they feel suits the character of the house.

Walls throughout the house are white, except where pine tongued and grooved board has been used. The only exception to the 'white walls only' rule is the hall, which is painted khaki and acts as a backcloth for the children's paintings.

The idea behind painting the hall in a deep shade was that it should provide a core of colour leading into neutrally coloured living areas. The front door is painted to match, which is a detail that many people overlook when planning their colour schemes. Ideally the front door should co-ordinate with the hall colours.

Upstairs, the house had a large front bedroom and another smaller one, with a staircase at the back. There are four flights of stairs between these rooms and the basement bathroom—this was another problem overcome in an ingenious way without spending a fortune.

At first the family had to make do with trudging up and down stairs, to and from the basement bathroom, but later they built a shower room with wc, washbasin and airing cupboard between the two upstairs bedrooms. They made space by demolishing the dividing wall between the rooms and taking a 'slice' out of each on a line with the chimney breasts. The doorway to the back bedroom now opens into a lobby which leads to the shower room. All walls are covered to avoid plastering and the job was completed very cheaply without any outside help except from a plumber.

The 'square' containing the shower room also incorporates a full-length wardrobe opening into the main bedroom. The doors are covered in hessian edged with pine in the same way as the living room units already described. They also match the wall of cupboards behind the bed which disguise a chimney breast.

The back bedroom is rather small as a result of building the shower room but the children use it only for sleeping as they have the basement and garden to play in.

Installing their own shower was the last step for the owners in converting the house into a comfortable and original home where every inch of space has been put to good use.

Making the most of it

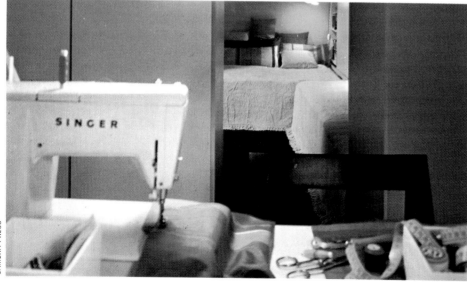

A limited amount of space can be a problem in a home—especially when the life style includes both the entertaining of friends and a need for quiet study—unless thought, originality and ingenuity are applied. Two married students, living in Bonn, wanted to make the most of the living space available to them and, with professional advice, tried to achieve both an attractive and practical home design.

The flat originally consisted of two rooms, kitchen and bath. The larger room measured $17\frac{1}{4}$ feet by 11 feet and was not only difficult to work with because of its size, but also because of the disadvantage of having four doors, which put wall space at a premium. The couple used this room for entertaining, dining, and studying so, quite understandably, they found that their furniture arrangement left them with a sense of congestion and over-crowding. The initial error in strategy resulted from using a complete wall surface as a cupboard for storing books and records—this meant that most of the remaining—and heavy—furniture was put on the other side of the room, leaving a sense of unbalance. The narrowness of the second room was further emphasized by placing the two beds next to one another, thereby creating no visual break in line.

The need for change was obvious. As well as requiring a freer flow of space and a better sense of balance, a second work/study area was to be built in the bedroom. The furniture was in good condition and, with the addition of a few inexpensive acquisitions, the relocation of furnishings, and the introduction of a new colour scheme, an entirely new look emerged.

The skilful use of colour can do more than any other single aspect of design to make a dull room bright, or a commonplace flat seem original and sophisticated. In smallish areas very bright colours are used in moderation so that they have the maximum impact without any irritating 'side-effects'. Muted greys and tans provide a restful background for the more hectic reds, oranges, and yellows—the 'sunshine' end of the spectrum—which form the eye-catching mural, and are echoed throughout the flat in the accessories such as the cushions and ashtrays. This gives a bright and vivid effect without being too overpowering.

The wall cupboard in the main room was taken out and the dining area put in its place.

Top left. *The desk unit, seating group and bedroom—co-ordinated by the brilliant touches of yellow, orange and red. A wall cupboard unit and bookshelves fill the space between the beds.*
Centre left. *The dining area now occupies the space where the wall cupboard used to be. The dramatic swirl of colour gives the room a distinctive character.*
Bottom left. *The shiny yellow paper in the bedroom makes it look larger and lighter.*

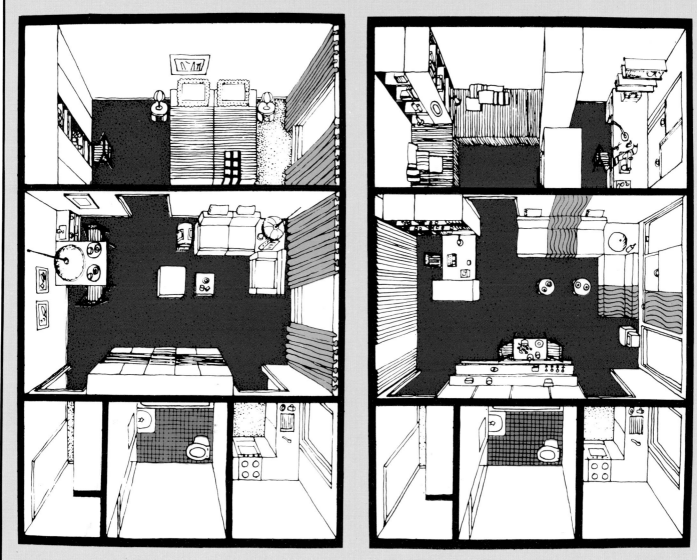

This was one of the most important changes because not only did it create a new living space, but also opened up the room by making a third focal point. The table is extendible and can seat six people. The shelves behind—easily assembled by a 'do-it-yourself' expert—are practical for storing china and add an intriguing pattern to an otherwise unimaginative wall.

The other two focal points are the sitting area and the working unit. The dramatic swirl of the yellow and rust colours reaching up to the ceiling give a distinctive character and a sense of co-ordination to the sitting area. The repetition of these colours in the dining area creates a good tie-in. The work unit has been cleverly constructed by its use of angles and planes. The high solid-looking vertical cupboards give a sense of privacy and make an interesting contrast to the other areas used for relaxation and entertainment.

The problem of narrowness in the bedroom was solved by projecting cupboards into the room and by rearranging the beds. The cupboards not only served as valuable storage space, but they also define a much needed sewing/work area. The beds are arranged in a head-to-foot fashion, brought together by

Above left. The original floor plan. Space in the bedroom was lost by bad placement of furniture. In the living room all the heavy pieces were put on one side of the room, leaving a sense of inbalance.

Above right. The new floor plan. The beds along the walls make the room look less tunnel like. The cupboards serve as room dividers. The strategic placement of the dining table gives the main room better balance.

shelves which provide head support. A warm and luxurious atmosphere is achieved through the use of light colours, lacquered wall paper and multi-coloured cushions which pick up the colour motif of the main room.

Wall lamps effectively create a warm and intimate feeling—the light reflects gently off the walls providing indirect lighting which gives little glare. Indirect lighting is best for a bedroom, or any room that requires a restful atmosphere. The familiar central pendant light tends to cast shadows, and provides a harsh overall lighting which does little to enhance any interior. Far better to use the many types of local lighting now available on the market, such as spotlights, downlighters or dimmer switches, if

you want to change the mood of a room. Subtle use of lighting can be the most effective way of creating an intimate atmosphere.

The sewing area is arranged in front of the window so that there is plenty of natural daylight to combat eyestrain. The privacy of this work area is assured because it is beyond the bedroom—the last place a visitor would wander into.

What originally appeared to be a cluttered and limited living area has been converted into a useful, elegant and comfortable home—and at a very nominal cost. The effect has been achieved through a selection of furniture with simple straight lines and a lightness both in appearance and actual weight. The strategic placement of furniture has created distinct areas of activity and well-balanced rooms. The colour scheme is rich and warm and, when combined with the various textures and building materials, a tasteful and consistent appearance results. The cupboards used for storage are distributed in such a way that they also function as room dividers and headboards.

A limited amount of space a problem? Not if imagination, a bit of know-how, and effort are applied. The home above is a living example.

English cottage, '70s style

The Negus family needed a country cottage. Just a simple, easy-to-run house that was functional but different, with exciting features both inside and out. Being unconventional people they had in mind something between a period cottage and a lighthouse. Since they could not find a house to these particular specifications ready-made, they decided to build their own and asked architects Leslie Gooday & Associates to design it.

The rectangular plot chosen for the site falls steeply from the road and then rises at the centre to an embankment, giving the architects considerable scope for their design. The extensive use of timber as a building material was a natural choice, and the final interpretation of features and materials was the result of a desire to recreate the spirit of the English cottage. The result is a rugged landscaped house in thickly wooded surroundings, merging with the natural environment.

Instead of planning the conventional ac-

commodation and accepted facilities of a house into a relatively confined space, the architects achieved a sense of freedom by allocating room areas first, without regard to their overall shape.

On the ground floor are the living room and dining area, which are separated from a spare bedroom by a folding partition. There are two bedrooms and a bathroom on the first floor at the back of the house. The kitchen, storeroom and carport are separate from the living quarters in a flat-roofed, single-storey section at the side.

The living room, around which the house was planned, finally determined its shape. It has a shallow ceiling slope, with its main rafters continuing out of the room, to be anchored by four concrete foundations in the hillside outside. Under the ceiling slope a window seat and plant trough run across the whole length of the south-facing windows in the wall and roof.

A timber spiral staircase to the first floor areas forms a major feature within the house. It was conceived and designed to form an economical and space-saving structure between the living area and the two bedrooms and bathroom.

A studio stove, placed in front of the staircase in the centre of the living room, provides a decorative focal point. To take full advantage of the heat dissipated from the flue pipe, a special conducting steel plate with copper rods was designed to be attached to the flue.

Timber light boxes containing decorative patterns of pressed fern leaves are suspended from the roof structure, and provide general additional light over the living area.

The interior of the house was designed to avoid redecoration by the use of low-key schemes provided by natural materials: plaster, varnished timbers, and a simulated aggregate

Opposite page. The house is landscaped to merge into the natural surroundings. Above. The sloping rafters in the living room are anchored in the hillside outside. Right. The studio stove in the living room, with the spiral staircase beyond.

finish in broken blacks, browns and pinks.

The floors are boarded throughout with pine. The ceilings and walls are finished with a simulated aggregate finish, except in the living/dining area, where insulation board has been used, and in the bathroom, which has narrow pine boarding.

The rugged organic character of this house is reflected and enhanced by the construction throughout, which uses a simple bolted 'carpentry' style, rather than conventional joinery methods.

Converting a vintage house

Sometimes a house has to be altered considerably in order to make the most of its potential, and to give it 'character'. But structural alterations can only work for a house if they are planned with foresight and imagination, and add something positive to its good looks and value which will last for years.

Diana Mather's house in Fulham, London, was ideal for re-planning: it has the solid foundations and sturdy structure that usually go with Edwardian terraced houses, and had rooms of good proportions which would flatter her chosen decor. She planned to use her talents as interior designer to add something extra to the house which would make it original and yet cosy enough to feel like a home.

She and builder Alan Rand decided to build a loft room with an elegant wrought iron spiral staircase leading up to it from the first floor landing. This would provide a private 'den' for her son, and the staircase would add a sense of spaciousness to the house as well as being a focal point in its own right.

There were structural problems to be dealt with : first—they had to support the new floor in the loft on top of the wall which separated the two first floor front rooms. And because only a dormer window was being installed in the rear slope of the roof it was impossible to fit a whole steel beam into the room to span from party wall to party wall. So due to the extra weight on the wall beneath, the load had to be transferred to ground floor level as far as the footings.

This massive upheaval was an excellent opportunity to knock the two main rooms on the ground floor into one large lounge. This was

spanned by a substantial reinforced steel joist with new concrete footings to spread the load, most of which was coming down from the loft room. And the wall immediately above it was discovered to be only a light wooden partition, so it was stripped of plaster and strengthened with wooden props.

In effect the weight of the new roof was carried by the whole house right down to the foundations so that no one spot would be forced to take the strain—which could be disastrous. It is always the best plan to discover the full implications of your structural alterations —before a wall buckles, or worse.

The new through room is welcoming, and is designed by Diana Mather to be restful to the eye. The colour scheme is predominantly composed of rich, warm browns with a white ceiling and white trim for a sharp contrast. A large shaggy rug in front of the period fireplace draws together several browns seen dotted around the room in accessories and gives the whole scheme a positive motif.

Floor-length hessian curtains in a soft mustard colour give the room a glow, especially when the curtains are drawn and artificial lighting is used to effect. A vivid bluey-green three seater settee looks just as comfortable as it is, and sets the mood of informal relaxation for the rest of the room.

The deliberate mixture of styles of furniture works well here—often period pieces and the starker lines of modern furniture flatter each other, especially if the tones of wood are similar, or there is another point of similarity which will bring the pieces together visually. Here the modern marble-topped table has the same 'chunky' look as the huge gilt-framed mirror

Far left. Colour contrast in the living room. The eye-catching green on the settee is set off by the subdued browns and golds.
Above left. The fireplace—a natural focal point—is enhanced here by the shaggy rug, gilt-framed mirror and attractive wooden bookshelves and cabinets.
Below left. The copper warming pan on the wall, and the jardinière tucked under the mirror, add unusual touches to the hall.
Above. The dark woods and aubergine walls give a masculine look to the dining room.

over the fireplace and emphasizes the solid look of the easy chairs and kneehole desk.

One special feature of the lounge is a timber-clad recess containing bookshelves. There are two tones of wooden strip, laid on to form an attractive symmetrical pattern in between the shelves so the whole unit looks like a handsome bookcase of a very high quality.

There is a deep brown fitted carpet which adds a note of luxury, and the impressive Victorian rocking chair was picked up for nothing.

The Edwardian flavour of the room is underlined by the jungly plants in a brass jardinière, and the framed prints in formal groups. It is the accessories which tend to give a room a character : an ultra modern room would contain characteristic objects made of chrome or plastic for example, and an Edwardian-style room needs pot plants and more sombre colours to achieve its point.

The dining room has aubergine walls with white window frames for contrast—white always adds crispness to an interior and seems to bring out the richness of any colour used with it. The dining furniture is all antique and its dark wood blends well with the brown cork-tiled floor, which is carried through to the kitchen.

Sharp lettuce green and white brightens up the kitchen which is at the back of the house, away from the sun. Fitted wall cupboards and a breakfast bar make the most of the space, and all the worktops are covered in sensible easily-wiped plastic laminate.

Diana Mather has made a positive feature of her hall. Too often halls are the poor relation in interior design—they are ignored on the grounds that nobody stays in them for very long. This hall is so well 'dressed up' that it invites you to linger ! There is an attractive polished wooden floor which catches the light from the fanlight. The wallcovering is composed of pinks, oranges and browns in an Art Nouveau pattern which gives an overall amber glow to the hall. And the expanse of wall provides an excellent background for a fine collection of old prints. A jardinière cut in half is set flush against the wall to maximize the effect of the foliage against the wallpaper.

The new spiral staircase rises dramatically from the first floor landing ; despite its sturdiness it looks delicate with its filigree pattern in wrought iron painted white. The landing was quite large, and the staircase fills in a dead corner.

The master bedroom used to be a bedroom plus a separate wc. The toilet has been extended to include a full bathroom suite taking a slice off the old bedroom, but still leaving a reasonably sized room. The bathroom is hidden behind a wall of cupboards a good practical point to note. There is a vivid mauve carpet—a positive move away from insipid pastel shades for bedrooms—and pink and mauve wallpaper. The bathroom suite is black.

A sunshine yellow curtain divides the new roof-room from the small landing, though it is only a formality as it's the only room up there. The walls have been rough-rendered and painted white, to reflect as much light as possible. An orange bedspread and yellowy-orange curtains stick to the theme of sunshine colours and gives an overall cheerful look to the room.

The house has not only been thoroughly renovated but given a whole new look which adds tremendously to its value and its appeal.

CLIVE CORLESS

An Edwardian conversion

Many people are finding that older properties provide more scope for imaginative treatments than brand-new housing. They can be purchased relatively cheaply, so that most of the budget is free for re-styling and adapting them for the future.

Mr and Mrs Waterlow bought an Edwardian house in Fulham, London, because it was reasonably priced and presented possibilities for future re-planning. They called in interior designers Farmer and Ore to re-design the house, and builder Alan Rand to carry out the conversion.

There was already a large through-room on the ground floor which the Waterlows use as a sitting room. One of the original fireplaces has been retained and provides an interesting focal point, helping to set off the Edwardian tone of the whole room.

A deep beige fitted carpet carries the eye from wall to wall, giving the room a spacious and luxurious look, and unifying what used to be two rooms. The furniture is mainly antique, with the exception of a small modern easy chair which has been covered in art nouveau patterned fabric to give it a period look.

The decor is composed of subtle shades of beige and mushroom to show off the darker browns of the antique furniture, and a dark brown beam which protrudes from the ceiling.

Camilla Waterlow used the texture and colour of fabrics to great effect in this room—often various textures such as velvet and the coarser weaves of hessian add a new dimension to an interior and enhance the subtlest colour schemes dramatically. Here the feeling is created by the use of velvet chair covers and the delicate weave of the William Morris pattern curtains in pinks,

blues and grey. The sofa is a wide two seater in a 1920s style which has been covered in a slate blue hessian.

It's the little touches that give this room a period flavour; a wash basin from an Edwardian wash-stand set provides an unusual plant holder. Another plant sits on top of an authentic turn-of-the-century plant pedestal. The floor length curtains are suspended from huge brass curtain rings on a bamboo pole, which makes a feature of the curtain tops and is different from the more common brass pole.

A pokey kitchen and dining room has been turned into a spacious and sophisticated kitchen-diner. Undoubtedly its focal point is a magnificent breakfast bar covered in marble-effect laminate in almost-black. It is placed so that diners are completely cut off from the sight of dirty pans in the kitchen half of the room. There is a handsome round dining table—another antique buy—surrounded by dining

CLIVE CORLESS

chairs covered by the owner's wife in a modern black and white fabric which adds a note of distinction. Aubergine and white floor length curtains in a fleur-de-lis pattern hang from more brass curtain rings. There is a black and white Spanish style rug as a centrepiece over terracotta rubber tiles.

The impressive half-timbered ceiling was already there when the present owners moved in—an unlooked-for bonus well worth keeping. The washable wallcovering is in shades of purple, and all the kitchen accessories tone with it. The total effect of a colour scheme is often lost if it isn't picked up in the smaller objects—plastic bowls in a kitchen or towels in a bathroom for example. And here the purples are also echoed in the seats of tall stools at the breakfast bar.

Whitewood wall units were turned into expensive looking storage simply by staining them a darker colour so they resemble pine panelling. Louvres at the front add to the expensive look. The working area fits neatly under the window that overlooks the garden and forms a handy U-shape, making an efficient and compact working area. All the worktops are covered in bright plastic laminate which matches the

Top left. A room with a bath ! Tucked away under the window, it effectively blends in with the other decor.
Bottom left. The bold maroon colour of the wall is picked up in the delicate Chinese mural and the print of the bedspread. The white cupboards and door contrast with the maroon.
Above. The kitchen and dining areas are practically divided by the high kitchen bar. The oriental carpet adds an elegant note without distracting, due to the simplicity of colours.

breakfast bar.

The master bedroom is something of a surprise. It incorporates a bath without a separating partition of any sort. Only a curtain confines the steamy area, but the idea has proved to be eminently workable (there is another bathroom for guests !) The 'bathroom' end of the room is tiled in pretty green, white and orange and has a fitted dressing table plus extra shelf space in a recess near the bath.

There are floor-to-ceiling cupboards along one wall, painted cream to tone in with the overall lightness of the decor. Unless you want to make an actual feature of obtrusive units such as cupboards, they are best painted in a light or

receding colour which will effectively camouflage them.

A large panel depicting a Chinese landscape overlooks the bed, and the Oriental flavour is echoed in a huge can chair in an antique Indian style. The fitted carpet is a soft oatmeal colour which gives the room a restful look, and provides an effectively subtle background for the white shaggy rugs. The attractive linen print bedspread was made by the owner's wife who added a deep fringe to add to the exotic look.

She also painted a bold abstract mural on one wall of her workroom in orange and purple. There are brown unsealed cork tiles on another wall. Floor cushions take the place of conventional seating to make the workroom a cosy and relaxed place.

The spare room has pretty coral-coloured walls, a fitted long-pile white carpet, brown and white floor-length curtains and fitted white cupboards. A small modern chair has been covered in brown and off-white fabric to make a neat focal point.

The whole house is highly imaginative, with a strong emphasis on the use of colour and texture. Yet from the outside this house looks very much like all the others in the terrace.

Rescued from rot

The work of renovating a run-down old house needs to be carried out by an owner with a good visual eye and the patience to see through the slow and laborious basic treatment to put the house back into good condition.

When this Edwardian terraced house in Fulham, London, was bought by its present owner, it was in a sorry state. It was virtually derelict and had been converted into flats. The ground floor had not been lived in for six or seven years, and there was a long list of defects, all caused by lack of good care over the years; from rising damp, rotten floor boards, and leaking pipes to damp in the roof.

The owner, a business consultant, could see the possibilities of the house, however. He was wise enough to realise that with time and patience he would be able to turn what was virtually a slum into a comfortable home. The proportions of the house were good, and it had the right number of rooms. His aim was to restore the place to its original function and to put in as many improvements as possible.

Before he even started to think about decoration, he very sensibly concentrated on the unseen part of the rehabilitation work that needed to be done in order to make the house sound for the future. So he began with

weatherproofing, treating the rising damp, renovating the roof, putting in new wiring, eradicating the insect-life and installing central heating, as well as new plumbing. He undertook all the unskilled work-jobs like clearing the site of old lino, furniture and rubble, and stripping the old wallpaper and paint. Work like installing the central heating and renovating the roof he had professionally done.

Houses like this one often have dark and narrow halls. The owner decided to make some unusual structural alterations here so that he could create a more spacious entrance. Now there is a pleasant hall-cum-dining room. The original wall between the hall and front room was removed, leaving a gentle sloping arch. The main reason for making an arch rather than removing the whole wall was to preserve the old ceiling and to make a subtle division between the meeting and eating areas. In fact, one of the best things about this house is the way all the old plasterwork and decorative cornices have been carefully preserved. They now add a definite style to the house, showing up with a fresh coat of white paint.

The old floorboards in the new enlarged hall were sanded and sealed. This was not only the cheapest but possibly the most attractive treatment. The original fireplace had been removed and the owner scouted round until he found one

LEONARDO FERRANTE

Top, above. The elegance and warmth of the dining room comes from the rich finish of the circular table and the pine floors. The intricate pattern of the wallpaper is an interesting contrast to the other areas of solid colour in the room. A graceful arch leading into the room is subtly echoed by the curves of the tables, the facing of the fireplace and the outline of the chair backs. *Above.* The clever construction of the hall invites the eye to travel two ways— up to the privacy of the first floor or that would fit in with the period of the house. The cast iron grate he moved down from an upstairs room, and the simple pine surround came from a demolished house.

Final additions were the French-style wallpaper in shades of brown and the smart tweedy curtains in an off-white colour, plus deep beige paint on one wall and carrying up the stairs. The furnishings also reflect the period style of the house and there are some good examples of wise auction sale buying both in the hall and in other parts of the house. It is well worth looking around auction sales for old furniture of this type. You can often find some real treasures as well as good inexpensive bargains, which, with a new coat of paint will look just right in a room with a period flavour—and will be cheaper to buy than new furniture for people on a budget.

The doors in this house are yet another example of how close attention to detail can add a great deal to the final effect. When he bought the house, the owner found all the doors had been covered with hardboard and plastic decorative strips. He removed all this covering and found the original sturdy pine-panelled doors still intact underneath. Patiently he scrubbed off the layers of paint, using caustic soda, so the doors could be returned to their original pine finish. This sort of treatment is well worth considering for similar old doors, but caustic soda should be used with great care. It will certainly give almost the best results of any of the paint stripping agents. However, make sure it does not come in contact with the eyes, and wear strong protective gloves.

A complete transformation has taken place in the rear part of the ground floor. Originally there was a cupboard under the stairs with a door leading down to the cellar. A narrow passageway beside the stairs led through to a small kitchen with a bedroom beyond it. Leading off the bedroom was a delapidated washroom with a lavatory and shower. One window bay was badly neglected and seemed to be coming away from the side of the house. The whole place was dark and depressing with an untidy small garden outside.

The owner wanted to bring in more light and a feeling of space. So he knocked out the interior walls, the cupboard under the stairs and the doorway through to this part of the house, to make a spacious sitting room with an open plan effect.

Access to the cellar is now through a trapdoor cunningly let into the carpet under the stairs. Now the whole of the ground floor is virtually open plan, apart from the kitchen, which gives a much greater feeling of space and light.

To add more light in his new sitting room, the owner put in big windows which lead out into the newly paved garden. This is an excellent idea because it makes the whole room seem larger and in the summer, the garden seems an integral part of the house.

The chimney breast in the new sitting room had been blocked up and there was a solid fuel boiler. In here, the owner wanted an open fire to sit by. So he designed a new and attractive fireplace with plain grey firebricks and a slate mantelpiece. An old fire basket was one of his most successful junk shop finds. This type of fireplace would be fairly simple for a good amateur bricklayer to make. It blends well with the atmosphere of the room and makes a pleasing focal point.

The colour scheme follows through the natural beige and white used in the hall. One of the chairs has been cleverly covered in one of the cheapest and most hard-wearing fabrics to be found—pillow ticking. Again the furnishings reflect the period style of the house.

The colourful orange kitchen was previously a bedroom, so the room had a complete rethink. Practical floor and wall units were made to measure, using inexpensive standard size pine-panelled and louvred doors. This way of making your own units is a particularly good one to remember. The frames and worktop can be fitted at little cost. The smart doors are good time and money savers and help to give the kitchen a professionally-made effect. There is a door leading out into the garden and the bright paint, combined with strip lighting under the wall cupboards and a collection of copper jelly moulds, make it a warm and friendly room for cooking.

Upstairs a small rear bedroom has been turned into a practical study painted an unusual terracotta colour. The old chimney breast has been cut away and turned into a neat and attractive bookcase. This has been cleverly done by putting an architrave round the opening and fitting bookshelves inside. Boldly patterned curtains and a collection of prints add to the masculine flavour of this comfortable working room.

Next to this is a smart bathroom which is in a slightly deeper shade of terracotta with lashings of white. In here the owner has used a professional decorator's trick. To get the glossy effect, he painted the walls first with ordinary emulsion paint—the same colour as he had used in the study—then he used a high gloss polyurethane seal on top. This has slightly darkened the emulsion paint but gives it a much more glossy finish than gloss paint only. A new bathroom suite was installed, and a smart blind at the window. Although this room is small and has been simply decorated, it shows how sophisticated a bathroom like this can look without costing the earth to re-decorate.

After years of neglect, this house is now sound and healthy once more. With its uncluttered decorations, it is a sophisticated home that shows what can be done with an old terraced house, using imagination, effort and know-how.

into the airiness and light ahead.
Above. *The kitchen is defined in terms of straight lines, squares and right angles— a striking change from the gentle curves in the other rooms. The strategic placing of lights softens the austerity of line, and enhances the texture of the louvred doors.*
Right. *The attractiveness of the living room lies in its contrasts—the armchairs are both light and heavy, the textures both soft (the moss velvet chair) and hard (the grey bricks of the fireplace).*

LEONARDO FERRANTE

COLIN WATMOUGH

Adapted for comfort

Top left. *The flat has an open plan look and the decor unifies it. The television has been cunningly built into the dividing wall. Adequate ventilation is provided by cupboards at the back.*

Houses specially built for disabled people are few and far between. And what specialized housing there is consists mainly of purpose-built modern homes. Often it may be more practical to adapt older property to suit the needs of a disabled person, and make the house easier and more comfortable for them to live in.

Converting this Edwardian house in West London proved a challenge for this wheelchair-bound bachelor. On a budget, he had to find a place that could be turned into a made-to-measure home on one floor. He knew the alterations he would have to do were major ones, so rather than find a house in good condition he chose one that was relatively cheap and in poor repair so that he could start from scratch.

An improvement grant was obtained from the local Council, and this helped to pay for the conversion.

Architects John Spence and Partners were called in to design the conversion. The ground floor became a self-contained flat for the owner and the first floor was turned into a separate flat that could be let.

The first job was to decide on the best arrangement of rooms in the flat, giving a skeleton shape for the architect to plan wiring, plumbing, and so on. They had to find out the right heights and widths for the various fitments, so the flat would be practical for the owner—and his wheelchair—to live in. Doors were too narrow for a start; the ground floor was on two levels and an efficient living unit had to be fitted into a pocket-sized space.

A wheelchair needs a certain amount of space for turning. The architect had to take its measurements into account during the planning of the flat, and particularly when it came to designing the kitchen and bathroom. Every inch was of great importance, so the whole flat had to be planned minutely.

Outwardly, it is a smart and well-organized bachelor flat but it has the inner bonus of being tailored to the owner's special needs in such a way that only he is aware of this.

For instance, his visitors may not notice the gently sloping brick path leads up to the front door and the missing front door step. This was specially converted so the owner can wheel himself into his home. The angle of the slope had to be carefully worked out so it was not uncomfortably steep.

One of the first major jobs was to make the flat on one level, so the floor in the rear rooms was raised about seven inches. The hall was made smaller and the staircase enclosed to make the entrance to the first floor flat. The old hall passage was removed, making more space for the living room and dining room.

Gas central heating was installed. To save space, a small brick house was built for the boiler outside. At the rear of the flat, the old kitchen, larder, and breakfast room has been turned into a kitchen and bathroom, with a passage leading to the bedroom. The old back staircase was removed to create extra space.

All the doors, except for the front door, are sliding ones. These are easier to manage if you are in a wheelchair. Aluminium angle corners

COLIN WATMOUGH

COLIN WATMOUGH

are fitted to protect doorways from bumps by the wheelchair—a good practical point.

To save the owner from going out to the front door every time goods are delivered, a tradesmen's hatch is discreetly fitted into a corner of the living room. A wide new opening between the sitting room at the front of the house and the dining room gives a spacious, almost open plan, effect. In fact, the flat has been designed to appear large and roomy even though it is in a fairly small house. For example: the old fireplaces in the sitting room and dining room were removed to make more space. The two rooms are comfortably furnished with a fitted carpet—mats are unsuitable for wheelchairs because they tend to get rucked up with the wheels.

The owner decided on the colour scheme after seeing the musty yellow colour of a book cover in a friend's house. He managed to get an exact match to this colour made up for him and then used the paint on the walls and ceiling of the sitting room and dining room, with the cornice picked out in sharp white.

One of the most original decorative touches in the flat is the neat way the television has been built into the wall—a good space saving idea for many cramped householders to copy. Originally the television took up more than its fair share of space in the living room. The owner found its case ugly and thought about

Middle picture. The specially wide French windows are ideal to allow the owner's wheelchair through, down the ramp and into the garden. The bedroom decor is composed of restful shades of subtle mauves, light browns and white.
Above. The bathroom boasts a very uncompromising colour scheme which suits a room used only for a short time. The floor is tiled in a Greek key pattern.

putting it in a cupboard. Then a friend of his, Nicholas Dimbleby, who is a young sculptor and artist, designed its new home. Together with a frame, the whole thing is now more of a picture than ungainly piece of furniture.

First Nicholas Dimbleby knocked a hole in the wall, between the sitting room and dining room, creating a recess. The TV was fitted on rails on the dining room side, so it can be pulled out easily for servicing. On the dining room side there is a whole wall of fitted cupboards and the back of the TV is hidden away neatly inside them.

The most ingenious room is the kitchen. Everything is fitted into a tiny area yet it is so neatly done that the kitchen looks quite spacious. None of the kitchen fitments are specifically designed for disabled people. They are standard units, which have been planned in such a way that they are easy for the owner to manage. For

instance, the sink is free standing, giving the owner space to manage washing up. Instead of using ordinary base unit cupboards under the worktops, the architect used shallower wall cupboards and open shelves, to make enough room for the owner to cook comfortably from his wheelchair.

The kitchen floor is tiled in practical vinyl, and is a pretty avocado colour. In the passage outside the kitchen a Greek key pattern in sharp white has been cut into similar shaped tiles, making an unusual decorative touch. The blinds pick out the avocado colour which is again echoed on the ceiling—adding another subtle touch. There are strip lights under the wall cupboards.

A sliding door shuts off the bathroom and bedroom from the rest of the flat so they can be used as a suite. Colours in the bedroom are restful mixture of aubergine and beige. The bold wallpaper has a matching blind and the beige background of the wallpaper is picked out in the paintwork. A large floor to ceiling mirror is placed on the side of a tall fitted cupboard. This reflects the passage and helps to create an illusion of space.

This flat is something of a model, because it shows how—with clever design and close attention to detail—an ordinary old 'semi' can be turned into a made-to-measure home of a special kind.

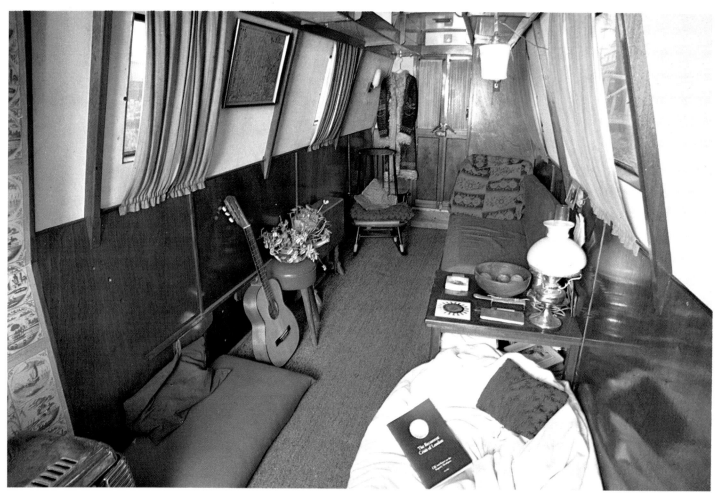

Above. The main living area of the boat shows how such a narrow interior can be organized to appear welcoming and smart. The sag-bag and large floor cushions add to the sense of informal comfort.
Below. The narrow boat 'Kent' has been re-painted in the traditional style to make an eyecatching home on the canal.

Living in boats

Living on board a boat is very much what you make it. As a general rule there are few restrictions — depending, of course, on the type of boat you want to live in. Even if living permanently afloat seems too restrictive, weekend boating is becoming increasingly popular.

The first governing factor is whether the boat you have chosen is connected to main services—if so, many of your problems end there. If not, your first job will be to fit your boat up with the equipment essential to everyday life.

You will need water—both for drinking and for washing with. Your main problem here will be where to site the tank, remembering that weight is always a problem afloat—particularly if the boat is still occasionally mobile. Tanks should be kept to a reasonable size, perhaps around 200 gallons, depending on the size of your boat.

Even for very brief stays you will need lighting and the use of other electrical appliances. Here again the size of the battery will be regulated by the amount of space available. Batteries are usually placed underneath the deck somewhere that is easily accessible for topping up and especially somewhere dry. Recharging is a simple matter—there are many compact generators on the market which are perfectly adequate for domestic use. Be sure to check the voltage of the appliances you will be using on board, though it is possible to buy vacuum cleaners and television sets which have specially adapted voltage.

Calor gas is probably one of the most practical methods of cooking and heating and can even be used for lighting. Remember though that gas is heavier than air, so it tends to sink down into the boat's bilges, where, despite its slightly unpleasant smell it can accumulate unnoticed and in extreme cases cause an explosion. Gas cylinders should always be kept in a well-ventilated place, preferably in a locker in the cockpit, or on deck where the fumes will disperse naturally. Make use of the many different models of gas and fire detectors which you should buy at the same time as your fire extinguishers.

Heating an enclosed area like a boat presents its own problems. Condensation is particularly bothersome in glass fibre or unlined metal hulls, but good ventilation should put that right. Ventilation is even more important if you use paraffin heaters because they give off small quantities of dangerous carbon monoxide.

Electrical heaters are ideal and fume-free, but not always feasible afloat.

Living on board a boat is in many ways very similar to caravan-living. Every inch of space must be put to good use, and you can't have too many drawers, lockers and useful odd corners. The spaces underneath beds and seats are perfect places for seasonal storage—summer clothes in winter and vice versa. Make sure that all storage space is well ventilated to prevent your clothes from getting mildewed over the months.

Unless your boat is of the sea-going variety, in Britain at least, you will be restricted to the chemical type of toilet—most inland waterways are very strict about them and give specific emptying instructions which must be adhered to.

Boats are fun, but for very small children they can abound in hazards. Fence in the topmost bunk bed and provide the children with safety harnesses if they are playing on deck. Fix them to a central point of the deck with a 'lead' just long enough for them to reach most parts of it, but not long enough to allow them to fall over the side. And the best safety measure is to make sure that everyone can swim.

As always, the kitchen—or 'galley'—is the focal point of any home, but in the confines of a boat you will be forced to exercise the maximum ingenuity. Most of your standard fitments should serve a dual purpose—for example a sink that turns into a work surface with the simple addition of a flap-down lid.

A young working couple have put these theories to good and practical use; they have bought and converted a 'narrow boat' which up to three years ago was still plying up and down the canals carrying coal. Immediately after this it was refurbished in the old traditional way, brightly painted and made into a period showpiece.

It has been attractively adapted into a permanent 'home', and, as everything was done on a shoestring it made the most of their ingenuity. The main living area was at first the hold. In its working life the 'Kent' had only a tiny cabin in the stern where the whole family used to live—in what must have been very cramped conditions.

Making the most of the kitchen space and lack of storage, the hatch through from the main area is surrounded by built-in shelves. The kitchen has all the basic essentials, lacking nothing that the ordinary household regards as standard. They have all the normal mains services including telephone.

Perhaps the most unusual and unexpected feature is the bath, this is very well disguised underneath an upholstered cushion. The front of the bath is panelled to match that facing all the sides of the boat. This helps to keep the bath hidden from view. The sleeping accommodation is small but gives the impression of being very comfortable: just a big bed with fitted drawers underneath and a built-in wardrobe.

The owners have chosen a narrow boat rather than the traditional barge, and lavished time and ingenuity on it so that the final effect is one of informal comfort.

Above. In cramped conditions every inch should be made to count, and here the room divider that separates the living area from the kitchen also contains shelves.
Below. *The tiny 'galley' or kitchen is in many ways ideal—everything is to hand, and the main living/dining area is only a step away.*

Above. *The eye-catching living area, colour co-ordinated in fresh green and white. Clean, simple lines and bold, abstract design create a striking and streamlined look.*

The modern look

When Formica purchased a turn-of-the-century terraced house in Richmond in 1972, it was in a dingy and dilapidated state—both inside and out. Formica undertook the job of a complete conversion and, after much careful and imaginative planning, there was a dramatic transformation, producing three separate, colourful and attractive flats.

The house consisted of three floors and a basement. Architect James Bath and his wife Valerie Bath, an interior designer, were called in to do the converting, decorating and furnishing. The architect's brief was to create three self-contained units, fully fitted and furnished, using Formica products wherever it was practical and sensible to do so.

The basement and ground floor became a roomy maisonette; the first floor a compact flat, designed for an older couple; and the top floor, a modern and streamlined flat which is featured here. Originally the top consisted of two rooms —one front, one back—and a central dividing corridor, with an access door at either end.

The architect decided on an open-plan scheme; in a space of only 140 sq ft (14.8 sq m), he had to fit lounge and kitchen/dining areas, a bedroom and bathroom. By removing hampering doors and partitioning walls

room were then devised. On one side is the spacious lounge and the staircase and on the other, the cooking, eating and sleeping areas. In the latter section a useful prefabricated unit was designed to serve a dual purpose: firstly, it functions as a room divider between the sleeping area and the kitchen/dining area and, secondly, it incorporates a complete array of kitchen fitments on one side and a bedroom storage/hanging cupboard on the other.

This prefabricated unit is an ideal example of how one item can be used to best advantage through intelligent forethought. Some partitioning was needed between sleeping and cooking areas as well as kitchen appliances and storage space for clothes. All these requirements were cunningly brought together in this well-organized unit. There is a fully-glazed door at either end of the wall unit which prevents heavy kitchen smells from getting into the bedroom, while also conveying freedom of movement, central to any open-plan scheme.

All the appliances are built in, including a handy eye-level wall oven, a modern hob and

Left. *A cheerful kitchen, tailored for convenience in a modern age. The central unit provides all the necessary fitments—oven and hob unit, mini-fridge, sink and cupboards.*
Below. *Opposite side of the kitchen. The attractive dining table—with its graceful bench seat—adds an unusual touch, while the Formica woodgrain finish eliminates bothersome scuffs and stains. An adjoining cupboard/shelf unit makes for easy serving.*

wherever possible, he created fluidity of space which gives the top floor flat a feeling of being larger than it actually is. An illusion of space, emerging from clever visual treatment in a conversion, can be as important as the actual amount of space available.

The first step was to take away the wall by the staircase—the internal wall of the original back room—making the central corridor into an 'island' surrounded by oceans of space. Advantage was taken of the fact that the two corridor walls couldn't be removed because of the support they provided for the loft ceiling. Most of the old lath and plaster was removed from the studding so the new laminate cladding could have a secure foundation.

Both ends of the 'island' were then closed in with durable laminate-clad panels, post-formed at the edges to avoid sharp corners and to create a streamlined effect—a feature of the interior design which is repeated throughout. A bathroom was then put into the 'island', maximizing on the old corridor space. Special ventilation was then provided to meet the British Building Regulations.

The new, long and narrow bathroom has a wc at one end, wash basin in the central area, and a shower unit at the other end. An outstanding feature of this room is the mock windows which help to eliminate a closed-in or confined feeling. The sky and floral scene which forms the mock window over the wc was incorporated in a panel of laminate by special 'artwork' processing during manufacture. The design is indestructible and makes for easy cleaning and care.

The areas on either side of the 'island' bath-

a small refrigerator. A waste disposal unit fitted into the sink overcomes problems of rubbish disposal. The practical laminate finish is designed with minimum cleaning and maximum visual appeal in mind.

Facing the kitchen unit is a dining table with a gracefully attached bench. The Formica woodgrain finish eliminates the need for a tablecloth —another labour-saving feature. In the alcove adjoining the blocked-up chimney breast, a useful cupboard unit, including a handy shelf, was built. No space could be wasted in designing this flat—every inch had to be utilized to the full.

On the bedroom side of the dividing wall unit are storage shelves and a built-in wardrobe which can be conveniently hidden by concertina-type doors when required. The low double bed here was made from blockboard and designed, again, for a multi-purpose role. There are two large storage drawers in the base of the bed and, at the head, there is a cupboard with sliding doors.

As the structural changes were being made,

Right. Making the most of a small bedroom area. The built-in bed is equipped with shallow cupboards and deep, roomy drawers. A shelf unit serves as a dressing table, set off by two mirrors framed in a cool green.
Below. Once a dingy corridor, now a compact bathroom. The mock window over the wc is livened up with a 'garden' design. Recessed shelves provide a useful storage area and a long mirror creates a feeling of space.

Valerie Bath was concentrating on the decorative aspects. Her brief was to utilize Formica laminate surfaces wherever practical, making this flat superb for easy maintenance. Her first decision was a colour scheme which would be consistent throughout the flat, resulting in a feeling of co-ordination and integration from one part to the next. Her choice was a fresh green and white, with splashes of warm brown and cheerful yellow accessories.

In the lounge area, the theme is simple and striking. The generous white sofa, with its smooth curves and modern look, sets the pace. The blind behind adds an eye-catching note because of the boldly zigzagging, jumbo-sized stripes in green. The green is then repeated in two tones—on the side wall and in the stereo speakers, attached to the wall as both decorative and practical items.

The lines are clean and simple—no fussy details here. The low white-surfaced table is in keeping with the general tone which is carried through the dining/kitchen area into the bedroom where the brown and white duvet cover creates an unexpected accent in colour. The floor here and throughout the flat is a Finnish birch plywood with a clear polyurethane hardwearing finish. No carpeting is required, just a scatter rug for the personal touch.

Formica has succeeded in producing a flat which is exceptional in two respects. Its interior design is unusual and unforgettable; and the materials used in construction and decoration are a great aid to the modern housewife who wants a home where housework and maintenance can be kept to a minimum.